EDUCATIONAL
LEADERSHIP
IN AN AGE
OF REFORM

Contributors

Frank Brown   Dean, School of Education, University of North Carolina at Chapel Hill   Urban education and politics of school governance

James A. Conway   Associate Professor, State University of New York at Buffalo   Organizational theory and staff development

Eleanor Farrar   Associate Professor, State University of New York at Buffalo   Educational policy studies and secondary education

Robert W. Heller   Professor, State University of New York at Buffalo Organizational theory and the school principalship

Stephen L. Jacobson   Assistant Professor, State University of New York at Buffalo   Personnel and educational productivity

Kofi Lomotey   Assistant Professor, State University of New York at Buffalo   Urban education and effective schooling

Mike M. Milstein   Professor, University of New Mexico   School leadership and organizational change

David A. Nyberg   Professor, State University of New York at Buffalo Philosophy of education and ethics

Albert J. Pautler   Professor of Education, State University of New York at Buffalo   Vocational education and instructional design

Hugh G. Petrie   Dean, Graduate School of Education, State University of New York at Buffalo   Philosophy of education and policy studies

Austin D. Swanson   Professor, State University of New York at Buffalo School governance and finance

EDUCATIONAL LEADERSHIP IN AN AGE OF REFORM

Edited by

Stephen L. Jacobson

State University of New York at Buffalo

James A. Conway

State University of New York at Buffalo

Longman
New York & London

Educational Leadership in an Age of Reform

Longman, 95 Church Street, White Plains, N.Y. 10601

Associated companies:
Longman Group Ltd., London
Longman Cheshire Pty., Melbourne
Longman Paul Pty., Auckland
Copp Clark Pitman, Toronto

Executive editor: Naomi Silverman
Production editor: Shirley Covington
Production coordinator: Ann P. Kearns
Cover design/illustration: Carla Bauer
Text art: Thomas Slomka
Production supervisor: Priscilla Taguer

Library of Congress Cataloging-in-Publication Data

Educational leadership in an age of reform / [edited by] Stephen L.
Jacobson, James A. Conway.
     p.   cm.
  Includes bibliographical references.
  ISBN 0-8013-0289-7
  1. Education—United States—Aims and objectives. 2. School
management and organization—United States. 3. School
administrators—Training of—United States. 4. Leadership.
I. Jacobson, Stephen L. II. Conway, James A.
LA217.E368 1990
370'.973—dc20
                                                  89-12986
                                                  CIP

ABCDEFGHIJ-MA-99 98 97 96 95 94 93 92 91 90

To Anita and Linda

Contents

Preface

In its 1983 report *A Nation at Risk: The Imperative for Educational Reform*, the National Commission on Excellence in Education (NCEE) warned that America's system of public education was "being eroded by a rising tide of mediocrity." This controversial report was one of several issued that year that collectively came to be known as the first wave of an educational reform movement. That wave has continued to grow as it has rolled across the nation's educational and political landscape for the past half decade.

The central concern of first-wave reformers was that economic growth depends on quality of education and that if our nation's schools did not improve quickly, the United States would lose its position of preeminence among the world's industrialized nations in commerce, industry, science, and technological innovation. This first devastating wave was followed by subsequent though successively less powerful waves of reform, each offering new recommendations to help reverse the perceived erosion in the quality of American education.

The second wave of the reform movement struck the educational shoreline in 1986 with the issuance of *Tomorrow's Teachers* and *Teachers for the 21st Century*, the respective reports of the Holmes Group and the Carnegie Forum on Education and the Economy. These reports argued that the initial recommendations of the first wave would provide only cosmetic changes in the educational enterprise and that lasting educational improvement was contingent on both a reconsideration of the quality of teacher preparation and a restructuring of the roles and opportunities available to individuals making teaching their career.

Leaders for America's Schools, the 1987 report of the National Commission on Excellence in Educational Administration (NCEEA), was the beginning of what may become the third wave in the tide of reform. Drawing on the recommendations of the earlier movements, this report raises important questions about educational administrators and their role in managing reform efforts in school improvement. Specifically, the report questions whether contemporary expectations of educational leadership need to be reconsidered, whether the preparation of future school leaders needs to be redesigned, and what the roles of federal, state, and local policymakers, teacher organizations, and particularly institutions of higher education should be in these changes.

This book examines the implications of these successive waves of reform both for the context in which future educational leaders will function and for the programs that will prepare those leaders. The intent of this book is to highlight critical issues, raise questions, and share informed concerns about the role of higher education in the preparation of school leaders. The work is a collective effort by past and present members of the Graduate School of Education at the State University of New York at Buffalo, a group deeply concerned with where the field of educational administration and its administrator preparation programs are going.

The reform movement challenges everyone involved in the delivery of educational services to reexamine the structure, content, and purposes of our schools. Those who seek to become future educational leaders and those who will prepare them must actively participate in this ongoing dialogue. We have arranged the book so that it will help current and aspiring administrators and faculty grapple with understanding the traditional hierarchy of roles in education and thereby prepare them to participate in an open discussion for determining more promising ends and better means for achieving them. It is for this audience—the students, professors, practitioners, and policymakers of educational administration—that this book is written.

PART I

The Context of Educational Reform

Part I presents three chapters that develop the context for change created by the three successive waves of reform discussed in the Preface. These chapters are not simply a rehash of the major reform reports but, rather, are a reexamination of their roots and their intent. In Chapter 1, "Reflections on the First Wave of Reform: Reordering America's Educational Priorities" Eleanor Farrar, a commissioned author for the National Commission on Excellence in Education (NCEE), takes a critical look at *A Nation at Risk* and the factors that triggered the initial wave of educational reform. In addition, Farrar examines a shift in educational priorities from equity to excellence and the factors that pushed educational reform to the forefront of the nation's political agenda.

In Chapter 2, "Reflections on the Second Wave of Reform: Restructuring the Teaching Profession," Hugh Petrie, a charter member of the Holmes Group and the dean of the Graduate School of Education at the State University of New York at Buffalo, discusses three issues fundamental to the second wave of reform and the implications of each for a new concept of educational leadership. Specifically, Petrie examines the past and future roles of teachers, the nature of the teaching-learning process, and the importance of context in education. The chapter underscores the emergent roles of teachers in the goal setting and governance of their organizations.

Finally, in Chapter 3, "Reflections on the Third Wave of Reform: Rethinking Administrator Preparation," Stephen Jacobson discusses key problems in educational administration as identified in *Leaders for America's Schools*, along with some of that report's recommendations for correcting these deficiencies. To foster an enlightened dialogue, Jacobson provides a historical overview as he examines the evolution of administrator preparation and the field's quest for a knowledge base. He shows that the current reform movement mirrors the evolution of educational administration in the university setting and that the critical issue in the reform of administrator preparation is the synthesis of theory-based research with field-based practice.

CHAPTER 1

Reflections on the First Wave of Reform: Reordering America's Educational Priorities

Eleanor Farrar
State University of New York at Buffalo

The decade of the 1980s brought major reform to public education and major revisions in the ways that the problems of schooling were defined and prioritized. The reforms of the early 1980s, often called the "first wave of reform," focused on student performance requirements and teacher quality. Between 1980 and 1986, nearly all states increased their requirements for high school graduation. Forty-four states required more courses for graduation, and 34 of these states increased their distribution requirements within subject areas. Forty-two states increased math requirements, mostly from one to two years of instruction. Thirty-four states initiated a science requirement or added an additional year of science study (Pipho, 1986). In addition, several states set minimum test results for graduation or grade-to-grade promotion, and others established minimum grade point averages for participation in sports and other extracurricular activities.

The first wave of reform also upgraded certification requirements, pay, and work conditions for teachers. By 1987, two-thirds of the states required state-prescribed, standardized tests for people entering a teacher training program or about to be certified to teach (Goertz, 1986). Permanent certification for teachers was ended in many states. Others tied certification renewal to further education or teaching performance. To attract more able teachers, several states raised starting salaries and gave across-the-board raises to teachers. Some states created alternative routes to teaching, permitting noncertified college graduates to teach if they took education courses toward formal certification. Other reforms included teacher career ladders and new training programs for administrators (Fuhrman, 1987).

3

In the last years of the decade, a second reform wave is tackling the more difficult issues of school structure and governance. The plan is to improve education by turning over more decision-making authority to faculty and administrators and by redesigning teacher education programs and school staffing patterns to reflect the central role that clinical training and experience play in professional practice (Carnegie Forum, 1986; Holmes Group, 1986). A third wave is gathering momentum to address the preparation of school administrators and their roles in schools where teachers have greater authority and where stratified teaching roles are being tried (University Council for Educational Administration [UCEA], 1987).

These varied reform efforts are bundled together under the rubric of the "educational excellence movement." They represent a significant departure from school reform agendas of the past 20 years, which began when the last "excellence" movement of the Sputnik era gave way to growing concerns about the access of poor and minority students to high-quality schooling. Education reforms spurred by President Lyndon Johnson's War on Poverty—ESEA Title I and Head Start, for example—were premised on the view that society was obligated to overcome the social and educational deficiencies caused by poverty and discrimination (Rawls, 1971). To that end, equity in education was defined in terms of compensatory services to promote equality of the outcomes of schooling.

The next reform movement began near the start of the 1970s and developed as a consequence of the civil rights movement and deeply troubling questions about the nature of authority and the knowledge taught in high schools. Formal education, formerly regarded as the solution to so many social problems, came to seem a major social problem itself. The critics argued that rigid, bureaucratic schools and an outmoded, traditional curriculum were obstacles to real learning. The result was a vastly expanded high school curriculum and radically new models of secondary schooling, including schools without walls and other alternative structures. Educational opportunity had been redefined again. Now equal opportunity meant the opportunity for all students to meet their own needs for education regardless of race, ethnicity, cultural preference, or ambition.

The excellence movement of the 1980s returned full circle to that of the late 1950s, but the reform focus in the 1950s was somewhat different. In 1959, James B. Conant urged giving attention to academically talented boys. He argued for stiffer academic requirements, tougher grading, and school consolidation to increase the range of advanced course offerings in small high schools (Conant, 1959). Like the current excellence movement, Conant's proposals had little to say about girls, the academically deficient, the poor, and schools in center cities. Whereas Conant's focus on talented boys anticipated later reforms aimed at particular groups of students, the current excellence movement proposes to upgrade educational quality for all students. The current movement is more ambitious and comprehensive in scope and begins to move beyond existing norms to toy with new ideas for recruiting and rewarding teachers.

Like current first-wave reform ideas, Conant's proposals were widely adopted, particularly the merger of small schools. In Illinois, for example, there were 646 high schools in 1945 but only 260 in 1961; in Iowa, where there were 819 high schools in 1955, by 1961 there were 562 (Hampel, 1986). Attention to science and math instruction also increased for a time under the auspices of the National Science Foundation, prompted in good measure by concern about America's technological strength in the cold war with Russia. (A March 1958 *Life* magazine article, "Crisis in Education," contrasted the schooldays of Stephen and Alexis, high school students in America and Russia in ways that intensified fears that American schools were easy. A reprint of the article today with Japan substituted for Russia would not seem dated.) The Conant report had a major impact on U.S. high schools despite the fact that Conant was forced to rely chiefly on persuasion to see his proposals carried through. The excellence reforms of the 1980s, by contrast, have been enacted by political entities empowered to mandate reform in local schools. The result has been an array of education reforms well beyond what Conant envisioned, reforms astonishing in both number and comprehensiveness and for the speed with which they have been enacted. Why did the 1980s reform proposals catch fire and spread as quickly as they did? How did the commission reports and studies that galvanized the movement define the problems of schools and propose to solve them? Why did state legislatures adopt some proposals and overlook others? And finally, what has been the impact of the early reforms? The remainder of this chapter addresses these questions by looking at the first wave of reform that focused on standards and teacher quality.

THE CONTEXT FOR REFORM

The 1980s excellence movement was spurred by three important changes in the environment of national education policy at the turn of the decade. First, the election of Ronald Reagan to the presidency in 1980 introduced a federal education policy that vastly differed from those of the preceding 15 years. Known as "the five D's," the Reagan agenda sought to eliminate the U.S. Department of Education (*disestablishment*), to *deregulate* federal education programs, to *decentralize* authority and responsibility to states and school districts, to reduce the place of education as a federal priority (*deemphasis*), and to reduce federal education spending (*diminution*) (Clark & Astuto, 1986). The Reagan education agenda sought to reduce every aspect of the federal role in education. At the same time, it encouraged the reform movement that was slowly gathering momentum. By abandoning the strong role federal government had played in education for the past 15 years, the first Reagan administration created, in effect, a vacuum in education leadership while simultaneously urging state governments and private enterprise to step in to fill the void.

A second change enabling the current reform movement to go forward was the willingness of state leaders—governors, legislators, and business executives—to take a more active role in education reform. Although state involvement in education had been developing for some time, the reduced federal role invited governors and legislatures to demonstrate leadership to their constituencies in an area that, according to the 1983 Gallup poll, the public was willing to support (McDonnell & Fuhrman, 1983). In addition, the state contribution to local education had been slowly increasing for nearly a decade. In 1983, state governments were paying, on average, half the total costs of public elementary and secondary education, which amounted to nearly a quarter of total state budgets (McDonnell & Fuhrman, 1983.) The draw of education costs on state budgets created a particular incentive for state leaders to pay more attention to the schools.

At the same time, the business community suspended its traditional opposition to tax increases to support education because of growing concern about the quality of the future workforce. The message from demographers indicated that lower birth rates meant a 20 percent decline in high school graduates entering the labor force between 1980 and 1990. Employers would have less choice of whom to hire. In addition, changes in the nature of work from manufacturing to service and high technology industries required a workforce well prepared in basic skills and able to learn new skills as required. Business recognized that tomorrow's workforce would be educated in public schools that were currently deficient (Timpane, 1984). The willingness of local business leaders to join forces with governors and legislators to move the reform agenda forward thus ensured that the reforms of the early 1980s would have strong leadership and would be based primarily in the states.

Finally, the current education reform movement gained considerable impetus from a series of national commission reports and privately funded studies that appeared early in the decade and set the tone and the agenda for the rush of reforms that quickly followed. The report of the National Commission on Excellence in Education (NCEE), *A Nation at Risk* (1983), was far and away the most influential. Others issued at about the same time and offering nearly the same recommendations included *Action for Excellence,* issued by an Education Commission of the States task force (1983); *Making the Grade,* a report of the Twentieth Century Fund (1983); and *Educating Americans for the 21st Century* issued by the National Science Board (1983). These reports were widely read and publicized in the press, but *A Nation at Risk* in particular hit the public with nearly the force of Sputnik; it galvanized public opinion to the need for reform in America's schools. Deliberately written in nontechnical but dramatic language, *Risk* drew wide public readership. It was in its fifth printing five months after publication, and more than 150,000 copies had been distributed. The report was also duplicated, distributed, and discussed by such diverse organizations as the American Association of School Administrators, which sent copies to its entire membership, and the Association for Computer Machinery, which mailed copies to its 63,000 members. The Iowa State Department of Education distributed copies to 60,000 state residents. One conservative estimate is that the report reached at least 4 million citizens, a number that would be larger if it were possible to calculate the number of people who shared copies or read newspapers that reprinted the report (Tomlinson, 1986).

The impact of *Risk* is hard to overestimate. It produced a firestorm of publicity for education in general while solidifying the excellence framework that guided the first wave of education reform in the 1980s. One of the great ironies of the NCEE is that it was convened to fill a vacuum created by the inability of the Reagan administration to advance its conservative education agenda (Finn, 1988). Still, *Risk* served as a lightning rod for growing national unrest about the condition of American schools. It also set the stage for a serious public discussion and press review of the scholarly critiques of secondary schooling by Boyer (1983), Goodlad (1984), and Sizer (1984) that were published shortly after and, which more than the earlier reports, helped shape the second reform wave of the 1980s.

PROBLEMS DIAGNOSED AND SOLUTIONS PRESCRIBED

Perhaps the most arresting diagnosis was offered by *Risk*, with its apocalyptic warning, now a household phrase, that "a rising tide of mediocrity" was "threatening our very future as a Nation and a people." The Twentieth Century Fund task force followed suit to warn that "Continued failure by schools . . . may have disastrous consequences for this nation." And the National Science Board group found that "alarming numbers of young Americans are ill-equipped to work in, contribute to, profit from and enjoy our increasingly technological society." Each of the reports asserts that we are in the midst of a national crisis caused by the schools' inability to turn out the kind of workers needed for an increasingly sophisticated economy.

The reports provided little solid evidence to back up these assertions: The NCEE cited several studies indicating that the Scholastic Aptitude Test (SAT) and other ability test scores declined during the 1970s, but its staff later admitted that it was forced to use data that were out of date or of uncertain validity because more timely education statistics were not available (Tomlinson, 1986). In addition, the studies were quick to assume that declining test scores were due to failures in the educational system. Other social and economic factors, such as increases in single-parent households and high unemployment rates, were not mentioned, although few would argue that such problems do not depress the test results of many students.

Many of the reports tell of declining support for public education, but once again the evidence is mixed. Surveys such as the Gallup polls indicate that public confidence in education is no lower than it is in Congress, in the military, or in most other public institutions. Moreover, the data on bond votes and expenditures for public schools show few signs of major decline. Teacher salaries did decline in constant dollars between 1976 and 1983, as did per-pupil expenditures, which declined by 8 percent between 1978 and 1983 after a huge increase of 45 percent between 1970 and 1978. When the commissions issued their reports, however, schools were less crowded, student-teacher ratios were lower, and per-pupil expenditures were much higher than they had been a decade earlier (Peterson, 1983).

A close look at the reports' recommendations reveals other problems. *A Nation at Risk* is a good case to examine, first because it was the most prominent of the reports published in 1983, and second because its recommendations are quite similar to those of the other reports. *Risk* identified problems and offered recommendations in five areas: stronger curriculum content; increased course requirements and higher standards for student performance in general; increased time for schooling in longer school days and the length of the school year; new approaches to attracting, training, and compensating teachers; and better leadership and fiscal support. With the exception of added time in school, the list is appealing and noncontroversial. On closer inspection, however, the recommendations are often vague, only weakly linked to empirical knowledge about teaching and learning, and noncommittal on implementation.

For example, the recommendations on curriculum content urge course requirements in English, math, social studies, science, and computer science (foreign language was only "strongly recommended") that would raise the graduation requirements in virtually all states. The great strength of these recommendations is that they force the elimination of many electives of dubious value from the curriculum by requiring students to take more "academic" courses. The problem, however, is that the curriculum is discussed in terms of outcomes, many of which we know little about how to implement. The report urges English instruction to equip students to "listen effectively and discuss ideas intelligently." Many teachers strive for this outcome, but little is known about how to teach these skills to teachers and how to teach teachers to cultivate them in students. The issue, then, goes well beyond what we usually think of as curricular content to what we know about teaching students and teachers the skills they must know to work effectively with academic content.

Recommendations on standards and expectations reassert the value of traditional grades and standardized tests of achievement to assess student performance. The NCEE ignores the issue of grade inflation or the difficulty of developing uniform, usable criteria for determining appropriate standards for grading. Four of the eight recommendations for raising standards deal with improving the quality of textbooks. Although one can hardly argue with this goal, *Risk* makes no mention of the market mechanisms that determine the content and levels of difficulty of textbooks. Nor, without some incentive, are for-profit publishers likely to develop special-interest texts for very small markets. Textbook publishers are one of the nonregulated, private "governments" that exert great influence on American schools (Cohen, 1978) and that have until recently shown little sign of responding to concerns about textbook quality and rigor. The NCEE's recommendations on standards did not move beyond textbooks to suggest that teachers particularly at the high school level, use primary source material, documents, and nonfiction trade books and magazines to supplement or replace inadequate texts.

Risk's recommendations on increasing the time students spend in school have been the most controversial and widely discussed; they are also perhaps the easiest to test empirically, although the NCEE's evidence on this point was thin: "In England and other industrialized countries, it is not unusual for academic high school students to spend 8 hours a day at school, 220 days per year." The report observed that by contrast, the typical U.S. school year consists of 180 six-hour days. The report's lack of evidence to support the assertion that more time in school leads to greater learning is particularly troublesome in light of the dollar cost such a policy would entail. By the same token, the recommendation for more assigned homework ignores the question of what constitutes useful homework rather than makework.

The recommendations on teaching deal exclusively with extrinsic incentives to improved teaching, such as increased salaries, eleven-month contracts, and evaluation systems to reward exceptional teachers and weed out the inadequate. Oddly, the recommendations ignore a substantial body of research across occupations and professions indicating the importance of intrinsic factors in work performance that are nurtured by supportive work environments, collaborative work arrangements, increased worker responsibility over work performed, and so on. The commissioners also seem to have overlooked recent studies that found no evidence that merit pay had a significant impact on the way teachers teach (Murnane & Cohen, 1986). The report also says nothing about teacher training; rather, it sidesteps that issue by proposing alternative avenues to certification and employment. *Risk* suggests that modest salaries are the main obstacle to improved teaching and that upgraded salaries will attract able people who might otherwise choose more lucrative occupations. In fact, the large number of teachers the nation's schools require make it highly unlikely that teacher salaries will rise to a level that is both affordable to districts and attractive to those seeking careers that pay well.

Finally, the recommendations on leadership do not discuss the issue of school governance or the appropriate domains of responsibility for school boards and superintendents. Again, training for administrators and for lay members of school boards is not mentioned despite increasing superintendent dissatisfaction with the disparity between knowledge about education issues and the management roles that members of school boards seek to play. In similar fashion, the report's recommendations on fiscal support assume that current school finance formulas and vehicles are well designed and equitable and that they provide adequate resources for school management and operations.

THE FIRST REFORM WAVE RECONSIDERED

The chief difficulty with the first-wave reports is their assumption that the existing educational system is basically sound, that schools can be improved by fine tuning and doing more of what they do rather than by redesigning the system. This is particularly paradoxical in the case of *A Nation at Risk*, whose commission was convened by an administration more critical of the educational establishment than any in recent memory. The commission's formula for pushing back the tide of mediocrity was to shore up the system with salary increases, more academic courses, higher standards, and more time in school—to wit, incentives and regulation. None of the commissions provided much hard or soft evidence as to why they thought that will work.

The reports assume that both the technology and the resources are available to implement their proposals. We do have much descriptive data on teaching and learning, and we have made great strides in our ability to test students and diagnose learning problems. But a great leap is required to suggest that we also know how to treat many learning deficiencies or have the political will to alleviate the learning deficiencies we understand. The issue is not just one of technology. Teaching new methods to the thousands of teachers who will be with us for some time yet is beyond the reach of all but the wealthiest districts.

What I have found problematic with the reforms—their premises that the education system is structurally sound and that the technology and resources are available to improve schools in the ways suggested—may be the very features that made them so attractive to states. The states had strong incentives to act: The federal government had created a vacuum of leadership; state dollars were supporting a growing share of district budgets; and the public and the business community were distressed about the condition of schools and willing to support tax hikes to support education. Once policymakers are motivated to act, however, the likelihood that they will is greatly increased if an easily understood solution exists for the problem. Governors and legislators needed both a reason and a framework to act. The 1983 commission reports gave them the framework (McDonnell & Fuhrman, 1983).

Unlike suggestions for organizational reform, the commissions' recommendations were politically palatable. They were presented in a way that made them sound simple, common-sensical, and appealing. The implication was that educators know how to make them work. Most enticing of all, they were reforms that could be mandated from the state house and passed down to local schools for relatively rapid implementation. Some reforms were extremely expensive, as when Arkansas poured millions of dollars into teacher training and California funded schools to devise their own improvement programs. But most states preferred to avoid reforms that could have long-term financial implications for state budgets and that might be awkward to repeal, such as longer school days and years or merit pay. Most states favored less costly approaches that increased graduation requirements, introduced testing for promotion and graduation, and made it harder for people to become certified as teachers.

IN CLOSING

Research on the first-wave reforms is just coming in, and the findings make interesting reading. A study of Texas, California, and South Carolina concluded that "educational excellence is not amenable to implementation by regulation or by scattering fiscal incentives. . . . Policymakers can manage what they control: macro-policy—funding, curriculum frameworks, teachers certification, textbook selection and the like. But they have limited control over daily events in schools" (Timar & Kirp, 1988). Findings of this sort are not surprising; the surprise is that states so quickly forgot, or did not heed, what is perhaps the single most important finding of educational research in the 1970s: that people who work on the front line of education—teachers and administrators—will be involved one way or another in decisions about what to do to improve the schools.

A number of states have backed away from reforms that were adopted quickly and then found difficult to implement. The issues involved in merit pay plans and teacher testing and recertification programs are now viewed, in the light of experience, as much more complex than was noticed at the outset. Still, the first wave of reform may leave a useful legacy. The commission reports and early reform efforts mobilized a broad-based coalition of educators, private citizens, elected officials, and business executives. Many have learned from that experience that education reform calls for more than mandates and new regulations. Whether the coalitions that came together to renew U.S. schools will stay together to develop long-term and more enduring strategies is now being decided as the second and third reform waves move forward.

REFERENCES

Boyer, E. (1983). *High school: A report on secondary education in America.* New York: Harper & Row.

Carnegie Forum on Education and the Economy. (1986). *Teachers for the 21st century,* New York: Author.

Clark, D., & Astuto, T. (1986). *The significance and permanence of changes in federal educational policy 1980–88.* Bloomington, IN: Policy Studies Center of the University Council for Educational Administration.

Cohen, D. (1978). Reforming school politics. *Harvard Educational Review, 48* (4), 429–447.

Conant, J. (1959). *The American high school today.* New York: McGraw-Hill.

Education Commission of the States. (1983). *Action for excellence: A comprehensive plan to improve our nation's schools.* Denver: Author.

Finn, C. (1988). Education policy and the Reagan administration: A large but incomplete success. *Educational Policy, 2* (4), 343–360.

Fuhrman, S. (1987, Summer). Educational policy: A new context for governance. *Journal of Federalism, 17,* 132.

Goertz, P. (1986). *State educational standards: A 50-state survey.* Princeton: Educational Testing Service.

Goodlad, J. (1984). *A place called school.* New York: McGraw-Hill.

Hampel, R. (1986). *The last little citadel.* Boston: Houghton Mifflin.

Holmes Group. (1986). *Tomorrow's teachers: A report of the Holmes Group.* East Lansing, MI: Author.

McDonnell, L., & Fuhrman, S. (1983). The political context of school reform. In V. Mueller, & M. McKeown (Eds.), *The Financial, Legal and Political Aspects of State Reform of Elementary and Secondary Education,* (pp. 43–64). Cambridge, MA.: Ballinger.

Murnane, R., & Cohen, D. (1986). Merit pay and the evaluation problem: Why some merit pay plans fail and a few survive. *Harvard Educational Review, 56* (1), 1–17.

National Commission on Excellence in Education. (1983) *A nation at risk: The imperative for educational reform.* Washington, DC: U. S. Government Printing Office.

National Science Board Commission on Precollege Education in Mathematics (1983). *Educating Americans for the 21st century.* Washington, DC: National Science Foundation.

Peterson, P. (1983). Did the education commissions say anything? *The Brookings Review, 2* (2): 4–5.

Pipho, C. (1986, December). Kappan special report: States move reform closer to reality. *Phi Delta Kappan, 68:* K1–K8.

Rawls, J. (1971). *A theory of justice.* Cambridge, MA: Harvard University Press.

Sizer, T. (1984). *Horace's compromise.* Boston: Houghton Mifflin.

Timar, T., & Kirp, D. (1988). State efforts to reform schools: Treading between a regulatory swamp and an English garden. *Educational Evaluation and Policy Analysis, 10* (2), 87.

Timpane, M. (1984, February). Business has rediscovered the public schools. *Phi Delta Kappan, 65,* 389–392.

Tomlinson, T. (1986). A nation at risk: Background for a working paper. In T. Tomlinson & H. Walberg (Eds.), *Academic work and educational excellence.* Berkeley: McCutchan.

Twentieth Century Fund. (1983). *Making the grade: Report of the Twentieth Century Fund task force on federal elementary and secondary education policy.* New York: Author.

University Council for Educational Administration. (1987). *Leaders for America's schools: The report of the National Commission on Excellence in Educational Administration.* Tempe, AZ: Author.

CHAPTER 2

Reflections on the Second Wave of Reform: Restructuring the Teaching Profession

Hugh G. Petrie
State University of New York at Buffalo

The common wisdom is that the first wave of educational reform, initiated by *A Nation at Risk* (National Commission on Excellence in Education [NCEE], 1983), was characterized by the imposition of top-down reforms that essentially asked us to do more of the same but to do it better. The second wave of educational reform, perhaps best exemplified by the Holmes Group Report, *Tomorrow's Teachers* (Holmes Group, 1986) and by the Carnegie Forum Report, *A Nation Prepared* (Carnegie Forum, 1986), was characterized by a recognition of the systemic nature of the educational enterprise and the necessity of putting the teacher at the center of educational reform.

But what does it mean to put the teacher at the center of educational reform? There are signs that it simply means we recognize that we have a long history of top-down, mandated reforms that have often been frustrated by the unwillingness of the teacher, once the classroom door is closed, to do what curriculum developers and policymakers say ought to be done. Some reformers also feel that teachers are somehow not up to the mark in terms of quality and performance and that we must somehow select them better, prepare them longer, test them harder, and get rid of the incompetents more cheaply. In short, there is much to suggest that teachers are to be put at the center of the reform movement simply in order to engage in another round of "teacher bashing."

However, there is another way to read at least some of the suggestions to be found in the second wave of reform. Under this alternative reading, the central role being proposed for teachers in a restructured teaching profession derives from questioning some fundamental assumptions about teaching, learning, and the organization of schools. It is in questioning these assumptions that some reformers have begun to develop a new vision of teachers and teaching, one that at least suggests, if not demands, a new concept of the role of teachers in schools. In turn, this new role for teachers has profound implications for our concept of educational leadership.

What I want to do in what follows is to explore three of these fundamental assumptions and how they are being challenged by some of the second-wave reformers. I will look at the concept of the role of teachers, the nature of the teaching-learning process, and the emerging appreciation of the importance of context in education. In each case I will contrast an older, often unstated concept of the situation with what is beginning to crystallize as one of the views contained in the second wave of reform. I will conclude with an analysis of what this new view suggests for a staged, or differentiated, idea of educational leadership, a discussion of a new notion of accountability, and a suggestion for a different kind of preparation for educational leadership.

THE ROLE OF THE TEACHER

A number of writers have commented on the contrast between conceiving of the teacher as a technician versus conceiving of the teacher as a professional. Schön (1987) speaks of the teacher as a reflective practitioner. Shulman (1987b) urges us to view the teacher as embodying the wisdom of practice. Giroux and McLaren (1986) see the teacher as a transformative intellectual. Brown (1988) and Bereiter and Scardamalia (1987) like to describe the teacher as a facilitator of knowledge-building activities by the learner. What seems to be common to all these ways of viewing the teacher is the highlighting of the role of professional judgment. Furthermore, this is not just the professional judgment that has always been present in cases of the teacher's deciding whether to give the unit test today or tomorrow, or whether to spend an extra five minutes reviewing the Civil War. Rather, this is a notion of professional judgment that requires the teacher to consider not only the best means to achieve some more or less clearly defined ends, but those ends themselves, the relations between a variety of means and ends, and which sets of means and ends are most appropriate in the circumstances.

This view of teacher as professional is to be contrasted with teacher as technician. Please note that I am not here conceiving of a technician as necessarily being without status. As I am using the term, an airline pilot is a technician because the job to be done is largely defined by external forces, and the skills necessary to perform the job, however complex they might be, are more or less directly causally related to the job at hand. Even pilots coping with unexpected emergencies act basically as superb technicians. They do what they have to do to fly their planes safely under extremely perilous conditions. However, if pilots were also to have a recognized stake in the very nature and organization of the airline industry, then they would be pushing at the limits of the strictly technical aspects of their job and would be considered more nearly as professionals.

The point is that a technical concept of teaching, or any profession for that matter, basically rules out a consideration by the practitioner of the fundamental goals and ends of the profession. Those are always taken as given, and best practice is then defined as the most efficient and effective use of means to those ends. A professional concept of practice, on the other hand, requires a constant movement back and forth between means and ends, not merely calculating effectiveness but also appropriateness in light of a historical and critical analysis of that practice as an evolving human activity.

Consider, for example, lesson planning. Some might argue that teachers now have a wide range of professional discretion to sequence and pace their lessons, to lecture or engage in discussion, to review or press on, to assign homework or a project, and so on. Is this not professional practice? Yes and no. Within a fairly tightly prescribed curriculum that must be "covered" and that is defined by the experts in the "disciplines" and that is packaged into self-contained 45-minute classes, and that is tested by "objective," often norm-referenced tests, there is, indeed, a fair amount of discretion.

But what of the teachers who are persuaded by Ted Sizer's (1984) notion that less may be more in terms of coverage? Can they easily decide to go into more depth in a particular topic, concentrating on giving the students not so much the actual information but *the tools* to pick up the information on the subject on their own? What of the teachers who would like to combine mathematics and science in the middle school to make them both come alive? Can they do any more than an occasional "interdisciplinary" project? What if a group of teachers in a school came to believe that they really need to spend whole mornings on an integrated notion of literacy, including reading, writing, speaking, and listening, rather than separate classes on English and drama and current events? Occasionally some school districts and buildings do allow for such teacher activity, but they are noteworthy precisely because they are so unusual.

I am trying to call attention to the fact that almost no teacher activity is concerned with considering fundamental goals of education or of balancing means and ends. Rather, most teachers are immersed in trying to practice effectively within a social institution basically defined by others. It is that kind of concern with effective practice and the technical means to engage in that practice that I am calling the technician model of teaching and which, I am suggesting, is to be contrasted with the emerging view of the teacher as reflective practitioner, a practitioner who is conscious of, concerned about, and active in defining the very nature of the profession, its purposes, and its goals. It is this view of teacher as reflective practitioner exercising professional judgment that is emerging from the second wave of reform.

THE TEACHING-LEARNING PROCESS

The second fundamental assumption that is being challenged has to do with the nature of the teaching and learning processes. Basically, there are two metaphors operating in most traditional concepts of teaching and learning. The most common is the notion of the teacher as someone in command of a variety of processes that, carefully chosen, will cause the desired learning to take place in the students. This is the factory model with the teacher as worker and the students' learning as product. Please note that not all factories are bad places. Some things are very usefully produced in factories—clothing, medicines, automobiles, computers, books, and so on. The point is that the factory is a place for the application of causal techniques by the workers in order to produce the intended product.

In obvious ways, the factory model of the teaching-learning process is related to the concept of teacher as technician, and, even if we think of teachers as very skilled technicians, like airline pilots, they are still fundamentally engaged in manipulating causal processes, which we call instructional techniques, to produce the desired learning in students. We even have appropriate quality controls on our use of these processes. We test students, sort them, grade them, and send them on to one or another future on the basis of the effectiveness of our instructional processes in causing the desired learning.

The second traditional metaphor for the teaching and learning process conceives of the teacher as therapist and the student as client. We speak, for example, of learning disorders and of providing appropriate services for the students. We diagnose difficulties with reading and prescribe appropriate cures. We sometimes even speak of the school as an appropriate place to center all the social services that our client students may come to need, from occupational counseling to nursery schools for teenaged mothers. In this metaphor schools are seen as treating pathologies in students that are sometimes severe, as when students have learning disorders, and that are sometimes relatively benign, as when ordinary students are helped to grow into well-rounded, socially responsible, job-holding adults.

These two views of the teaching and learning process are to be contrasted, I believe, with the emerging view of the process as one of joint meaning-making. This approach sees knowledge not as somehow in the possession of the teacher, waiting to be transmitted to the student or to be used to treat the students' problems, but as mutually constructed by teacher and student in order to make sense of human experience. The notion is not one of "anything goes." Certain constructions of knowledge are neither possible nor coherent. The earth is not flat, for example. At the same time, however, it is clear that the knowledge one can have of various situations depends on one's point of view and purposes.

Viewing teaching as causing learning or as treating some sort of learning or social or psychological deficit leads to different kinds of knowledge than does viewing teaching as facilitating the construction of meaning by the student. Consider, for example, the different ways in which each of these metaphors might construe the making of "mistakes" in a word problem in algebra. Under the causal view, a mistake by a student is a kind of quality control problem. Either the teaching process chosen was inappropriate, or the material (i.e., the student) was somehow defective, or something intervened in the process to frustrate its natural conclusion. In any event, the product, the student learning, did not turn out as intended and the situation must be corrected. We might try to improve our instructional processes by using educational research to determine which teaching techniques work best and then trying to put those techniques into the hands of teachers along with appropriate information on how they are to be used. We might try to improve the raw material by asking more of the teachers in the system below us. "If only the elementary teachers had done their jobs!" Or of the parents. "If only parents would give kids the support they need!" Or of the social-cultural system. "If only kids didn't watch so much television!" Or we might try to see what kinds of interference occurred in the process. "Were the kids distracted by being hungry? Then we will feed them breakfast." Under the causal view of teaching and learning, student mistakes are aberrations in the productive process and need to be corrected.

Consider the metaphor of student as client. Here the mistake is taken as some kind of deficit. Perhaps it is individual. The student cannot learn because he or she simply does not have the aptitude for algebra. Then let us put the student into a vocational track that does not require algebra. Alternatively, the student may have a learning disorder. Let us treat it with appropriate "pull-out" programs. Or, perhaps, the deficit is social. The student comes from a poor background. Let us enrich it by means of a Head Start program or by means of remedial classes. Here the emphasis is not so much on the defective production processes as on the remediation of perceived deficits in the student. Once those deficits are removed, the mistakes will, it is believed, no longer occur.

Contrast both of these approaches with viewing the mistake through the lens of meaning-making. The first result is that the "mistake" may not even look like a mistake anymore. Under the view that knowledge is constructed, seeing a certain move in solving an algebra problem as a mistake depends on the standard and traditional interpretation of the problem. There may be other ways of construing the problem. The first thing the teacher might do would be to ask whether there is some way of making sense of the problem that would have led quite logically to the mistake. By exploring with the student why he or she is approaching the problem in this way, the teacher can begin to determine whether this is just a careless error that the student would also acknowledge, or whether it represents a reasonably coherent alternative framework for making sense of the problem. If it is the latter, that framework can also be explored to determine its connection with the more traditional framework. The mistake can be used as a springboard for exploring both the student's meaning-making frameworks and, in the more advanced cases, even for alternative explorations into the nature of mathematics itself (Borasi, 1986). Conceiving of teaching and learning as meaning-making is, then, the second new approach suggested by the second wave of reform.

CONTEXT IN EDUCATION

The third assumption I wish to explore is the role of context in education. Conventional wisdom has it that context plays a very small role in teaching and learning. After all, we have statewide syllabi and curricula adopted for use in all schools in the state, rich and poor, urban, suburban, and rural. Some large states have statewide textbook adoption policies that in turn influence the range of textbooks available for everyone. John Goodlad in *A Place Called School* (1984) paints a dismal picture of the sameness of schools across the country. In our teacher preparation programs we provide either general theory with the hope that students will learn to apply it to concrete situations, or we teach nontheoretical recipes, which turn out to be just as general and context-independent as the theory. We look for what works with the idea somehow being that we can find the magical formula or recipe or theory that will then more or less automatically apply itself to concrete situations.

The reality, however, is that education is a practical activity that takes place in concrete individual situations. Even when this fact is recognized, too often we tend to act as if the problem is that we just need to learn how to apply general theory to concrete situations. The difficulty with this view is that it tends to generate an infinite regress. If what we need to solve the problem of knowing how to apply theory to practice is some more knowledge, say, of recipes, then we will need another level of knowledge that tells us when the situation is the kind for which it is appropriate to apply the recipe and when not. But that process has no logical end. As more and more scholars of education are beginning to realize, we need a kind of knowledge that is rooted in action rather than in cognition (Schön, 1987; Petrie, 1981).

This kind of knowledge is basically good judgment. The essence of judgment is the ability to reconcile *in practice* competing principles or maxims. Furthermore, this reconciliation takes place within the social context of a community of practitioners engaged in and reflecting on their problem-solving efforts. Judgment is *not* a series of propositions but a process leading to action. It is not procedural or technical in the sense of following explicit rules laid down by someone else. Rather, it is value-laden, and in some cases it is the values themselves that are changed or the emphases given to competing values that are altered. It is the ability to adapt to the concrete situation with all its particularity that marks the teacher with good judgment.

Let me sketch two examples of how this notion of judgment in particular contexts is beginning to influence thinking about educational reform. The first comes from Lee Shulman's work on pedagogical content knowledge (1987b). Shulman claims that recent research on general pedagogy inevitably fails to account for what appear to be real differences in the kinds of instructional judgments made by expert teachers in various subject areas. It is, of course, useful to know about the effects of direct instruction, higher-order questioning, and the like. However, it is equally important to realize that the knowledge used by a third-grade mathematics teacher to make instructional judgments will likely be heavily dependent on that teacher's knowledge of the content being taught and will, therefore, differ essentially from the knowledge used by a high school social studies teacher in making instructional judgments in teaching about the Civil War.

In short, Shulman is pointing out to us that the context provided by the subject matter being taught has a significant influence on good teaching. Indeed, Shulman's team has pilot-tested assessment protocols for the National Board for Professional Teaching Standards using the pedagogical content knowledge approach (Schulman, 1987a). Preliminary results indicate that perhaps for the first time real teachers believe that they are being appropriately assessed by means of exercises that really do measure the effectiveness of the teaching in which they engage. This is in sharp contrast to other teacher tests such as the National Teacher Examination (NTE) which seem to have little connection at all to effective teaching (Haney, Madaus, & Kreitzer, 1987).

A second area in which the importance of context is becoming more and more apparent lies in the growing concern over the problem of educating at-risk youth. The issue here revolves around the demographic facts that the number of youth historically at risk of not benefiting from education is on the upswing. These youth comprise the majority of dropouts; they are often poor, of minority background, of limited English proficiency, and have seldom even received the benefit of traditionally conceived "good" educational practices. These are the students with whom our educational system has had the least success in the past, yet such youth will comprise a growing percentage of our school-aged population in the future. The context provided by the social, ethnic, racial, gender, and economic backgrounds of these children will have to be taken into account by teachers who wish to teach them.

The growing numbers of these students are providing a very different context for schools than the more traditional suburban model that so many policymakers seem to have in their heads. Nor is it obvious that what is needed are standard or even different instructional techniques that will reach these children. Indeed, some critics suggest that the institution of schooling as currently organized is inherently incapable of providing successful experiences for these students (Ogbu, 1988; Coleman & Hoffer, 1987). In a sense, the meaning-making intended by the schools is incompatible with the meaning-making in the culture of these at-risk students where doing well in school is equated with "acting white." The whole context of schools, the cultures represented by schools, the cultures represented by at-risk students, and the society in which they all reside pose fundamental questions about the kind of sense-making that the schools may be able to assist their students in performing. The emerging view of the teacher, then, requires an appreciation of the role of context in education, from that provided by the subject being taught to that provided by the social, economic, and political milieu in which we find ourselves.

A NEW VIEW OF EDUCATIONAL LEADERSHIP

What, then, are the implications for educational leadership of a vision of teachers as reflective practitioners exercising professional judgment, facilitating meaning-making rather than causing learning, adapting to a variety of contexts affecting schooling, and committed to understanding, participating in, and influencing the debates surrounding the purposes of teaching and schooling? Are current concepts of educational leadership adequate? How might they be changed? Can we continue to think of educational leaders solely as administrators, or must teachers take over a considerable part of the leadership of education?

It seems clear that if teachers are to be viewed as reflective practitioners exercising professional judgment, educational leaders will not tell such professionals what to do. There will not be detailed syllabi externally imposed. Bureaucratic rules and regulations will be kept to a minimum. Structures will be developed that allow a broad range of discretion and influence, not merely in how to teach the syllabus once the classroom door has been closed, but in the very construction of those syllabi. The leadership will be the leadership associated with groups of semiautonomous professionals rather than the leadership associated with hired help. Relationships will probably look more like the collegial models of higher education or the associations of professionals in accounting or architectural firms, or like health maintenance organizations rather than like industrial labor-management arrangements.

If teachers are to be conceived of as facilitating meaning-making rather than causing learning, then educational leadership will be concerned less with techniques of teaching and with making certain that teachers display those techniques, and more with the quality of life in classrooms and the opportunities for teachers and students alike to engage in meaningful activities as part of the learning process. If teachers are to be models of meaning-making for their students, then educational leaders will have to model joint meaning-making with the teachers. Educational leaders will help provide the resources that teachers and students need to engage in meaningful learning rather than monitoring to see if certain instructional techniques are being implemented. Educational leaders will work collaboratively with teachers to make schools sensible places to be rather than institutions disconnected from the real world.

If teachers are to be conceived of as making adaptive judgments in context rather than applying generalized theories or recipes, leaders will need to encourage experimentation, risk taking, and alternative teaching styles. Educational leaders will have to insist that all children can learn, especially the disadvantaged, and provide the support that will allow teachers to foster the learning of all students. Leaders will need to appreciate the powerful contexts created by their own school buildings, the teachers, and the students. Mentoring programs for new teachers, peer coaching for experienced teachers, and collaborative learning will need to be nurtured and supported to begin to use the school context in positive ways rather than ignoring its effects. Resources will need to be made available for alternative ways of trying to reach the mutually agreed-on goals of the school. Educational leaders will need to devise clear and acceptable ways of measuring progress toward those goals and mechanisms for taking corrective actions when the goals are not being reached.

Given this new vision of what teachers are like, it is not hard to see why there have been calls for a more differentiated structure of teaching and a more staged version of educational leadership. It is not easy to envision the kind of professionalism being called for on the part of teachers being inculcated solely within a college or university program for teacher education. Still less is it a professionalism that is amenable to hierarchical control by a principal or superintendent or state-level commissioner of education who somehow can direct every move of the teachers and know how to evaluate every judgment and adaptive change made in thousands of different contexts. It is much more nearly the view of a profession of reflective practitioners who practice together and who learn together through their joint enterprise.

It is extremely unlikely that any one person called a superintendent or principal can embody all the virtues required of the educational leaders of tomorrow. It is much more likely that what will be necessary is a profession organized in stages. There will be student teachers. There will be neophytes in the teaching profession, apprenticed perhaps to more experienced teachers who also show a propensity for working with other adults as well as with children in the continual learning required of the schools of the twenty-first century. There will be expert teachers, perhaps certified by the new National Board for Professional Teaching Standards, with expertise in a variety of specialized teaching functions—subject matter specialties, special education, mentoring, evaluation, instructional supervision, and the like. The hard and fast distinction between the classroom and the principal's office will of necessity begin to blur simply because reflective professionals will need to perform some of the traditional administrative tasks and administrators will be unable to perform all of their traditional tasks without significant input from people more expert than they in certain areas.

Take, for example, the job of evaluating and assisting new teachers. As soon as one acknowledges the idea of pedagogical content knowledge, it immediately becomes apparent that no one secondary principal can possibly know all that is required to evaluate and assist biology teachers, mathematics teachers, music teachers, English teachers, and so on. General pedagogical principles are of limited value, and observational checklists give no credence whatsoever to the objective of meaning-making with students. What will be required are expert teachers in these fields who can not only deliver effective instruction to children but who can also assist their colleagues in becoming more effective. Such "lead teachers" will themselves engage in continual learning and improvement of their craft, not through the typical half-day workshop in which they listen to some "expert" present the latest "technical" quick fix, but through continual self-renewal and collegial interactions.

Or take another example. If we wish to promote higher-order thinking skills among all our children and if we take seriously the challenges presented by the demographics of the at-risk student population, we will be unable to reach our goals with centrally mandated uniform syllabi that must be covered. Instead, we will need to allow a good deal of freedom and flexibility to teachers in setting appropriate goals for the kinds of students they have. They will need to select their own textbooks and supplement them as needed with a variety of material. The standardized norm-referenced tests so beloved by central office and state-level administrators will need to be seen as essentially inimical to the long-term goals of the schools (Koretz,

1988). It is becoming clearer and clearer that such tests do not adequately assess either students' or teachers' performance, achievement, or skills, and they serve neither the purpose of improving the curriculum and instruction nor the purpose of accountability.

Accountability

It will be asked just what kind of notion of accountability is presupposed by the view of teacher as reflective practitioner exercising professional judgment. After all, it might be argued by defenders of more traditional arrangements for schooling that the view I have been propounding is one that seems to deny accountability altogether. Whatever other problems there may be with current structures of schooling, at least they have the virtue of locating responsibility for learning in clear and identifiable places. The state is responsible for the education of its citizens, the local school board has the legal responsibility for implementing that education in local districts, the superintendent is clearly responsible to the elected school board, and the principals and teachers responsible in turn to the superintendent. If we don't like the results, we can throw the appropriate rascals out. What I am proposing is a system in which it would appear that anything goes.

Our current accountability system is built on regulations and structures that presuppose the idea of a teacher as a technician, faithfully following detailed syllabi prepared by others and evaluated by administrators who often know less about the content involved than do the teachers. What I have been suggesting, however, is the idea of a teacher as a semiautonomous professional subject to the judgments of other professionals as reflected in the standards and policies set by those professionals. Such a concept suggests that we obtain true professional accountability through regulating the qualifications of who will be counted as a professional, rather than through micro*managing* what the professional does. It is the way in which we treat professionals in other fields, from accountants to doctors, from architects to psychologists. It is the way that we might consider treating teachers.

Nevertheless, there are serious issues facing a professional system of accountability as opposed to the highly centralized and bureaucratized system we now have. I would like to touch on just two of these—the central role of credible assessment in such a system and the question of whether teacher unions are inimical to a professional system of accountability that works in the public interest.

Let me turn first to assessment. Establishing a system of accountability that focuses on the qualifications of the people allowed to be called professionals requires a heavy dependence on the assessment mechanisms used to make such judgments. Not even doctors or lawyers, let alone teachers, can simply ask the public to trust them in their individual judgments. There must be credible and rigorous assessment procedures, including tough entrance standards to challenging preparation programs that are periodically reviewed for their effectiveness, state and national examinations to check on the quality of graduates, supervised internships, and, most important of all, performance evaluations that go far beyond simple-minded behavioral checklists. We do not presently have such assessment procedures, although the National Board for Professional Teaching Standards is committed to trying to create them.

It is also clear that significant changes will be needed in the traditionally negative union response to calls for professional responsibility. Such a reaction may be justified in an "us versus them" system in which schools are hierarchically organized and managed. It is wholly inappropriate in schools organized around more professional norms. Teachers will have to evaluate other teachers. Teachers will have to give up seniority rights that enable the most experienced teachers to have the easiest assignments and novices the hardest. Imagine, if you will, the newest doctors performing the most advanced surgery while the experts perform the appendectomies and tonsillectomies. Or imagine the new associates in law firms trying the most difficult cases while the senior partners do the legal research. A truly professional teaching corps will need to give the most challenging tasks, the hardest classrooms, to the most competent and experienced teachers.

Fortunately, there are some indications that traditional attitudes are changing. The recent contracts approved in Rochester and New York City appear to recognize the necessity for a professional form of accountability. Teachers in Toledo have been evaluating other teachers for several years now with no apparent ill effects on union solidarity and some beneficial effects on the quality of teaching being conducted there.

The idea of accountability in the new concept of schools is an accountability of processes and procedures that seem to give us promise of moving closer to our societal goals while allowing for the continual criticism and refinement of those goals and the means we employ to reach them. In a clear sense, that is the core notion of professionalism in any field. The professionals are not technical experts whom the rest of us are simply supposed to trust. Rather, professionals are people well educated in their field, who understand the tentative nature of their knowledge and expertise, who are constantly learning with and from each other, who hold and enforce high standards of performance, who can explain and justify their claim to expertise to the rest of us, and who stand ready to modify their profession in the light of emerging human and social needs.

Preparation for Educational Leadership

This notion of professionalism also carries with it a radically different notion of the proper kind of preparation for educational leaders at all levels. In the 1987 report of the National Commission on Excellence in Educational Administration (University Council for Educational Administration [UCEA], 1987), the debate seems to be over whether and to what extent administrator preparation should be based on theoretical approaches to administration or on practical experiences in supervising and administering. The concept of teachers and the kind of leadership they will require that I have been urging suggests that this way of framing the issue is largely misguided. Focusing on administrative theory will result in an empty formalism as appropriate to a business organization as to a school, whereas focusing on practice will likely lead to a fragmented collection of recipes and rules of thumb with no understanding of the basis of the rules or sense of when to break them.

What is required as an absolute prerequisite to any kind of preparation for educational leadership is the kind of truly liberal education often promised by our colleges and universities but all too seldom delivered in this day and age (e.g., Study Group, 1984; Association of American Colleges, 1985). The ideas that the goals of education are essentially open to debate and that the essence of teaching and learning is meaning-making strongly suggest that educational leaders must have a strong grounding both in social philosophy and in general curricular and epistemological issues of teaching and learning. Philosophy, history, sociology, political science, cognitive psychology—these and other such general subjects are the absolute prerequisites for educational leaders.

It is, however, important to note two things. First, educational leaders also must have some acquaintance with general administrative theories and specialized school knowledge, such as school law, labor relations, and the like. But educational leaders need not master such subjects—they would have to know too much. Rather, they will have access to experts in those fields who *can* provide the mastery, and they must know when to call on these experts. Educational leaders will also need the good judgment to know when a problem calls for the use of technical, expert knowledge and when it requires going beyond a merely technical solution. That kind of judgment is precisely what should result from a liberal education.

SUMMARY

I have asserted that the second wave of educational reform has indeed put the teacher in a central role. However, I have been arguing that this role is central not simply because teachers are somehow in the middle of things.

Rather, I have been urging that under one interpretation of several of the important thrusts in the second wave of reform, the very concepts of teachers and teaching are undergoing radical revision. This revision in turn requires that we question our notions of educational administration and educational leadership.

I considered three features of the emerging reconceptualization of teachers and teaching:

1. The teacher as reflective practitioner exercising professional judgment in varying contexts.
2. Teaching and learning as meaning-making rather than as some sort of causal production of something in the learner by the teacher.
3. The importance of context in teaching, from the context of the subject being taught to the context of the demographic and social character of our society in the twenty-first century.

In discussing these features, I illustrated how they call for a fundamental rethinking of teaching, learning, schooling, and the social organizations and arrangements we have developed to perform these tasks.

I suggested that thinking about teachers and teaching in these ways calls for a new vision of educational leadership, one concerned less with micromanaging teaching and more with facilitating the work of semiautonomous, reflective practitioners exercising professional judgment. Leading professionals is simply different from leading hired hands. This new vision of educational leadership strongly suggests a rethinking and reordering of the educational leadership tasks in our schools. No sharp distinction between administrators and teachers is likely to be useful in tomorrow's schools.

The idea of teacher as reflective practitioner exercising professional judgment also carries with it important implications for two other issues—accountability and the preparation of educational leaders. With respect to accountability, we need to shift to a notion of the accountability of professionals. This is an accountability that relies much less on clearly defined tests of agreed-on outcomes and much more on rigorous processes for recruiting, preparing, and monitoring the professionals in the system. In particular, I contrasted these professionals who take responsibility not only for the means of their activity but also for debate over the ends of their activity with technical "experts" who essentially disclaim responsibility for the uses to which their expertise is put. I suggested that true professionals are and must be accountable to society for the practice of their profession, from their technical expertise to the justification for that profession within society itself.

Finally, I proposed a kind of preparation for educational leaders that presupposes a truly liberal education. There would, of course, have to be some work in school-specific areas and organizational theory, and significant practical internships. However, the core education for leaders in tomorrow's schools would consist of a thorough grounding in the knowledge most worth knowing in our society and in the skills and propensity to critically reevaluate what is most worth knowing. Educational leaders must not only know what to do and how to do it and have the skills to be able to do it, they must cultivate the ability to recognize in a variety of contexts what they ought to do. In short, educational leaders will be leaders because they have acquired the wisdom to exercise good professional judgment.

REFERENCES

Association of American Colleges. (1985). *Integrity in the college curriculum: A report to the college community.* Washington, DC: Association of American Colleges.

Bereiter, C., & Scardamalia, M. (1987). Knowledge telling and knowledge transformations in written composition. In S. Rosenberg (Ed.), *Advances in applied psycholinguistics: Vol. 2. Reading, writing and language learning.* Cambridge: Cambridge University Press, 142–175.

Borasi, R. (1986). *On the educational roles of mathematical errors: Beyond diagnosis and remediation.* Unpublished doctoral dissertation, State University of New York at Buffalo.

Brown, A. (1988) *Interactive learning environments.* Paper prepared for Tomorrow's Schools Project. East Lansing, MI: Holmes Group.

Carnegie Forum on Education and the Economy. (1986). *Teachers for the 21st century.* New York: Author.

Coleman, J., & Hoffer, T. (1987). *Public and private high schools: The impact of communities.* New York: Basic Books.

Giroux, H., & McLaren, P. (1986). Teacher education and the politics of engagement: The case for democratic schooling. *Harvard Educational Review, 56*(3), 213–238.

Goodlad, J. (1984). *A place called school.* New York: McGraw-Hill.

Griffiths, D. (1988). *Educational administration: Reform PDQ or RIP.* A UCEA Occasional Paper. Tempe, AZ: University Council for Educational Administration.

Haney, W., Madaus, G., & Kreitzer, A. (1987). Charms talismanic: Testing teachers for the improvement of American education. *Review of Research in Education, 14.*

Holmes Group. (1986). *Tomorrow's teachers: A report of the Holmes Group.* East Lansing, MI: Author.

Koretz, D. (1988). Arriving in Lake Wobegon: Are standardized tests exaggerating achievement and distorting instruction? *American Educator, 12*(2); 8–15, 46–52.

National Commission on Excellence in Education. (1983). *A nation at risk: Imperative for educational reform.* Washington, DC: U.S. Government Printing Office.

Ogbu, J. (1988). Class stratification, racist stratification, and schooling. In L. Weis, (ed), *Class, race, and gender in American education* (pp. 163–182.) Albany: SUNY Press.

Petrie, H. (1981). *The dilemma of enquiry and learning.* Chicago: University of Chicago.

Schön, D. (1987). *Educating the reflective practitioner.* San Francisco: Jossey-Bass.

Shulman, L. (1987a). Assessment for teaching: an initiative for the profession. *Phi Delta Kappan, 69*(1): 38–44.

Shulman, L. (1987b). Knowledge and teaching: foundations of the new reform. *Harvard Educational Review, 57*(1); 1–22.

Sizer, T.R. (1984). *Horace's compromise: The dilemma of the American high school.* Boston: Houghton Mifflin.

Study Group on the Conditions of Excellence in American Higher Education. (1984). *Investment in learning: Realizing the potential of American higher education.* Washington: National Institute of Education.

University Council for Educational Administration. (1987). *Leaders for America's schools: The Report of the National Commission on Excellence in Educational Administration.* Tempe, AZ: Author.

CHAPTER 3

Reflections on the Third Wave of Reform: Rethinking Administrator Preparation

Stephen L. Jacobson
State University of New York at Buffalo

Just as the currents and tensions created by *A Nation at Risk* (National Commission on Excellence in Education [NCEE] 1983) and the other major reports of the first wave of educational reform were instrumental in producing the second wave of reform, so too did the issues generated by *Tomorrow's Teachers* (Holmes Group, 1986) and *Teachers for the 21st Century* (Carnegie Forum, 1986) provide the impetus for a third wave: the reform of administrator preparation. The Holmes and Carnegie reports gave scant attention to the role of the administrator in their respective visions of a restructured teaching profession, but when they did, as Griffiths (1988a) notes, they made it exceedingly clear that the present order of things had to change:

> The existing structure of schools, the current working conditions of teachers, and the current division of authority between administrators and teachers are all seriously out of step with the requirements of the new profession. (Holmes, 1986, p. 67, cited in Griffiths, 1988a, p. 7)

> *In such schools, the teachers might hire the administrators, rather than the other way around.* (Carnegie, 1986, p. 61, cited in Griffiths, 1988a, p. 7) (Emphasis added.)

This last provision, which Griffiths (1988a, p. 7) has called "Al Shanker's pet idea," perhaps best exemplifies the extent to which reformers of the second wave would alter traditional administrator/teacher roles. Not surprisingly, opposition to the implementation of changes that might hasten the reconfiguration of traditional job roles has come primarily from principals' unions. Maeroff (1988, p. 84), for example, reports that the Council of Supervisors and Administrators in New York City filed a grievance against the city's teachers' union in order to block lead teachers from being allowed to train new teachers, and in Rochester the principals' union actually sued both the district and its teachers' union in a failed attempt to prevent a mentor teacher program. In both cases, representatives of the districts' administrators were acting to preserve what they perceived as their membership's traditional and rightful roles and to prevent the usurpation of those roles by "empowered" teachers. As Ted Elsberg (1986) president of New York City's principals' union argued, "We already have master teachers working with those entering the system, they are the principals, assistant principals and other supervisors who have the preparation, the training, the experience, and the licenses for the job" (Maeroff, 1988, p. 84).

Unfortunately, not everyone, many administrators included, appears to be as confident about the level of requisite skills that Elsberg suggests administrators bring with them to the job. Of particular concern is the adequacy of the graduate preparation and training that most administrators receive. In a nationwide survey of district- and building-level school executives conducted by the University of Buffalo (UB) and reported in *The Executive Educator* (Heller, Conway, & Jacobson, 1988), 51 percent of 1,123 respondents rated their graduate training as either fair or poor, with training in the areas of school finance and community relations receiving especially poor grades from all levels of administrators. Almost half of those sampled (46 percent) believed that the current requirements of graduate preparation programs are not sufficiently rigorous to meet the demands of educational leadership. As a result, fewer than 10 percent (6.6 percent) viewed their graduate school preparation as the most beneficial training for their current job. Instead, on-the-job training was rated as the most significant element in administrator preparation by a majority (60.5 percent) of the respondents. In fact, 90 percent of the respondents identified a practicing school administrator as their primary mentor, whereas professors of educational administration and their theory-based approach to preparation were more commonly singled out for criticism in the respondents' comments (Heller et al., 1988):

> I do not believe the professors at my school of graduate study were well enough prepared to instruct me in the field of educational administration. They had little practical experience.
>
> Too many professors have never worked in a public school. They have no perspective on the problems, let alone the solutions.
>
> Graduate school preparation needs to be more realistic and practical and less theoretical.

> Practitioners should teach these courses, not . . . college professors who
> are not on top of central office problems. (pp. 19–20)

The concerns expressed by these school executives mirror many of the problems in administrator preparation enumerated in *Leaders for America's Schools* (University Council for Educational Administration [UCEA], 1987), the report of the National Commission on Excellence in Educational Administration (NCEEA) that heralded the beginning of the third wave of educational reform.

The purpose of this chapter is to introduce the reader to this most recent wave of reform. The key areas of concern identified in *Leaders for America's Schools* are examined, as well as some of the commission's recommendations for addressing them. To better understand the present state of administrator preparation, the chapter also examines what Culbertson (1988) has called educational administration's "quest for a knowledge base," and how this quest has affected the evolution of training in school administration. I will show that the evolution of the current educational reform movement mirrors in many ways the evolution of educational administration in the university setting and that the present call for reform in administrator preparation is really an attempt to create a more cohesive synthesis between theory-based research and field-based practice.

THE THIRD WAVE: REFORMING
ADMINISTRATOR PREPARATION

In *Leaders for America's Schools* (UCEA, 1987), the NCEEA made explicit the logical connection between its own mission and those of the earlier reform reports,

> The evolution of reforms over the past few years has progressed from cosmetic changes in course requirements to radical restructuring of the school environment. The new roles envisioned for teachers in reports of both the Holmes Group and the Carnegie Task Force on Teaching as a Profession draw education into a broader field of management research from which it has been isolated for too long. At the same time, these reports identify the unique setting of the school workplace, envisioning how teachers could respond to greater autonomy and professionalism. Yet, the reforms cannot be successful without strong, well-reasoned leadership from principals and superintendents. (p. 6)

The NCEEA identified 10 major deficiencies in the present state of administrator preparation (pp. xvi–xvii); deficiencies that need to be corrected immediately if, as Griffiths (1988a) has warned, educational administration is to "reform pretty damn quick or rest in peace." Next follows a listing of these deficiencies and some observations about each:

1. *The lack of a definition of good educational leadership.* "The complete administrator," argues Achilles (1988, p. 41), "knows *what* to do, *how* to do it, and most important of all, *why* an action is appropriate." Achilles contends that: (a) "what administrators do" relates to *administration as a science* and should be the subject of *research and theory-testing*; (b) "how administrators do what they do" relates to *administration as a craft* and should be the subject of *practice and theory-using*; and finally, (c) "*why* administrators do what they do" relates to *administration as an art* and should be the subject of *conceptualization and theory-building.*

   Achilles contends that at present even the best administrator preparation programs unfortunately usually provide no more than two components of this essential trinity.

2. *The lack of leader recruitment programs in the schools.* The route to educational administration is typically determined through self-selection. There is no systematic mechanism through which individuals with the potential for educational leadership are identified, encouraged, and/or financially supported by their school districts or professional organizations to enter into administrator preparation.

3. *The lack of collaboration between school districts and universities.* A perceived schism between field-based practice and theory-based preparation led the NCEEA to recommend greater cross-fertilization between the field and the academy, with superintendents and principals used as professionals on campus, and professors of educational administration keeping their skills up to date by substituting for school administrators on leave.

4. *The discouraging lack of minorities and women in the field.* The NCEEA reported that although the number of women superintendents increased slightly (from 1.7 percent to 3 percent since 1970), the percentage of women principals nationwide actually declined (UCEA, 1987, p. 11). Data from New York's State Education Department are far more encouraging in terms of principalships for women, revealing increases from 20.1 percent to 28.9 percent at the elementary level, 6.7 percent to 13.6 percent at the junior high level, and 6.4 percent to 11.5 percent at the senior high school level in the five years between 1981 and 1986 (State Education Department [SED], 1982, 1987).

   In terms of minority representation, Valverde and Brown (1988) report that between 1974 and 1982 there was an increase in the proportion of minority administrators, with the greatest gains having been made by blacks, Hispanics, and Asians, in that order. Valverde and Brown suggest that a reported increase in the pool of black teachers (Weinberg, 1977) may presage a further increase in the number of minority administrators, particularly in large urban districts. In fact, of those who responded to the *The Executive Educator/UB* 1988 survey, 3 percent of superintendents, 10 percent of high school principals, 13 percent of junior high/middle school principals, and 11 percent of elementary principals identified themselves as members of a minority group (Heller et al., 1988).

Although these figures suggest that the field is becoming more representative of the general population than in the past, the NCEEA's concern for greater female and minority participation in administration cannot be ignored.

5. *The lack of systematic professional development for school administrators.* The report notes that, as part of their certification criteria, few states mandate that educational administrators either upgrade their skills or keep abreast of changes in the field on an ongoing basis. In New York, for example, an individual awarded permanent certification requires no further demonstration of professional competence by the state throughout the duration of his or her administrative career. The potential danger of this laissez-faire approach is brought into focus when one realizes how long administrators typically remain in education. Demographic analyses of the *Executive Educator/UB* survey revealed that 72 percent of the superintendents, 66 percent of the high school principals, and 54 percent of the elementary principals had more than 20 years of service in education. Indeed, 22 percent of the superintendents had been in education for more than 30 years (Heller et al., 1988). What this means in many cases is that administrators who were trained in the 1950s and 1960s are leading our schools into the 1990s, yet the public has no assurance that these administrators have ever upgraded their skills. With this in mind, it is perhaps not surprising that the NCEEA recommended that, "school administration licenses require renewal, to be granted on the basis of successful performance and continuing professional development under the quality control of the state licensure board" (UCEA, 1987, p. 27).

6. *The lack of quality candidates for preparation programs.* To the extent that scores on the Graduate Record Examination (GRE) provide an accurate reflection of administrative potential, then the report card on candidates for educational administration is alarming. The NCEEA reports that school administrators scored higher only than candidates in home economics, physical education, and social work among a total pool of candidates for 94 careers (UCEA, 1987, p. 10). When one considers that educational administrators come almost exclusively from the ranks of the teacher workforce and that disturbingly low standardized test scores have previously been reported for teachers (NCEE, 1983; Sykes, 1983; Weaver, 1979), then the poor test results of aspiring administra-

tors should come as no surprise. Nevertheless, as Griffiths, Stout, and Forsyth (1988b, p. 290) argue, these low GRE scores signal a potential problem, "Lest some think too much emphasis is placed on the intellectual criterion for educational administrators, they should be reminded that there are no recorded examples of good dumb principals or successful stupid superintendents."

The lack of quality candidates for administrator preparation is only exacerbated by the fact that there are presently 505 programs offering courses in school administration in the United States. As Cooper and Boyd (1988, p. 262) note, "Schools of education depend upon a steady flow of trainees to maintain their programs." As a result, the lack of quality candidates has led many preparation programs to lower their admissions standards. Peterson and Finn (1985, p. 51) contend that, "If entrance requirements exist at all, they are not very competitive and most applicants are accepted." Quite simply, for too many administrator preparation programs, *any body* is better than *no body.*

The NCEEA has recommended, therefore, that universities "prepare fewer—better", and that only those fewer than 200 graduate programs that the NCEEA believes have the "resources and commitment" to provide excellence in administrator preparation be allowed to continue to do so (UCEA, 1987, p. 24).

7. *The lack of preparation programs relevant to the job demands of school administrators.* Criticisms over this issue are legion, coming primarily but not exclusively from practicing administrators (recall, for example, the survey comments reported earlier). Among the professoriat, Pitner (1988) critiqued administrator preparation and identified four key discrepancies between graduate training and the job demands of practice that can be classified as follows:

   i. *Differences in time constraints.* The student of administration is taught to carefully reflect upon solutions to potential problems, whereas the administrator's work day is more often characterized by snap decisions covering a multitude of disjointed issues.

   ii. *Differences in role.* The student of administration functions in a subservient role, whereas the practicing administrator assumes a superordinate position within the organizational hierarchy.

   iii. *Differences in communication.* The student of administration is trained to communicate through the written word, whereas in daily practice the administrator typically depends on face-to-face verbal communications.

   iv. *Differences in affective relationships.* The student of administration functions in an environment in which ideas and rationality are prized and feelings are largely irrelevant, whereas the administrator's world is far more volatile, an environment in which "angry parents, excited students, and aroused employees may combine to overload administrators with emotional barrages" (p. 377).

Bridges (1977) perhaps best summarizes the feelings of many when he concludes that *graduate training may in fact be dysfunctional* in the preparation of school administrators.

8. *The lack of sequence, modern content, and clinical experiences in preparation programs.* Perhaps the most telling criticism of graduate training is the dearth of programs that offer aspiring administrators a well-supervised clinical sequence. Recall that a majority of the respondents in the *Executive Educator/UB* survey rated on-the-job training as the most significant part of their administrative preparation. In fact, more than two-thirds (68.4 percent) of these practicing administrators believed that an administrative internship would be a very useful experience, yet, surprisingly, almost two-thirds (64.7 percent) had never participated in an internship, and of those who had, less than 10 percent (6.7 percent) had served a full year.

9. *The lack of licensure systems that promote excellence.* The commission's concern in this regard is a negative by-product of the "One Best Model" that Cooper and Boyd (1988) suggest the evolution of administrator training has produced. Primarily credit driven, the "One Best Model" approach to administrator certification uses numbers of courses taken as a proxy for knowledge and skills possessed. Instead, the commission recommended, "Standards should be written in terms of skills, knowledge, and attitudes considered desirable for educational administrators, not in numbers of courses. Merely accumulating course credits should not be a 'back door' entrance to school administration" (p. 26).

10. *The lack of a national sense of cooperation in preparing school leaders.* To correct this problem, the NCEEA recommended the creation of a National Policy Board on Educational Administration, a body similar in purpose to the National Board for Professional Teaching Standards proposed by the Carnegie Task Force (Carnegie Forum, 1986), and whose function it would be to:

Monitor the implementation of the Commission's recommendations, conduct periodic national reviews of preparation of educational administrators and professors, encourage the development of high quality programs for preparation of educational administrators, produce white papers on critical national policy issues in education, hold forums for discussions in educational administration, and generally ensure good communication across interest groups about policy concerns (p. 14).

Objections to the Commission's Report

Before examining the evolution of training in school administration and the field's quest for a knowledge base (i.e., the antecedent conditions to the Commission's report) it is important first to note that the Commission and its report were not without detractors. Gibboney (1987, p. 28) for one, viewed the report as "deficient and inadequate": "How can it speak seriously about reform when it resurrects and builds on the same trivial courses in management and administration that have been taught for several decades? This is not even old wine in new bottles; it is more like Mississippi river water in tin cans."

Particularly disturbing to others was the Commission's recommendation that those universities "unable to accept the spirit of excellence" described in its report should cease preparing administrators (UCEA, 1987, p. 23). One criterion for excellence established by the Commission was that a university should have no fewer than five full-time faculty engaged in administrator preparation (p. 24). It should be noted that the consortium of universities affiliated with the UCEA, the organization that sponsored the Commission, have a median of eight educational administration faculty members as compared to only four at non-UCEA institutions (McCarthy, 1988). Clearly, UCEA institutions are more apt to meet the Commission's criteria than their non-UCEA counterparts.

Faculty members at smaller institutions, institutions whose administrator preparation programs would be closed if the recommendations of the Commission were implemented, view the UCEA and this report in the same light as they viewed the Holmes Group and its report—that is, as further evidence of a continuing attempt by academe's professional-bureaucratic elite, a group Spring (1988) calls the "knowledge brokers," to consolidate their power:

> Knowledge brokers influence decisions about who receives research support, the types of research that are considered acceptable by the research community, and the types of research that are published in scholarly journals. (p. 18)

> In the mid-1980's, under the leadership of Judith Lanier, dean of the college of education at Michigan State University, the Holmes Group was formed for the purposes of reforming and dominating teacher education. One self-proclaimed objective of the group is to organize the major research universities into a national lobbying group. (p. 18)

The facts that Judith Lanier was also a member of the National Commission on Excellence in Educational Administration and that many UCEA institutions have joined the Holmes Group further fuels the perception of some persons that educational reform is simply an exercise in power politics by the knowledge brokers. Browder (1987), for example, characterizes the recommendations of the Commission as an attempt by UCEA institutions to gain a monopolistic control over administrator preparation.

ADMINISTRATOR TRAINING AND THE QUEST
FOR A KNOWLEDGE BASE

Cooper and Boyd (1988) examined the evolution of administrator training in education and concluded that over the past half-century, a mandatory, state-controlled, university-based, credit-driven, certification-bound "One Best Model" has evolved. Cooper and Boyd contend that "the programmatic content of the One Best Model now rests on an intellectual paradigm borrowed from social psychology, management, and the behavioral sciences," while "the philosophical base of the One Best Model . . . is an abiding belief in empiricism, predictability, and 'scientific' certainty, taught by professors steeped in this approach" (p. 252). But educational administration's programmatic and philosophical grounding in the sciences has not always been the case, as Culbertson (1988) documents in his examination of the field's quest for a knowledge base. Indeed, it has been this quest that has resulted in the six-phase evolution of administrator training described by Cooper and Boyd.

Cooper and Boyd call the first phase the "Philosopher-statesman (or the happy amateur)" phase, a period that spanned the last quarter of the nineteenth century. During this initial phase, administrator training was informal, based primarily on one's experience as a teacher; there were no special degrees or licenses. Culbertson (1988) notes that during this period the scope of inquiry was extremely broad, based primarily on speculative philosophy and practiced by men who valued ideas and pure reason more than data, men who sought to "develop generalizations that educators and managers could apply in practice" (p. 6).

The first quarter of the twentieth century witnessed educators attempting to develop a science of school management that moved administrators "away from philosophizing about the 'essences' of phenomena and toward studying the observable characteristics of phenomena" (Culbertson, 1988, p. 7). The underlying perspective during this period was positivistic, drawing heavily on the tenets of "efficient" scientific management as applied to business. Indeed, the titles Cooper and Boyd apply to the second, third, and fourth phases of administrator training nicely capture the extent to which the "cult of efficiency" reordered the orientation of the field (i.e., the administrator as educational capitalist, as business manager, and as school executive, respectively). It was during this period that formal, university-based, degree-granting programs and state licensing in educational administration began.

During the second quarter of the twentieth century, scholarship in educational administration was broadened by the introduction of concepts drawn from social sciences such as psychology, sociology, anthropology, and political science. Dewey's philosophy of pragmatism was particularly influential at this time, and the focus of inquiry was the study of administrative functions within democratic contexts. This fifth phase in the evolution of administrator training prepared the aspiring administrator to be a social agent whose role it would be to mediate "between classroom learning-teaching and the purpose or function of schools" (Callahan & Button, 1964, p. 91). For the prospective administrator, human relations became as important as scientific management.

But, by the 1950s, many were dissatisfied by the limitations of this pragmatic approach to educational administration and felt that the introduction of logical positivism to the field would facilitate the development of an administrative science. Getzels (1952, p. 235, cited in Culbertson, 1988, p. 15) laid the groundwork for change when he argued, "Systematic research requires the mediation of theory—theory that will give meaning and order to observations already made and that will specify areas where observations still need to be made. It is here that we would place the root of the difficulty in administration: there is a dearth of theory-making."

The subsequent "theory movement" marked a profound transition in both the quest for a knowledge base and the evolution of administrator training: "At last, school administration had evolved into the possibility of academic respectability within the academy, on a rough par with business management and public administration studies" (Cooper & Boyd, 1988, p. 260).

Now the administrator would be prepared as a behavioral scientist (Cooper & Boyd, 1988) who would study what administration is, as opposed to what administration ought to be. Theory would encourage description, explanation, and prediction, as opposed to prescription, which to that point had been more characteristic of administrative research (Culbertson, 1988).

Yet, as each phase sows the seeds of the next, so too over the past twenty years has the logical positivistic underpinnings of the theory movement given way to the more humanistic perspectives of phenomenology and critical theory. Critics, such as Greenfield, Foster, and Bates, ". . . have attacked the root assumptions of the theory movement . . . and turned their backs on it" (Culbertson, 1988, pp. 20–21). Greenfield (1988), for example, argues:

> What the angels of systematic reasoning and administrative science must comprehend is that issues great and small—whether to die for love of one's country, whether to close a school in the face of falling enrollments, whether to stop smoking today—are decided by people who bring all their belief, passion, habit, frailty, or nobility to the choice that faces them. Whatever the choice before them, they are unlikely to make it on the basis of a calculated, fact-driven rationality alone (p. 146).

In his description of this alternative perspective, Foster (1988) writes:

Critical theory, further, unabashedly endorses such values as liberation and equity, and sees the role of the social sciences not just in defining more appropriate control systems for running organizations but, more importantly, in self-reflective activity designed to recognize systems of domination, and, in so doing, to increase the possibility for a truly democratic regime (p. 73).

Culbertson (1988) contends that the holistic approach to inquiry that these authors endorse brings the field full cycle:

In speculative philosophy the "is" and the "ought" were closely connected; thereafter, positivism separated them; pragmatism in turn put them back together; logical positivism subsequently rent them asunder; recently, critical theories have sought once more to reunite them (p. 21).

Nevertheless, the impact of the behavioral science approach to administrator preparation remains, most notably reflected in the "abiding belief in empiricism" of the educational administration professoriat, who for the most part received their own preparation during the halcyon days of the theory movement. As this professoriat struggled to win the respect of others within the academy, they moved further from those in practice. As their research interests became more narrowly focused, their findings became more tangential to the needs of practitioners. As a result of their insulation from the field, the value of the research produced by educational administration's professoriat diminished in importance not only to those in practice but even to those others within the academy they had struggled so hard to impress. Note, for example, Bok's (1987) remarks about the relative contributions of educational research:

Educational research . . . suffers from the fact that it is useful only insofar as it can be applied successfully in real schools and classrooms.

The prevailing view is that scholars have contributed little to improve practice in the schools. (p. 52)

This schism between research and practice is the fundamental cause underlying the present call for administrator preparation programs and the faculties that guide them to reconsider what they are doing and where they are going. Which brings us back to the educational reform movement and, more specifically, to the reform of administrator preparation.

COMING FULL CIRCLE: RETHINKING ADMINISTRATOR PREPARATION

Petrie (in Chapter 2) points out that the reforms of the first wave "essentially asked us to do more of the same, but do it better," whereas the second wave was characterized by "a recognition of the systemic nature of the educational enterprise." It is interesting that in less than a decade the reform movement has mirrored in many ways the evolution of educational administration. The first concerns addressed by both were to increase efficiency and to improve productivity in education, with management practices from business serving as models for schools to emulate (e.g., the hotly debated notion of offering merit pay incentives to teachers).

Just as the proponents of positivistic, scientific management sought to mold educational administration in the image of the business world, reformers of the first wave felt that our schools could search for educational excellence in much the same manner as Peters and Waterman (1982) sought it in the corporate sector. And, just as scientific management evolved into the more pragmatic study of administrative functions within democratic contexts, reformers of the second wave realized that educational excellence would be unattainable without a restructuring of the enterprise itself.

Now reformers of the third wave, having considered the implications of a restructured educational enterprise, are recommending that the "is" and the "ought" of educational administration be once again more closely connected. Theory building and theory testing need not be dismissed from the preparation of administrators. Indeed, aspiring administrators should be encouraged to study the art and science of administration in order to improve the craft of administration. A deeper understanding of what administrators do and why they do it can only improve how administrators do what they do. Therefore, practice must become an equal partner with research in the preparation of educational leaders.

To accomplish this marriage of research and practice, Bok (1987) suggests that schools of education devise a mixed strategy that recognizes both the centrality of research within the university setting and the centrality of school practice within the field of education and that makes schools the centerpiece of educational research while, at the same time, recognizing that focusing exclusively on schools may cause the field to become ". . . too confined and too insulated from other fields of learning that could offer useful insights" (p. 50).

Bok's mixed strategy is obviously not an easy strategy. Nevertheless, changes in the field probably make it the most appropriate way to go. Griffiths (1988b, p. 35), for example, notes that although public schools appear presently to be in the middle of a organizational design continuum postulated by Kanter (1983) to range from "traditional," mechanistic structures to "emerging," organic structures, schools are gradually becoming more organic, emerging organizations. Teacher empowerment, site-based management, shifting political agendas, and the explosion of information and communication technologies (issues to be addressed in subsequent chapters) are key factors that are shaping these emerging organizations, organizations that "require educated, sophisticated career employees who perform complex and intellectual tasks often using electronic and biological technologies in an environment where there is considerable overlap between workers and managers" (Griffiths, 1988b, p. 34).

If implemented, the reforms of the second wave would simply hasten a transition that is already in progress. The challenge of the third wave is to get educational administrators, both in the professoriat and in the field, to study these changing environments and then to develop cooperatively the kinds of programs needed to prepare the individuals who will lead them.

Even without being implemented, the Commission's recommendations will have an important impact if they cause faculty and students within administrator preparation programs to simply reflect on what they are doing and how well they are doing it. Although the professoriat's response to reform will probably not be as demonstrative as that of the school administrators described earlier, some will undoubtedly feel threatened by the implications of these potential changes. Nevertheless, the first swell of this latest wave in educational reform is on us and those of us in educational administration must begin to consider how we intend to respond when this wave crests.

Recall that the purpose of this chapter was to introduce key issues identified in *Leaders for America's Schools*, as well as to enumerate some of the Commission's recommendations for addressing these problems. In addition, the chapter has provided a brief overview of the evolution of training and thought in educational administration. I hope the chapter has raised more questions than it has answered (e.g., How can administrator preparation develop a more successful balance between research and practice? What will be the roles and responsibilities of future administrators? How should leadership be defined? Where will future educational leaders come from?).

In the final section of this book, we attempt to answer these questions, but only after first examining a number of important undercurrents in contemporary education, each of which may have a profound effect on the structure and organization of future American schools. Specifically, the issues of teacher empowerment, school-based management, the changing politics of education, and the effects of electronic technologies are examined. In light of these undercurrents, we will try to develop an appropriate role for university training in the preparation of America's future educational leaders.

REFERENCES

Achilles, C. (1984). Forecast: Stormy weather ahead in educational administration. *Issues in Education, 2,* 127–135.

Achilles, C. (1988). Unlocking some mysteries of administration and administrator preparation: A reflective prospect. In D. Griffiths, R. Stout, & P. Forsyth (Eds.),

Leaders for America's Schools: Final Report and Papers of the National Commission on Excellence in Educational Administration (pp. 41–67). San Francisco: Mc-Cutchan.

Bok, D. (1987, May-June). The challenge to schools of education. *Harvard Magazine,* pp. 47–57, 79–80.

Boyan, N. (Ed.). (1988). *Handbook of research on educational administration.* White Plains, NY: Longman.

Bridges, E. (1977). The nature of leadership. In L. Cunningham, W. Hack, & R. Nystrand (Eds.), *Educational leadership: The developing decades.* San Francisco: McCutchan.

Browder, L. (1987). *A commentary on* Leaders for America's Schools. Paper presented at the National Conference of Professors of Educational Administration, Chadron, NE.

Callahan, R., & Button, H. (1964). Historical change in the role of the man in the organization, 1865-1950. In D. Griffths (Ed.), *Behavioral science and educational administration.* Chicago: University of Chicago Press.

Carnegie Forum on Education and the Economy. (1986). *Teachers for the 21st Century.* New York: Author.

Cooper, B., & Boyd, W. (1988). The evolution of training for school administrators. In D. Griffiths, R. Stout, & P. Forsyth (Eds.), *Leaders for America's schools: Final report and papers of the National Commission on Excellence in Educational Administration* (pp. 284–304). San Francisco: McCutchan.

Culbertson, J. (1988). A century's quest for a knowledge base. In N. Boyan (Ed.), *Handbook of research on educational administration* (pp. 3–26). White Plains, NY: Longman.

Elsberg, T. (1986, December 24). New York "Master Teacher" plan is self-defeating. [Letter to the editor]. *New York Times.*

Foster, W. (1988). Educational administration: A critical appraisal. In D. Griffiths, R. Stout, & P. Forsyth (Eds.), *Leaders for America's schools: Final report and papers of the National Commission on Excellence in Educational Administration* (pp. 68–81). San Francisco: McCutchan.

Getzels, J. (1952). A psycho-sociological framework for the study of educational administration. *Harvard Educational Review, 22*(4), 235–246.

Gibboney, R. (1987, April 15). Education of administrators: "An American Tragedy," *Education Week,* p. 28.

Greenfield, T. (1988). The decline and fall of science in educational administration. In D. Griffiths, R. Stout, & P. Forsyth (Eds.), *Leaders for America's schools: Final report and papers of the National Commission on Excellence in Educational Administration* (pp. 131–159). San Francisco: McCutchan.

Griffiths, D. (1988a). *Educational administration: Reform PDQ or RIP.* A UCEA Occasional Paper. Tempe, AZ: University Council for Educational Administration.

Griffiths, D. (1988b). Administrative theory. In N. Boyan (Ed.), *Handbook of research on educational administration* (pp. 27–51). White Plains: NY: Longman.

Griffiths, D., Stout, R., & Forsyth, P. (Eds.). (1988a). *Leaders for America's schools: Final report and papers of the National Commission on Excellence in Educational Administration.* San Francisco: McCutchan.

Griffiths, D., Stout, R., & Forsyth, P. (Eds.). The preparation of educational administrators. In D. Griffiths, R. Stout, & P. Forsyth (Eds.), *Leaders for America's schools: Final report and papers of the National Commission on Excellence in Educational Administration* (pp. 284–304). San Francisco: McCutchan.

Heller, R., Conway, J., & Jacobson, S. (1988, September). Executive educator survey. *The Executive Educator,* pp. 18–22.

Holmes Group. (1986). *Tomorrow's teachers: A report of the Holmes Group.* East Lansing, MI: Author.

Kanter, R. (1983). *The change masters.* New York: Simon & Schuster.

Maeroff, G. (1988). *The empowerment of teachers: Overcoming the crisis of confidence.* New York: Teachers College Press.

McCarthy, M. (1988). The professoriate in educational administration: A status report. In D. Griffiths, R. Stout, & P. Forsyth (Eds.). *Leaders for America's schools: Final report and papers of the National Commission on Excellence in Educational Administration* (pp. 317–331). San Francisco: McCutchan.

National Commission on Excellence in Education. (1983). *A nation at risk: The imperative for educational reform.* Washington, DC: U.S. Government Printing Office.

Peters, T., & Waterman, R. (1982). *In search of excellence.* New York: Harper & Row.

Peterson, K., & Finn, C. (1985, Spring). Principals, superintendents and the administrator's art. *The Public Interest,* pp. 42–62.

Pitner, N. (1988). School administrator preparation: The state of the art. In D. Griffiths, R. Stout, & P. Forsyth (Eds.). *Leaders for America's schools: Final report and papers of the National Commission on Excellence in Educational Administration* (pp. 367–402). San Francisco: McCutchan.

Spring, J. (1988). *Conflicts of interest.* White Plains, NY: Longman.

State Education Department. (1982). *Public school professional personnel report: New York State 1981–82.* Albany, NY: Author.

State Education Department. (1987). *Public school professional personnel report: New York State 1986–87.* Albany, NY: Author.

Sykes, G. (1983, March). Teacher preparation and the teacher workforce: Problems and prospects for the 80's. *American Education,* pp. 23–30.

University Council for Educational Administration. (1987). *Leaders for America's schools: The report of the National Commission on Excellence in Educational Administration.* Tempe, AZ: Author.

Valverde, L., & Brown, F. (1988). Influences on leadership development among racial and ethnic minorities. In N. Boyan (Ed.), *Handbook of research on educational administration* (pp. 143–157). White Plains, NY: Longman.

Weaver, T. (1979, September). In search of quality: The need for talent in teaching. *Phi Delta Kappan, 61:* 29–46.

Weinberg, M. (1977). *A chance to learn: A history of race and education in the U.S.* New York: Cambridge University Press.

PART II

The Undercurrents of Reform

Part II examines four of the more significant issues in education that function as undercurrents to reform. Specifically, the four chapters that comprise this part examine empowerment and educational authority, the restructuring of school governance, the politics of educational leadership, and the impact of emerging educational technologies.

In Chapter 4, "Power, Empowerment and Educational Authority," David Nyberg offers a philosophical perspective on whether empowerment is an asset or a hindrance to reform. The chapter looks at the concept of power in education and explores its companion notion of empowerment—whether it's the empowerment of teachers, students, or communities—and the potential implications for educational authority and leadership.

In Chapter 5, "Restructuring School Governance," Kofi Lomotey and Austin Swanson examine the findings of the literature on effective schools and consider its implications for urban and rural schools. The effective schools movement has focused almost exclusively on the urban elementary school, and as a result, has left aside the great numbers of urban secondary and rural school districts that make up America's public education system. Yet there are many lessons to be learned from schools that exist at the extremes of this demographic continuum. This chapter redresses that deficiency as it describes alternative levels of educational governance and the importance of decisionmaking at the building level.

In Chapter 6, "The Language of Politics, Education, and the Disadvantaged," Frank Brown examines the broad political structures that educational leaders must confront. All too often the student preparing for educational administration develops a myopic vision of schools and looks only inward at the problems of school management. This chapter shows the need for more global awareness as it examines the tasks of leadership in education as a function of many forces, including state and

45

federal mandates, court-imposed actions, and the context of the community itself. To develop his perspective, Brown focuses on attempts to better educate poor and disadvantaged minority students within our urban educational systems.

In Chapter 7, "The Impact of New Technologies on Schools," Austin Swanson puts into words the apprehensions we have all felt about the current explosion of information and communication technologies. As he elaborates on that concern, he examines one perspective on ways in which these technologies may reshape educational delivery systems and, consequently, the roles, functions and preparation of educational leaders. This is a chapter wherein the reader's dream of education's future may be as valid as the author's. Both alert us to the need for a more reasoned entry into an uncertain future.

CHAPTER 4

Power, Empowerment, and Educational Authority

David A. Nyberg
State University of New York at Buffalo

The purpose of this chapter is to introduce a philosophical perspective on the question whether empowerment of communities, teachers, and/or students is the right course to pursue for the improvement of public education. Another way to put the question is to ask, "Who ought to share authority for public education in a democratic society?" The fact that such questions are raised at all is a matter of concern to those who presently enjoy positions of official administrative status in education because they believe that if others gain in power or authority, then they themselves must necessarily lose in proportion the power and authority they have now. The concern is real, although the belief on which it is based—that for every gain in power there is an equal loss—may be false. Of course, the questions would not have been raised in the first place unless others had serious concern about the wisdom, fairness, and efficacy of the current actual distribution of power and authority in public education. The questioners believe that a shift of empowerment and a redistribution of authority will improve the moral character of education and will solve many practical problems in schools. Again, the reality of the concern cannot be denied, but is the belief that empowerment will necessarily improve the situation correct?

These questions deserve scrutiny by experts in educational administration, teaching, school culture, curriculum, political and organizational theory, psychology, and philosophy of education. My aim for now is a modest one. I shall play the philosopher's role of doubter and hunter—doubter of propositions, hunter of assumptions—in an attempt to achieve a clearer understanding of the concepts, the values, and the issues at stake. Philosophical work of this kind is bound to be somewhat inconclusive, but it can be important for pointing out questions that have not been asked before; for grasping what is believed to be important but is hard to manage; and for seeing flaws in research programs and results.

The chapter begins with a look at the concept of power from several different angles, a synthesis of characteristics common to all the views, followed by an elaboration of a theory of power for education. The second section focuses on the nature and limits of educational authority in democratic society and highlights the special obligations of professional educators. The concluding section fleshes out the psychological, social-political, and instrumental aspects of empowerment both as a means and as a goal in education, and closes with a note about recasting the debate over empowerment (which has been polarized by the antagonistic notions of autonomy and accountability) in the language of cooperation.

THE CONCEPT OF POWER

Bertrand Russell (1938, p. 12) was right in saying that "the fundamental concept in social science is power, in the same sense in which Energy is the fundamental concept in physics." The first point to be drawn from Russell's observation is that we can't understand social life, including our own personal lives, without the concept of power. The second point is that power is morally neutral, like energy. Either can be used by good and bad people for good and bad reasons in producing good and bad results.

Power plays a role in everyone's life, and it clears the air to say so. It is a great hypocrisy not to face this fact, especially if one is an educator with responsibilities for preparing the young to live a decent life in this world. Interest in the study of power is aroused by such questions as, "Why does X respond to these circumstances in *this* way rather than that? Is there someone or something that causes X to respond in this way? Can the cause, if there is one, be controlled? If causing X to respond in this way can be controlled, what are the different ways we can do it? What is the ethical nature of such control?"

Many definitions of power have been proposed in a literature that is too vast to summarize here. By way of introduction to the variety, consider these few examples: Thomas Hobbes (1968 [1651], p. 150), "The Power of a Man, (to take it Universally,) is his present means, to attain some future apparent Good"; Bertrand Russell (1938, p. 35), "Power may be defined as the production of intended effects"; Harold D. Lasswell and Abraham Kaplan (1950, p. 76), "Power is a special case of the exercise of influence: it is the process of affecting policies of others with the help of (actual or threatened) severe deprivations for nonconformity with the policies intended"; Adolph A.

Berle (1969, p. 37) offers five "natural laws" of power: (1) power invariably fills any vacuum in human organization; (2) it is invariably personal; (3) it is always based on a system of ideas; (4) it is exercised through institutions; and (5) it is invariably confronted with a field of responsibility"; Rollo May (1972, p. 99), "Power is the ability to cause or prevent change."

These definitions contain much truth and much potential for contradiction. Here and elsewhere power is variously seen as a personal trait or motive or "drive"; a gift or vision of charismatic leadership for which there is no satisfactory rational account; a curse of institutional corruption and greed. Power is sometimes treated as an end in itself, sometimes as a means to other ends. Its root is seen at times in force alone, or in manipulation, or in the vaguer notion of "influence." Class structure has been credited with the final determination of power, as has the controlled exchange of goods and services at all levels of social life. It has been argued both that power and authority are inextricably related and that the two are categorically separate.

By now I hope to have raised some doubts about what exactly we are referring to when we use the term *power*, or its derivative, *empowerment*. In an attempt to organize the confusion, I'll summarize in general terms three major divisions among power theories and then propose a concept of power meant to be particularly useful in the field of education.

Three Major Views of Power

Steven Lukes (1974) provides an illuminating categorization of competing views of power, subsequently elaborated and applied in field research by John Gaventa (1980), as proof of the categories' utility. The account that follows relies to a great extent on these two works.

The One-dimensional View. The one-dimensional view is essentially that of the pluralists, notably Robert Dahl (1957, 1961, 1968, 1970) and Nelson Polsby (1959, 1963). Dahl wrote (1957, p. 202), "My intuitive idea of power is something like this: *A* has power over *B* to the extent that he can get *B* to do something that *B* would not otherwise do." In a community, then, one studies power by examining "who participates, who gains and loses, and who prevails in decision-making" (Polsby, 1963, p. 55). The emphasis is on the *observable* influence some have over others; the focus is on *behavior* "in the making of *decisions* on *issues* over which there is an observable *conflict* of (subjective) *interests*, seen as express policy preferences, revealed by political participation" (Lukes, 1974, p. 15).

The Two-dimensional View. The limitations of the pluralist view were noted by Bachrach and Baratz (1962, 1963) who presented a more complex view of their own in which power is exercised "not just upon participants within the decision-making process but also towards the exclusion of certain participants and issues altogether" (Gaventa, 1980, p. 9). Bachrach and Baratz (1962) argue that all organizations develop a "mobilization of bias . . . in favor of the exploitation of certain kinds of conflict and the suppression of others. . . . Some issues are organized into politics while others are organized out" (p. 8). Thus the study of power must not be limited to who gets what, when, and how; it must be broadened to include who gets left out, and how. Although the critique is well aimed, Lukes (1974) argues, it is not radical enough. It is still too committed to behaviorism—the study of overt, actual behavior—especially as decisions in situations of conflict. Like the pluralists, the behaviorists' methodology is too individualist in its concern for conscious, deliberate decisionmaking. In this concern, both views follow Max Weber for whom power meant "the probability of individuals realising their wills despite the resistance of others" (Lukes, 1986, p. 20).

In addition, the two-dimensional view still insists on actual conflict as essential to power. Lukes (1974) argues that an effective use of power is to prevent conflict by securing compliance through agreement of desires and beliefs, by preventing people from feeling grievances in the first place.

The Three-dimensional View. Lukes (1974) himself puts forward the three-dimensional view, which has at its center the proposition that "*A* exercises power over *B* when *A* affects *B* in a manner contrary to *B*'s interests" (p. 34). The means for the exercise of such power go well beyond those of the first two views. To summarize: *A* may exercise power over *B* by "influencing, shaping or determining his very wants" (p. 23); "this may happen in the absence of observable conflict, which may have been successfully averted," but it requires "a contradiction between the interests of those exercising power and the *real interests* of those they exclude" (pp. 24–25); and this exercise of power must allow for "consideration of the many ways in which *potential issues* are kept out of politics, whether through the operation of social forces and institutional practices or through individuals' decisions" (p. 24).

By "not restricting power to individuals' actions, the three-dimensional definition allows consideration of the social forces and historical patterns involved in . . . the 'engineering of consent' amongst the subordinate classes" (Gaventa, 1980, p. 13).

At this point one can begin to see the outlines of three views of empowerment that correspond to these three views of power. In the one-dimensional view, empowerment means acquiring the ability to affect public/political debate on issues resulting from conflict of interest (an example might be running for a seat on the school board in a regularly sanctioned election). In the two-dimensional view, empowerment means acquiring the capacity to determine which issues will be highlighted in the public/political arena in the first place, and to influence the way people perceive their own subjective interests in relation to those issues (e.g., using the local newspaper for calling attention to the wide discrepancy between administrators' and teachers' salary scales, then linking this to the superintendent's arguments *for* a school tax increase and *against* hiring new faculty to reduce class size, thereby cornering the superintendent into defending what to the public looks like a conflict of interest). In the three-dimensional view, to become empowered means to raise one's consciousness about how historical, material, and class forces have shaped one's subjective interests, and how in consequence one's real interests have been suppressed. An example is coming to understand, perhaps through selective reading in history and philosophy, the potential for unfairness and injustice inherent in electoral schemes controlled by established institutional hierarchies that inevitably serve their own interests under the guise of freedom and/or equality, then putting this understanding to use in exposing the ways powerholders can control access to information.

The Common Core of Power

These views of power are different in many important ways, and they each have weaknesses that will not be explored here. They are not presented as the full picture of power theory but as a good general categorization of the range of thinking in the field of power studies. Basic to all views of power is bringing about consequences, usually but not necessarily of some significance, by some agent—which could be a person, a class or group, or a system.

Two questions identify and separate power theories in a slightly different way from the way used so far: (1) What is the place of intention in the exercise of power? That is, does it make sense to talk about the "unintended bringing about of consequences" within social systems, by "structural determinants" rather than by individuals or groups, as an exercise of power? Or is this some other kind of influence different from power? (2) Must conflict be present for power to come into play, or can power sometimes exist as a collective, cooperative capacity to realize group aims? If conflict is necessary, then eventually power is measured by determining who wins and who loses; if one gains power it is always at the other's expense. But if conflict is not necessary, then power is at least sometimes measured by determining how well a group, by working together rather than individually, achieves its common goals (Parsons, 1963a, 1963b; Arendt, 1970).

A THEORY OF POWER FOR EDUCATION

In proposing a theory of power for education (Nyberg, 1981a, 1981b, 1982), I have opted for a view that is at once compatible with the principles of democracy (spelled out in the next section) and equally important, one that is teachable. In my view, it makes the best sense to speak of power as a kind of influence that comes about as a result of intended action but that does not require the presence of conflict to come into play. In this way we avoid some of the conceptually befuddling problems of the three-dimensional view. For example, how can one identify the (alleged) mechanism of an exercise of power that may involve inaction (a nonevent), be unconscious, and be exercised by "collectivities" or "systems" as a matter of structural determinism that leaves out any consideration of responsibility? To my way of thinking, finding power is largely a matter of finding responsibility—in the causal sense primarily but in the moral sense, too.

Let us begin with the proposition that *whenever at least two people are related in some way relevant to at least one intended action, power is present as a facet of that relationship.* The minimum necessary conditions of power are two people and one plan for action. (Most of the time more than two people will be involved, and more than one plan will be in effect, which means that power is more complex than I am making it out to be here. I simplify for the sake of initial understanding.) We now can say that whenever a person (group) succeeds in getting others to help, or at least not to interfere with accomplishing a plan, then power is at play. If this much is correct, then it follows that power has three aspects: social, psychological, and instrumental.

The Social Aspect

If we accept the proposition that power is present whenever at least two people are related through a plan for action, and if we accept the further proposition that all individuals inevitably stand in organized relation to (many) others as plans are in fact carried out, then we can begin to see that organization (both formal and informal) is intimately bound to power. Where there is organization, there is power also; where there is power, there is also organization. Power is always social because it always involves two or more people who are related formally or informally to a plan, probably in some kind of hierarchical organization that involves some kind of delegation by the planner.

Hierarchy and delegation are the key characteristics of the social aspect of power. *Hierarchy* is a tendency to organize for leadership in concerted action. Michels (1959) says that this tendency is activated whenever a group exceeds half a dozen or so in number, and he calls it the "iron law of oligarchy." To act in concert requires some number of individuals and separate parts for them to play, and it requires agreement as to plan. In other words, it requires both delegation and consent. The idea of delegation, or division of labor, is the heart of hierarchy, and it is close to the heart of power, too. One who has a plan *and* has others who can help carry it out has power. The effectiveness of delegation depends on a group's acceptance of its leader(s) and consent to the plan, at least as it affects individual obligations, which takes us to the next aspect of power.

The Psychological Aspect

The psychological aspect of power is best understood as having two interactive parts: intention and consent. My first proposition about the nature of power is that it requires a plan for action. A *plan* is an intention plus an idea of how to carry it out. Here I differ with Lukes's three-dimensional view, which allows for influences brought about by structural determinism (the class structure, for example) to count as instances of power. In that view, virtually everything that happens in the world, intended or not, counts as power. Because nothing is excluded, the concept loses all analytic usefulness and logical force. I am happier calling this larger empirical category *unintended* influence, thus keeping it distinct from the better defined category of power as intended influence, while not diminishing the importance of either. This distinction is of interest for education if educators want to teach practical knowledge about power with the aim of doing something about its actual distribution.

Having a plan is one part of the psychological aspect of power; the other part is consent to that plan. The writers of the Declaration of Independence understood the crucial role of consent in government and in the lives of citizens, phrasing the point unforgettably:

> We hold these truths to be self-evident: that all men are created equal; that they are endowed by their Creator with certain inalienable rights; that among these are life, liberty, and the pursuit of happiness. That, to secure these rights, governments are instituted among men, *deriving their just powers from the consent of the governed* [my italics]; that, whenever any form of government becomes destructive of these ends, it is the right of the people to alter or abolish it . . .

The power of a governing order is great, but that power is grounded in majority consent that may be withdrawn, if well enough organized, at any time. In this way, one can argue that the withdrawal of consent is a form of control over power. It is the power over power.

The nature of consent is such that we often give it without thinking much about it. Like Mithradates, who trained himself to tolerate poison by taking small quantities over a long time, those who give their consent to power claimants often do so through a gradual habituation to minor acts of obedience, or "adjustments." This is a kind of self-deception—this passive consent to the way things are—and is perhaps the greatest single enemy of freedom, as well as the tyrant's best friend. His worst enemy then would be education about the nature of power relations and the dynamics of consent and its withdrawal—that is to say, empowerment.

The Instrumental Aspect

Power is a means to other ends; it is not an end in itself. People do not seek power merely in order to have power. They seek it in order to use it for getting something (done) that they value. In fact, power cannot be understood apart from effects and consequences brought about through intentional concerted efforts. People may attempt to exercise power, like Glendower (in *Henry IV*, part 1) who boasts that he can "call spirits from the vasty deep," but they are put in place when, like Hotspur, we reply: "Why so can I, or so can any man; But will they come when you do call for them?"

The Four Forms of Power

Force. In addition to these three aspects of power, we can identify the four forms it can take, or its four basic mechanisms. The first, which is the most obvious and least interesting, the most primitive and least stable, is force. The actual or threatened use of physical harm can be used to extort consent (obedience, in this case) from the otherwise unwilling. Power gained by force is costly and inefficient because unwilling, hostile consent must be maintained under constant surveillance—a situation that requires a large investment of resources. As Milton put it in *Paradise Lost*, "Who overcomes by force, hath overcome but half his foe."

There is a strong cultural tendency in America to equate or identify power with force, perhaps because force is so blatant, so easy to recognize, and relatively easy to understand. Hence, since we don't like force and it frightens us, we don't like power and it frightens us, too. Although force is undeniably a form of power, it is not the only one. There are three others that are much more interesting and relevant to the concerns of educators.

Rhetoric, or Storytelling. In power the central idea is to win consent to a plan. A person who is good at using words to turn ideas into images in the minds of listeners and readers is a person of great potential power. A storyteller is someone who uses words to create a sense of meaning or a frame of reference to use for interpreting events. Stories and storytellers purvey their power by creating ways of thinking about certain plans. The aim is conditional assent; the means is creating a belief in the plan itself. Although it is clear that politicians use this form of power to win elections, raise taxes, and make war, it is less clear—but no less true—that scientists use it to introduce new theories and explanations of the nature of things, be they microphysical quarks or astrophysical blackholes, and metaphysicians tell imaginative stories about quintessences, gods, and devils. Teachers use their own stories, too, in helping students interpret events: the Dark Ages, the Enlightenment, the Cold War, are the names of a few.

As a caution it should be mentioned that lying belongs here, as do other forms of deception, but so do motivation and lofty inspiration. Whether one makes intentionally inaccurate statements or accurate ones, whether one speaks an imagined truth or a proven one, whether one aims at another's vulnerabilities or strengths—in all these cases, if one is trying to enlist the cooperation (belief) of the other person for purposes of accomplishing a plan, then one is using this form of power.

Exchange and Bargaining. This mechanism of power is most easily understood and commonly recognized as an offer of reward for services made within the rules of some pattern of economic exchange. The reward need not be money, but it must always be something valued by the one who performs the service, just as the service must be valued by the one who offers the reward. In short, this form of power involves offering or withholding rewards to people in order to make social conditions more consistent with a particular plan. In power relations of this sort, consent is bought. In education, this form of power can be seen in the assignment of teachers to certain schools, classes, and extra duties, in public recognition for targeted achievements such as high test scores or football scores, and in favored dispositions such as cheerfulness and willingness to volunteer. Teachers themselves use this form of power in the assignment of grades, promotions, honors, recommendations, and the like in exchange for hard work, high achievement, and good behavior. This is the currency of the system. All behavioral modification programs are based in this form of power.

Trust and Mutual Commitment. I have argued that power is present in all social situations in which at least two people are related through a plan for action. The task in such power relations is to secure consent to the plan and cooperation in putting it into effect. Now imagine two (or more) people who have the same plan, who share all information relevant to that plan, and who have achieved a balanced trust with each other. Consent is assumed and needs no enforcement; time, energy, and attention can be concentrated on the tasks required and not dissipated in surveillance management. The kind of organization that achieves these characteristics is very powerful, indeed. As consent approaches complete willingness, based on informed judgment, and invigorated by a personal motivation to accomplish the plan in question, then delegation and consent mingle into a sort of mutual cooperation that requires no vigilance, incentive, or coercion.

The application of this form of power to education would begin with a reconsideration of the ways in which educators (teachers and administrators) learn to work with each other, with students, and with school community members. At present there is too little emphasis on learning how to develop trust, to share information, and to work cooperatively on plans that are genuinely and personally held to be mutual by all involved parties. This is where the question of empowerment becomes a useful focus.

EDUCATIONAL AUTHORITY

The idea of empowerment has as much to do with authority as it does with power. Having had a glimpse at the logic and the mechanisms of power, it is time to look at authority and some of its special characteristics in democratic education in order to get a better grasp of what empowerment means.

What Is Authority?

Like many short questions, this one has a long answer (Krieger, 1973; Lukes, 1978; Watt, 1982). For present purposes, let it suffice to say that authority is a kind of influence that falls between the use of force on the one hand and open rational persuasion on the other. Authority is a term of internal relation; its exercise is a matter of getting people interested (motivated) to do or believe something you want them to do or believe, without having to resort to sanctions or to self-justifying discussions. This is the case in both kinds of authority, commonly distinguished as (1) being "in" authority over some realm of conduct by virtue of one's office; and (2) being "an" authority in some subject by virtue of one's knowledge and achievement. In the end, authoritative utterances (whether commands, such as "Stop talking and take out your books, or assertions, such as "W. Jackson Bates has written the best biography of Keats") are effective only if the person who speaks is respected by the person(s) who listen. When we speak of authority we should say, as Carl Friedrich does (1958): "The communications of a person possessing (authority) exhibit a very particular kind of relationship to reason and reasoning. Such communications, whether opinions or commands, are not demonstrated through rational discourse, but they possess the *potentiality of reasoned elaboration*—they are worthy of acceptance" (p. 35). In a sense, then, one is accepted as authoritative if one is believed to be in possession of the capacity for reasoned elaboration: One is an authority on the think-so of somebody else. We cannot overemphasize the role of expectation in maintaining authority relations. So much of what happens in the world happens because people expect it to happen. People in positions of authority know this—or they should. So should the rest of us.

Authority helps us conceive of the unity of society in two ways. On the one hand, society needs shared, common beliefs, taken on the principle of authority—on trust and without debate; it is the presence of shared values that makes authority possible. On the other hand, it is because individuals in society do not share all, or enough, common beliefs that an authoritative framework of rules that allow individuals to pursue their own ends is needed; it is the absence of shared values that makes authority necessary. In both cases, it may be said that authority is that which makes it possible for people who differ to cooperate (Friedman, 1973).

In a sound organization, power and authority will be kept from drifting too far apart.

Who Should Share Educational Authority?

The answer Plato gave in the *Republic* was that the state, viewed as a kind of family, should have it all. The family state claimed exclusive authority over education, which was seen as "a means of establishing a harmony . . . between individual and social good based on knowledge . . . by teaching all educable children what the (sole) good life is for them and by inculcating in them a desire to pursue the good life above all inferior ones" (Gutmann, 1987, p. 23).

John Locke proposed a radically different answer in the form of a state of families, "which places educational authority exclusively in the hands of parents, thereby permitting parents to predispose their children, through education, to choose a way of life consistent with their familial heritage" (Gutmann, 1987, p. 28).

A third extreme view was argued by John Stuart Mill, along with other liberals who criticize all educational authorities "that threaten to bias the choices of children toward some disputed or controversial ways of life and away from others. Their ideal educational authority is one that maximizes future choice without prejudicing children towards any controversial conception of the good life" (Gutmann, 1987, pp. 33–34).

Amy Gutmann (1987) has proposed a fourth view which sees educational authority in democratic society as a public trust shared by citizens, parents, and educational professionals:

> Unlike a family state, a democratic state recognizes the value of parental education in perpetuating particular conceptions of the good life. Unlike a state of families, a democratic state recognizes the value of professional authority in enabling children to appreciate and to evaluate ways of life other than those favored by their families. Unlike a state of individuals, a democratic state recognizes the value of political education in predisposing children to accept those ways of life that are consistent with sharing

the rights and responsibilities of citizenship in a democratic society. A democratic state is therefore committed to allocating educational authority in such a way as to provide its members with an education adequate to participating in democratic politics, to choosing among (a limited range of) good lives, and to sharing in the several sub-communities, such as families, that impart identity to the lives of its citizens. (p. 42)

In such a trust, with educational authority broadly distributed among citizens, parents, and professional educators, claims to authority will inevitably come into conflict. It is a distinguishing feature of democracy that such conflict is made the basis for public debate, the result of which is better understanding of education and of each other than we would likely achieve if we had taken Kant's advice "to depend entirely upon the judgment of the most enlightened experts" (Kant, 1960, p. 17).

Still, not all conflict over education ends so happily of its own accord. Sometimes conflict needs structured resolution, or guidance, according to principles that are valued and shared by the participants. What might these principles be? Gutmann (1987) answers this question by arguing that the central purpose of democratic education is to teach every educable person the skills and dispositions required for participating in critical deliberation, or what she calls "conscious social reproduction" of democratic forms of life. This constitutes the threshold obligation of democratic society for each person's education. The core activity of public debate on any issues—including those to do with education—is governed by two, and only two, principles. The first is the principle of *nonrepression*, which "prevents the state, and any group within it, from using education to restrict rational deliberation of competing conceptions of the good life and the good society. Because *conscious* social reproduction is the primary ideal of democratic education, communities must be prevented from using education to stifle rational deliberation of competing conceptions of the good life and the good society" (pp. 44–45).

The second principle is *nondiscrimination*. "For democratic education to support conscious *social* reproduction, all educable children must be educated. The effect of discrimination [against racial minorities, girls, and other disfavored groups of children] is often to repress, at least temporarily, the capacity and even the desire of these groups to participate in the processes that structure choice among good lives" (p. 45).

In democratic education, professional educators—both teachers and administrators—have a responsibility to uphold these two principles by cultivating in all students the capacity for rational deliberation and by resisting attempts by the state or by local communities, or by other educators, to exercise their respective authority in a manner that would violate one or both of these principles.

POWER, AUTHORITY, AND EMPOWERMENT

The debate over teacher empowerment has polarized into a debate over autonomy versus accountability. Teachers say they want to take control of their own professional lives; those who now control teachers say they want to hold teachers more accountable for the results of their work. There is a whiff of irony in the conservative voice that calls for stronger teacher authority over students (as a means to greater accountability) but is silent on the issue of teacher authority in the educational institution with regard to curriculum, methods of instruction, testing, hiring and promotion, parents' role in schooling, other links with the community, fiscal priorities, purchasing, and so on.

This situation is not new . . .

> the argument for keeping authority at bay is always substantially the same. We must preserve a minimum area of personal freedom if we are not to 'degrade or deny our nature.' We cannot remain absolutely free, and must give up some of our liberty to preserve the rest. But total self-surrender is self-defeating. What then must the minimum be? That which a [person] cannot give up without offending against the essence of . . . human nature. What is this essence? What are the standards which it entails? This has been, and perhaps always will be, a matter of infinite debate. (Berlin, 1969, p. 126)

Obviously this debate will not be resolved here, but we might be able to change its course a bit by introducing into it a language of empowerment based in an understanding of power and authority that focuses attention on the importance of intention and planning while emphasizing cooperation (concerted action) rather than conflict. Instead of polarizing autonomy and accountability, these two notions should be brought together as complementary attributes of empowerment.

Good teachers make for good schooling. The opportunity and responsibility to shape conditions of teaching make for good teachers. Involvement in decisions about conditions within which they work is at the heart of teachers' power. Decades of research in management, institutional morale, social psychology, and organizational development have left no reasonable doubt that participation in forming the goals and being kept well informed about progress and problems with planned institutional activity often lead to increased commitment, effort, cooperation, and improved attitudes about work among those who do the work. More recently, the Effective Schools research has shown that similar factors contribute to positive school culture and performance. Purkey and Smith (1985) identify thirteen such factors that interact in effective schools:

1. School-site management and democratic decisionmaking.
2. Strong leadership from administrators, teachers, or teams of both.
3. Staff stability.
4. A planned, coordinated curriculum with in-depth study.
5. Schoolwide staff development.
6. Parental involvement and support.
7. Schoolwide recognition of academic success.
8. Maximized active learning time in academic areas.
9. District support for local school efforts.
10. Collaborative planning and collegial relationships.
11. Sense of community.
12. Clear goals and high expectations commonly shared.
13. Order and discipline established through consensus.

It is not difficult to see how teacher, community, and to an extent, student empowerment are crucial contributing factors to the school administrator's dream—an exemplary effective school. To realize this dream, administrators would do well to put aside questions such as, "Who can (adversely) affect the interests of whom if teachers (community, students) are further empowered: who can then *control* whom?" They should ask instead, "In this school, who can secure the achievement of collective goods?" A shift to this question requires believing that conflict is not a necessary precondition for power to come into play, and it requires giving up the related idea that power is necessarily a zero-sum game in which power must be measured by determining who wins and who loses, who gains at whose expense.

Empowerment of Others without Loss

Assisting in the empowerment of others need not imply loss of power for self. Parents surely understand that raising a child is an empowering activity of the first order. Successfully nourishing a child into becoming a confident, capable, autonomous person produces an asset for the family, not a deficit or detraction. Having such a child does not weaken a parent; just the contrary. Everyone gains and no one loses.

Similarly, one can think of teaching itself as an empowering activity that does not imply any loss of power for the teacher. The teacher derives power from being an authority in a subject, by mastering certain knowledge and skills. Knowledge is a resource that is not depleted or impaired when it is applied in service of a goal, or when it is shared—given—to others. Therefore, teachers may teach what knowledge they have, share all they know on a subject, without losing their own knowledge or giving up their claims to subject authority. Students who gain knowledge thereby become to some degree empowered themselves. This is the purpose of teaching. Could it also be considered the purpose of educational administration?

Empowerment for Teachers

Empowerment for teachers is the sum of three factors: psychological, social-political, and instrumental.

The Psychological Factor. If we have learned anything from psychological research about human nature, it is that people need to think well of themselves in order to be happy and mentally healthy. Thinking well of oneself is partially contingent on at least some others thinking well of one, also. Power is derived from the kind of self-respect that comes from being respected and from being a competent and effective person. Authority in teaching depends, as it does in every other activity, on the respect of others.

The Social-Political Factor. Power is derived from holding office as a teacher, from the nature of one's relations with others as they are shaped by that office, from awareness of the social-political environment, and from one's ability to think critically about it. C. Wright Mills (1959) put the point well: "Insofar as such decisions [about arrangements and conditions of work] are made (and insofar as they could be but are not) the problem of who is involved in making them (or not making them) is the basic problem of power" (p. 40).

The Instrumental Factor. Power is derived from one's capacity to extend a positive influence from self to the larger context of other individuals, one's institution, and the community. In teaching, this capacity is based in expert subject authority, as well as in knowledge about teaching (which I suggest includes knowledge about power).

In the field of education now, there is a problem with the nature and distribution of knowledge about teaching (Garrison, 1988). The problem comes from the fact that there are two kinds of knowledge. The first comes from formal scientific research. Teachers are left out of the production and the distribution of this kind of knowledge. The second is the result of informal inquiry and experience, the lore of the craft as produced and shared by practicing teachers. This kind of knowledge often leads teachers to discredit the first kind of knowledge (for example, the image of the "mindless" teacher in Madeline Hunter's program of mastery teaching presently so popular with some boards of education and superintendents; another example, the teacher-proof, "de-skilling" curriculum packages of all sorts). One has to ask who is actually empowered by the first kind of knowledge and the "great ideas for reform" derived from it. Elmore and McLaughlin (1988, p. v) conclude after their survey of the literature of educational reform policies that "educational reform has historically had little effect on teaching and learning in classrooms." The knowledge base of teacher empowerment, it would seem, will not come from formal research. It will come, and this is part of the message of empowerment, from the teachers themselves, who respectfully request that we respectfully listen to them.

THE OBLIGATION AND THE RISK

At bottom, what does empowerment mean? It means to share authority. And this in turn means to provide others with the knowledge and the skills of rational discourse and inquiry needed to gain access to the sources of social goods. It means also to provide help in developing the will and the dispositions (positive self-regard, dignity, initiative) needed to act on such knowledge and skills. This idea is not a luxury for teachers if we wish to cultivate a democratic education for a democratic society—it is an obligation. But it is an obligation with risk.

The risk is that in achieving greater teacher empowerment, which is the key condition in any reasonable plan to strengthen the teaching force in schools, there is a chance that teachers (and to a lesser degree, empowered students) will use their capacity in ways not consistent with administrative-bureaucratic, or larger state interests. To invite improvement in teaching as a profession through empowerment is to accept the risk of transformation in anticipated but unintended ways (Carlson, 1987).

TIT FOR TAT: COOPERATION AS A WINNING STRATEGY

I can't resist a short concluding note taken from Robert Axelrod's fascinating book, *The Evolution of Cooperation* (1984). Axelrod organized a tournament for decision theorists, computer scientists, artificial intelligence experts, and others wherein the point was to solve the Prisoner's Dilemma. This famous philosophical dilemma involves two players and allows for three options: Both players can cooperate and hope for a limited mutual gain; one of the players can exploit the other in hopes of a larger personal gain; or neither cooperates and each takes his chances alone. Of all the solutions offered, it was the simplest one that was the winner. "Tit for Tat won the tournament, not by beating the other player but by eliciting behavior from the other player that allowed both to do well" (p. 112). The strategy was this: Start with cooperation, then do what the other player did on the previous move. In the tournament the players would make several moves over a period, so that one player benefited from the other player's cooperation. The trick was to encourage that cooperation. "Tit for Tat" showed that a good way to encourage cooperation is to make it clear that you will reciprocate (p. 123). This is a much more positive and constructive interpretation of "tit for tat" than the putative sense of "getting even."

The lesson to be drawn from the tournament is that cooperation emerges because our ability to remember and take history into account plays a role in determining *how* we shall meet again, when we know *that* we shall indeed meet again. The great enforcer of power, authority, and cooperation—perhaps morality itself—is the probability, or the need, that we will meet again. Knowledge of the other, plus expectation of further intercourse, transact together to produce cooperation.

Thus, for all concerned parties, cooperation is the most highly recommended practical strategy for achieving empowerment and the benefits for effective schooling that come with it.

REFERENCES

Arendt, H. (1970). *On violence.* New York: Harcourt Brace Jovanovich.

Axelrod, R. (1984). *The evolution of cooperation.* New York: Basic Books.

Bachrach, P., & Baratz, M. (1962). The two faces of power. *American Political Science Review, 56,* 947–952.

Bachrach, P., & Baratz, M. (1963). Decisions and non-decisions: An analytical framework. *American Political Science Review, 57,* 641–651.

Berle, A. (1969). *Power.* New York: Harcourt Brace Jovanovich.

Berlin, I. (1969). *Four essays on liberty.* London: Oxford University Press.

Carlson, D. (1987). Teachers as political actors. *Harvard Educational Review, 57*(3), 283–307.

Dahl, R. (1957). The concept of power. *Behavioral Science, 2,* 201–205.

Dahl, R. (1961). *Who governs? Democracy and power in an American city.* New Haven: Yale University Press.

Dahl, R. (1968). Power. *International Encyclopedia of the Social Sciences, 12,* 405–415.

Dahl, R. (1970). *Modern Political Analysis* (2nd ed.). Englewood Cliffs, NJ: Prentice-Hall.

Elmore, R., & McLaughlin, M. (1988). *Steady work* (Document #R-3574). Washington, DC: Rand Corp.

Friedman, R. (1973). On the concept of authority in political philosophy. In R. Flathman (Ed.), *Concepts in social and political philosophy.* New York: Macmillan.

Friedrich, C. (1958). Authority, reason and discretion. In C. Friedrich (Ed.), *Nomos I: Authority.* Cambridge, MA: Harvard University Press.

Garrison, J. (1988). Democracy, scientific knowledge, and teacher empowerment. *Teachers College Record, 89*(4), 487–504.

Gaventa, J. (1980). *Power and powerlessness: Rebellion and quiescence in an Appalachian valley.* Urbana: University of Illinois Press.

Gutmann, A. (1987). *Democratic education.* Princeton, NJ: Princeton University Press.

Hobbes, T. (1968 [1651]). *Leviathan.* New York: Penguin.

Kant, I. (1960). *Education.* Ann Arbor: University of Michigan Press.

Krieger, L. (1973). Authority. In P. Wiener (Ed.), *Dictionary of the history of ideas,* Vol. 1, 141–162. New York: Scribner.

Lasswell, H., & Kaplan, A. (1950). *Power and society: A framework for political inquiry.* New Haven: Yale University Press.

Lukes, S. (1974). *Power: A radical view.* London: Macmillan.

Lukes, S. (1978). Power and authority. In T. Bottomore & R. Nisbet (Eds.), *A history of sociological analysis.* New York: Basic Books.

Lukes, S. (1986). *Power.* Oxford: Basil Blackwell.

May, R. (1972). *Power and innocence: A search for the sources of violence.* New York: Norton.

Michels, R. (1959). *Political parties: A sociological study of the oligarchical tendencies of modern democracy.* New York: Free Press.

Mills, C. (1959). *The sociological imagination.* New York: Oxford University Press.

Nyberg, D. (1981a). *Power over power: What power means in ordinary life, how it is related to acting freely, and what it can contribute to a renovated ethics of education.* Ithaca: Cornell University Press.

Nyberg, D. (1981b). A concept of power for education. *Teachers College Record, 82*(4), 535-551.

Nyberg, D. (1982). Does education need a concept of power? *New Education, 4*(2), 3-16.

Parsons, T. (1963a). On the concept of influence. *Public Opinion Quarterly, 27,* 37-62.

Parsons, T. (1963b). On the concept of political power. *Proceedings of the American Philosophical Society, 107,* 232-262.

Polsby, N. (1959). The sociology of community power: A reassessment. *Social Forces, 37,* 232-236.

Polsby, N. (1963). *Community power and political theory.* New Haven: Yale University Press.

Purkey, S., & Smith, M. (1983). Effective schools: A review. *Elementary School Journal, 83*(4), 427-452.

Russell, B. (1938). *Power: A new social analysis.* New York: Norton.

Watt, E. (1982). *Authority.* New York: St. Martin's Press.

CHAPTER 5

Restructuring School Governance: Learning from the Experiences of Rural and Urban Schools

Kofi Lomotey and Austin D. Swanson
State University of New York at Buffalo

American schools range in degree of complexity from small rural schools serving the countryside and villages to huge urban schools in central cities of large metropolitan areas. In the middle of the continuum are moderately sized suburban schools.

Suburban schools seem to have relatively few problems with respect to academic achievement, discipline, and teacher quality when compared with their urban and rural counterparts. Thus, the spotlight of educational reform has focused most sharply on urban and rural schools as the weak links in America's educational system. On the surface it would appear that these two categories of schools are the antithesis of one another. In many respects this is true; the problems of one are not necessarily the problems of the other. In fact, many of the strengths of urban schools are weaknesses of rural schools and vice versa. This leads one to wonder whether a comparative analysis might provide useful insights for developing public policies that would help improve the effectiveness of each set of schools. The purpose of this chapter is to compare the characteristics of urban and rural schools, to look at their strengths and weaknesses, and to consider policy alternatives for improving their effectiveness through restructuring school governance. The implications for the practice of school administration are substantial.

Urban schools are in an increasing state of deterioration (National Commission on Excellence in Education, 1983; Lomotey, in press). In speaking of this critical state, the Carnegie Foundation (1988) concluded in their report, "An Imperiled Generation: Saving Urban Schools," that:

America must confront, with urgency, the crisis in urban schools. Bold, aggressive action is needed now to avoid leaving a huge and growing segment of the nation's youth civically unprepared and economically unempowered. This nation must see the urban school crisis for what it is: a major failure of social policy, a piecemeal approach to a problem that requires a unified response. (p. xv)

Rural education also faces serious problems. Curricular offerings are at best limited, and it is difficult to attract well-qualified professionals to work in rural areas. Rural schools are criticized for being too small and too remote from the mainstream of American life to provide a relevant education for those required to attend them. They are viewed as being expensive and inefficient. The malady has been diagnosed as smallness; the dominant policy solution for all of this century has been to consolidate rural schools, casting them in the image of their urban counterparts.

Much of the existing scholarship on rural education is unsophisticated (DeYoung, 1987). In recent years, however, research on rural education has become more refined as it has taken into account total cost and socioeconomic status of pupils and included additional criteria such as achievement, pupil self-image, and success in college. Research into the problems of urban education done during the mid-1960s through the mid-1970s was not very helpful from the perspective of educational policy since it pointed to the family as having the overwhelming influence on a child's success in school and attributed little to the impact of the school itself. The recent effective schools research has been much more useful. It has found some urban schools that have been unusually successful with at-risk children and has concentrated on identifying those characteristics that explain their success (Edmonds, 1979; Lomotey, 1987; Venezsky & Winfield, 1980; Weber, 1971).

RURAL AND URBAN SCHOOLS: AN ASSESSMENT

In this section, the characteristics of typical urban schools, effective urban schools, and rural schools will be studied in juxtaposition. The characteristics of special interest are the nature of the populations served, pupil achievement, school culture, leadership and decisionmaking, and finance. These characteristics will be considered separately at first, followed by a discussion of their interrelationships.

Nature of Pupil Population

On measures of socioeconomic status such as family income and education level, both rural and central city communities score low. In central cities, these populations are highly conspicuous. In rural areas, the poor are dispersed, integrated, and frequently "invisible."

Socioeconomic statistics for 1983 for the United States, for central cities in metropolitan areas over and under 1 million in population, and for nonmetropolitan areas make the point clear (U.S. Commerce Department, 1984a, 1984b). Without exception, nonmetropolitan areas rank below central city and United States medians on averages related to income and education. Central cities in metropolitan areas with more than 1 million in population rank below central cities in smaller metropolitan areas which, except for the percentage of college graduates, rank below United States statistics. Both categories of central cities exceed the national proportion of persons completing four or more years of college. However, central city populations are bimodal owing to the presence of the affluent and the very poor. Since the affluent in central cities often send their children to private schools, the reported statistics probably overstate the wealth and education of parents sending their children to public schools.

Poverty in urban schools tends to be multicultural whereas in rural areas the poor are more likely to be of one ethnic group. Forty-six percent of central city students in public schools are African-American, 23 percent are Hispanic, and 5 percent are Asian-American. More than 100 language groups are represented in urban schools (Council of the Great City Schools, 1987). In contrast, 91 percent of the rural population is white compared with the national average of 85 percent. The percentage of whites for the northern tier of states is even higher because rural African-Americans and Hispanics are concentrated in the South and Southwest. Ninety-one percent of the nation's 6.4 million nonmetropolitan African-Americans live in the South (Fratoe, 1980). Most of the rural Hispanic population live in the five southwestern states (Fratoe, 1981). Poverty in rural areas affects all ethnic groups except that the pockets of poverty are ethnically distinct. The same is true for effective urban schools (unlike many typical urban schools) because they, too, tend to be ethnically homogeneous (Rosenholtz, 1985).

Pupil Achievement

The achievement level of pupils attending urban schools is a critical problem. In a recent National Assessment of Educational Progress (NAEP) survey, 17-year-old urban students scored significantly below the national average. Concurrently, the urban school dropout rate is approaching 50 percent. In the Chicago public schools, a system labeled by some as the worst in America, 13,000 pupils drop out of school each year (Council of the Great City Schools, 1987). Pupil achievement levels in effective urban schools are not as high as those in suburban and rural schools, but they are considerably higher than those achieved in typical urban schools (Lomotey, 1989).

Except for African-Americans and Hispanics, achievement is not as depressed in rural schools and may even be a source of pride because the performance of pupils attending rural schools approximates national and state norms (Coleman, 1986). In New York State, for example, elementary pupils in districts with enrollments under 1,100 pupils (mostly rural) tend to achieve only slightly below the average for suburban districts in reading, writing, and mathematics, and well above all categories of cities and for the state as a whole (New York State Education Department, 1986). At the secondary level, rural achievement levels are similar to those of suburban districts and exceed those of all city categories and state average performance. This is not an aberration of a single year but is consistent over the 20 years that the tests have been given (New York State Education Department, 1967). The better achievement of suburban children can be explained in part by the predominance of upper- and upper-middle-income families in those communities who, research shows, tend to achieve at higher levels. Socioeconomic differences alone cannot explain the achievement gap between rural and urban children, however. Similar evidence on the success of rural schools in terms of pupil achievement has been found elsewhere (Bidwell & Kasarda, 1975; Coleman, 1986; Sher & Tompkins, 1977; Turner & Thrasher, 1970; Ward, 1988).

Not all children fare well in rural schools, however. Fratoe studied the educational status of African-Americans (1980) and Hispanic (1981) children in nonmetropolitan areas. The high school completion rate for these minority populations was not only below the completion rates for whites but also below that for similar groups in metropolitan areas. The functional illiteracy rate for nonmetropolitan African-Americans is nearly three times that of metropolitan African-Americans and five times that of nonmetropolitan whites.

School Culture

School culture is the pattern of beliefs and expectations of the members of the school community that guide their predominant attitudes and behaviors. School culture affects everybody's ability to function cooperatively and productively. Between-school differences in pupil achievement and behavior have been shown to be a function of school culture (Rutter, Maughm, Moritmore, Ouston, & Smith, 1979).

In addressing the issue of the unwholesome culture of many schools, the report of the Carnegie Foundation (1988) observed:

> Overcoming anonymity—creating a setting in which every student is known personally by an adult—is one of the most compelling obligations urban schools confront. Young people who have few constructive relation-

ships with adults need a sense of belonging. They need positive encounters with older people who serve as mentors and role models for both educational and social growth. Building community must be a top priority if students in urban schools are to academically and socially succeed. (p. 24)

Many urban schools lack purpose and coherence. They are "running" rather than "being run." They often have a negative physical appearance. They are characterized by a lack of coherent instructional programs and regular routines (Carnegie Foundation, 1988; Lou Harris and Associates, 1988). Cusick (1983) and others have argued that the high level of ethnic diversity in the student populations of these typical urban schools works against the establishment of consensus on common norms within the school and contributes to their characteristic indiscipline. There is no sense of community. In too many instances, students are unable to establish meaningful relationships with teachers; they are often left on their own to succeed or fail. Furthermore, little or no effort is made to enable students to understand the connection between their schooling and their life outside the school. Many teachers do not believe that inner-city youth can perform adequately. Attitudes and comments of these teachers frequently cause discomfort, fright, and confusion among the students. All these factors contribute to the low level of academic achievement in urban schools.

The Institute for Educational Leadership found many urban teachers who wanted better relations with their students (Lou Harris and Associates, 1988). The teachers claimed their efforts were hampered by disciplinary problems, classes of large size, lack of time for individual interaction, disruptive busing policies, and lack of student participation in extracurricular activities. The study concluded that a productive work environment for teachers includes good physical conditions, a supportive administration, and opportunities to work in collaboration and to influence policy, curriculum, and instruction.

In those urban schools that have been found to be effective in boosting academic achievement, schools are being run. There are order and discipline, a positive physical appearance, a coherent structure to the instructional program and preplanned routines (Venezsky & Winfield, 1980; Weber, 1971). In effective urban schools, there is congruence among school goals, classroom instruction, and test content, and there is regular consultation between principals and teachers to discuss achievement. Instruction is individualized (Jackson, Logsdon, & Taylor, 1983; Lomotey, 1989; Weber, 1971).

The culture of effective urban schools is characterized by a pervading expectation of high academic achievement (Wellisch, Macqueen, Carriere, & Duck, 1978; Jackson et al., 1983; Rist, 1970). Teachers are supportive and task-oriented, zeroing in on academic deficiencies of students. They set challenging, yet attainable, goals, and they encourage all pupils to try harder.

Furthermore, the effects of high expectations are carefully monitored through systematic evaluation of pupil progress (Brookover & Lezotte, 1979; Jackson et al., 1983; Weber, 1971).

Rural schools are characterized by not only a strong sense of community within the school itself but also a strong sense of being a part of the external community and an extension of the family. It is this factor that has been identified as overcoming the many admitted weaknesses of rural schools (Barker & Gump, 1964; Coleman, 1986; Newman, 1981). It is also the fear of losing that sense of community that causes much of the rural population to oppose schemes of school consolidation.

In urban and suburban schools, there is a great emphasis on competitiveness to prepare pupils for survival in the economic and academic institutions of urban environments. In rural areas, most organizations, not only schools, are small and tend to be quite personal, and businesses are frequently family proprietorships. These personal and familial relationships carry over into the schools where there is a culture of acceptance, cooperation, and mutual support (Skelly, 1988). Indeed, many of the innovations of the current educational reform movement, including individualized instruction, peer tutoring, cross-age grouping, and community involvement, have always been practiced in many schools (Barker, 1986).

Coleman (1986) hypothesizes that "district ethos," defined similarly to "culture," may account for the strong and unexpected negative relationship he found between pupil achievement and expenditure per pupil.

> In particular, it [district ethos] seems capable of explaining the unexpectedly strong academic performance of small and rural districts, despite their traditional frugality with public funds. Secondly, it provides a useful linkage between classrooms, schools, and school districts, helping explain relationships known to exist between effective schools and central offices. (pp. 95–96)

Leadership and Decision Making

Leadership in urban schools is in turmoil partly because principals have little control over the curriculum, the hiring of staff, and fiscal matters. Most critical decisions are made at the district level with limited input at the school level. The structure is highly bureaucratic, contributing to many of the problems that arise in these schools. The Carnegie Foundation (1988) report observes:

> Teachers in urban schools . . . have little control over their work. They are three times as likely as their counterparts in non-urban school districts to feel uninvolved in setting goals or selecting books and materials. They are twice as apt to feel they have no control over how classroom time is used or course content selected. (p. 6)

Lack of a sense of control over school matters also extends to parents. The neighborhood or other designated school is the only option for most parents because of regulations, although central-city districts increasingly are permitting parents some choice through open enrollment policies and magnet schools. The typical neighborhood school is viewed by members of its immediate community as a foreign institution, placed there by an external power and having little to do with the neighborhood itself.

Effective urban schools operate within the same bureaucratic structure as do other urban schools, but the principals and teachers, through creative insubordination, have been able to effect meaningful changes and meet the specific needs of their students. Effective urban schools are characterized by strong leadership manifested primarily in principals who have assumed control whether or not they have been granted formal authority. Several researchers (Brookover & Lezotte, 1979; Edmonds, 1979; Lomotey, 1989) have observed that principals of effective urban schools tend to be confident in the ability of their children to learn, committed to seeing that all their pupils receive what is necessary for success, and have a compassion for and understanding of their students and the communities from which they come. The principals of effective schools make an effort to participate in neighborhood affairs and encourage parents to become involved in the education of their children.

Leadership in rural schools has not been studied to any great extent. Given the fact that rural schools are often training grounds for teachers and administrators in small cities and suburbs, professional leadership often has a fleeting quality and tends to be inexperienced. Continuity in program is frequently provided by lay and teaching personnel rather than administrators. When there is only one school in a district, as is frequently the case in rural areas, school-based decision making and school-based budgeting are long-standing traditions. Decision making tends toward the informal, giving consideration to the uniqueness of each case.

The rural school is seen as an integral part of its community by the educating professionals, students, and other community members. School board members in most rural districts are elected and are readily accessible to any member of the community. Because the school is one of the community's primary social and cultural centers, school activities are given extensive coverage in the local media. School athletic teams receive the attention given to professional teams in urban areas. The school band is an essential element in any community celebration. The school play and musical concerts are frequently the only cultural events to take place in the community.

Curriculum and Staff

The curriculum of most urban schools is very diverse, making available to students an extensive selection of courses in a wide variety of disciplines.

This diversity gives the appearance of providing enriched academic experiences not available in rural schools. Without proper guidance, however, the diversity often results in what Powell, Farrar, and Cohen (1985) have referred to as "the shopping mall high school."

Effective elementary urban schools have deliberately limited their curricula, focusing on the basic skills of reading, writing, and arithmetic. The assumption is that, once the foundation is laid, students will be more likely to continue in an academically successful pattern. In focusing on basic skills, these schools also give careful attention to intergrade consistency—that is, a given reading or mathematics program is used throughout the elementary grades, program changes are not made from grade to grade.

The presumed inferiority of small rural schools is rooted in their limited curricula. Even this argument may be overblown, however, particularly at a time when greater emphasis is being given to the development of basic skills. An analysis by Monk (1984) of a random sample of New York State school districts pointed to some differences in curricular offerings and teacher qualifications between large and small districts. Opportunities to study science, especially by students not bound for college, are fewer in small districts, but opportunities to study mathematics and English do not relate to district size. Opportunities to study a foreign language are greater in small districts than in large districts. Despite the availability of courses in science, math and foreign languages, students in small districts are less likely to enroll in them. Opportunities to study advanced courses are virtually nonexistent in small districts.

Monk and Haller (1986) report no significant change in class size or in the number of course offerings as school size increased beyond 400 pupils in grades 9 through 12, but they report, "the curricular offerings of the very smallest secondary schools . . . are seriously deficient" (p. 62). They found that larger schools offer more courses; however, "never did more than 12 percent of the students enroll in courses that are denied to their peers in the smallest high schools" (p. 59). The greater variety of courses offered by large schools tends to be at the introductory level, not at the specialization level. They speculate that this is a means of avoiding small class enrollments. On the basis of their analysis, Monk and Haller question the wisdom of reorganizing school districts for the sake of offering a richer curriculum. In a much earlier study, Barker and Gump (1964) reached similar conclusions. However, although small schools may offer a reasonably broad curriculum, individual students experience difficulty in scheduling desired courses because there is usually only one section of each course available and numerous schedule conflicts. This is not a serious problem in large schools because of multiple sections.

Mathematics, English, and foreign language teachers in small districts tend to have less training and experience than teachers in large districts

(Monk, 1984). There are more first-year teachers in small districts, and teachers are more likely to teach outside their area of certification. Sher and Tompkins (1976) also observed that highly educated teachers are more likely to obtain a position in a consolidated or larger school system than are teachers with less education.

The Council of Great City Schools (1987) points to the staffing problems of urban schools. They report that the shortage of teachers is 2.5 times as great in urban districts as it is for other districts. The shortage is particularly acute for African-American and Hispanic teachers, leaving the increasingly multicultural urban school student population without sufficient culturally similar role models. Moreover, current teachers in these groups report plans to leave the teaching profession at a rate significantly higher than that of white teachers (Lou Harris and Associates, 1988).

Financing

Urban school districts are typically fiscally dependent on city government, making education just one department among many that must compete for funding. In rural areas, school districts are often organized as special units of local government. As such, they may determine their own programs and budgets, and they levy taxes in support of their operations independently of other local governments. The tax levy of such rural school districts is frequently subject to voter approval, however.

Professional salaries in central cities tend to be competitive with most other districts in their metropolitan areas, but working conditions may not be. In addition to school culture considerations, teachers are likely to face very large classes, the only exception being teachers of special education classes. The net result is an overall per-pupil expenditure at about the state average. The state-local financing is supplemented significantly by federal categorical aid programs in central-city school districts.

Professional salaries in rural districts are low by any standard (Ward, 1988). Class size at the elementary level is about the same as for suburban districts, but they are much smaller at the secondary level. Rural districts tend to have very narrow property tax bases, severely constraining their ability to raise money locally and making them highly dependent on state aid for operating revenues. As a result, their per-pupil expenditures are typically well below the average for their state. Although the nature of their pupil populations qualify them for federal categorical aid, it is difficult for them to take advantage of such aid because they do not have specialized staff members to write the proposals.

The discussion of the condition of typical urban schools, effective urban schools, and rural schools is summarized in Table 5.1. The populations served by urban and rural schools tend to be poor; in urban areas, they also

TABLE 5.1. SUMMARY OF COMPARISONS OF TYPICAL URBAN SCHOOLS, EFFECTIVE URBAN SCHOOLS, AND RURAL SCHOOLS

Characteristic	Typical Urban Schools	Effective Urban Schools	Rural Schools
School and District Size	Very large and unwieldy: typically over 1,000	Same as typical urban schools	Small: most high schools > 400: frequently K–12 configuration
Nature of Pupil Population:			
Socioeconomic status of students	Low	Low	Low
Cultural diversity of pupils	Highly heterogeneous and increasing	Poor and minority	Tend to be ethnically homogeneous
Pupil Achievement	Well below national average	Fair; improving; emphasized throughout school	High relative to urban schools
School Culture:			
Achievement expectations	Low	High	Low
Sense of community	No sense of community: unconnectedness between school and life of students	Developing sense of community; nurturing; challenging; compassionate	Nurturing; relaxed (laid back); focal point for student and community activities
Achievement evaluation	Traditional teacher evaluation	Systematic; emphasized by administrators and teachers	Teacher evaluation: report cards
Discipline	Inconsistent and poor; violence; vandalism; disorder	Good; orderly; preplanned routines	Orderly; self-monitored
Leadership and Decision Making:			
Leadership	Poor: limited power	Strong administrators employing creative insubordination	Frequently weak and inexperienced: school boards frequently involved in administrative decisions
Decision making	District level: highly bureaucratic	Same as typical urban schools	School board and administrators

TABLE 5.1. SUMMARY OF COMPARISONS OF TYPICAL URBAN SCHOOLS, EFFECTIVE URBAN SCHOOLS, AND RURAL SCHOOLS (Continued)

Characteristic	Typical Urban Schools	Effective Urban Schools	Rural Schools
Community relations	Very limited; parents feel disenfranchised and no sense of ownership	Somewhat greater than in typical urban schools	Strong; school is center of social and cultural activities
Curriculum and Staff:			
Curriculum	Very diverse; many offerings	Fewer offerings than typical urban schools: emphasis on basic skills	Basic skills: enrichment limited scheduling difficulties
Staff	Fair; poor attitudes; no sense of ownership; moderate and increasing salaries	Fair; good attitudes; greater sense of ownership; salaries same as typical urban schools	Acceptable; many locals; sense of ownership
Financing	Moderate	Moderate	Low

tend to be composed largely of African-Americans and Hispanics. Urban districts are large, as are the schools they operate; governance is formal and impersonal, epitomizing the bureaucratic tradition. Rural school districts tend to be small, frequently operating only one school that serves all grades; governance tends toward the informal and personal with strong community participation. Effective urban schools and rural schools tend to be ethnically homogeneous.

The average achievement of urban children is well below that of suburban and rural norms, but some urban schools are more effective than others. These have developed a nurturing school culture that demonstrates care and respect for the individual and sets high achievement expectations that are carefully monitored. The effective urban school establishes linkages with the community surrounding the school and motivates teachers through involvement and example. Strong professional leadership appears to be key to their success.

Strong professional leadership and high expectations are not typically characteristic of rural schools, but aside from that, there are striking similarities between effective urban schools and rural schools (Jacobson, 1988; Reed, 1985). Rural children tend to achieve at or above state averages in spite of the limitations of their curricula. The relative success of rural schools in terms of pupil achievement has been attributed to their nurturing environment fostered by smallness and community involvement. Rural schools do not typically have a formal monitoring procedure for pupil progress, but because of their smallness, children do not get "lost"; their uniquenesses are well known to teachers and administrators. In rural areas, the prerequisite climate seems to arise naturally out of the rural context; in urban areas, the necessary climate seems to be dependent on professional leadership.

SCHOOL CULTURE, SIZE, AND GOVERNANCE

What size should a school be? Barker and Gump (1964) were not specific, but they provided a useful guide as they concluded their classical work with these words:

> The data of this research and our own educational values tell us that a school should be sufficiently small that all of its students are needed for its enterprises. A school should be small enough that students are not redundant. (p. 202)

Conant's study of the American high school (1959) was more specific. For a school not to be too small, Conant recommended that it have 100 graduates per year. This corresponds with the conclusions of Monk and Haller (1986).

Newman (1981) reports the optimum size of secondary schools to range between 500 and 1,200 pupils. Student participation in school activities and general interaction among them is greatest in that range; vandalism and delinquency are lowest.

> [T]he opportunity that small schools provide for sustained contact among all members is a significant safeguard against alienation. The larger the school, the more difficult it is to achieve clear, consensual goals, to promote student participation in school management, and to create positive personal relations among students and staff. (p. 552)

In his comprehensive national study of *A Place Called School*, Goodlad (1984) observes:

> Most of the schools clustering in the top group of our sample on major characteristics were small, compared with the schools clustering near the bottom. It is not impossible to have a good large school; it is simply more difficult. . . . What are the defensible reasons for operating an elementary school of more than a dozen teachers and 300 boys and girls? I can think of none. (p. 309)

Concerning secondary schools, Goodlad writes:

> Clearly we need sustained, creative efforts designed to show the curricular deficits incurred in very small high schools, the curricular possibilities of larger schools, and the point where increased size suggests no curricular gain. . . . The burden of proof, it appears to me, is on large size. Indeed, I would not want to face the challenge of justifying a senior, let alone a junior, high of more than 500 to 600 students (unless I were willing to place arguments for a strong football team ahead of arguments for a good school, which I am not). (p. 310)

Boyer's (1983) report of the Carnegie Foundation's study, *High School*, notes that research over the past several decades suggests that small schools provide greater opportunity for student participation and greater emotional support than larger ones. Acknowledging the difficulty of knowing the exact point at which a high school becomes too large, he proposes that schools enrolling 1,500 to 2,000 students are good candidates for being reorganized into smaller units using a school within a school concept. Turning to the issue of the small high school, Boyer raises the question:

> Can a small school provide the education opportunities to match the social and emotional advantages that may accompany smallness? We believe the preferred arrangement is to have bigness *and* smallness—a broad education program with supportive social arrangements. (p. 235)

In summary, there is no clear agreement on the optimum size of a school, particularly at the secondary level, and the criteria for optimally sized schools continue to change. Optimum size is a function of desired standards, available technology, and governing structures, but bigness is no longer viewed as a virtue.

The current school reform movement has set significantly higher academic standards. Standards have also changed because of federal and state policies on affirmative action, education of the handicapped, and occupational education. The need to meet these new standards is often cited as a reason for supporting the consolidation of small schools and school districts.

The creation of regional service units lowered the minimum functional size of school districts by making it possible for many small districts to jointly provide specialized programs and services none could provide alone. Intermediate units largely provide occupational education and education of the severely handicapped. They also provide certain administrative, instructional, and technological services (e.g., joint purchasing, mainframe computers, staff development, graphic laboratories, curriculum consultants, and hardware and software support groups).

Developments in educational technology have affected the definition of optimal school size in the past and are likely to continue to do so in the future. For example, the policy of rural school consolidation was viable only after the development of the school bus and paved highways. Realization of the full potential of many emerging technological developments, such as teleconferencing and computerized information systems, will occur only through networking at the regional, state, and national levels. School districts, large or small, can't do it alone, but when the supporting infrastructures are built, optimal school size may be greatly reduced.

For decades, the conflict between the ideal of providing for individual needs and the practice of standardization has plagued the educational community. School district consolidation has assumed that individual needs can be met only by providing an increased number of standardized programs. Studies of size have generally assumed that the variety of programs identified by separate classes truly measures diversity of opportunity for learning. This can be a fallacious assumption. Compare, for example, the one-room schoolhouse to the comprehensive urban high school. In the one-room schoolhouse, one teacher served 30 or more students at different grade levels and taught a variety of subjects. Older children helped younger children, and much learning was done independently. The diversity in program derived simply from the diversity of the children and the flexibility of the teacher. But one cannot say that because one teacher served a group of 30 children that only one program existed.

The comprehensive urban high school, however, assumes that the greater the number of program offerings, the richer the program for the student. Yet, just the opposite may be true. With size comes specialization and more rigidly defined curricula. Teaching becomes compartmentalized into departments and special topics or courses within departments. Once size forces departmentalization and specialization within programs, then organizational constraints do indeed require a greater number of programs to provide enrichment. A large school may offer more pieces of an educational program, but if the pieces are standardized, they may also be fragmented. When education is fragmented, building understanding of a broader picture requires more fragments. In this context, a greater variety of programs might be necessary for quality education, but the availability of a greater variety of pieces by no means guarantees a quality education for individual students.

Both rural and urban schools are finding it difficult to meet the higher standards of the current school reform movement. The bureaucratic nature of urban schools and school districts, derived primarily from their large size, appears to be a major impediment to reform for all but the most stalwart. On the other hand, the smallness of rural schools severely limits their options in providing new curricula. A nurturing school culture and community involvement seem to be achieved more easily in small schools than in large ones; yet, it is easier to provide diversity in large schools than in small ones.

In the past, providing diversity in curriculum and support services at an affordable cost were the primary justifications for large urban schools and rural school consolidation. Now, the disadvantages of bigness and the virtues of smallness have been well documented. Additionally, technological advances characteristic of the information age have made it possible for any individual in almost any place to access curricular diversity easily. These developments combine to impel a reassessment of the large-school policies of central cities and state school consolidation.

Smallness facilitates but does not assure the nurturing school climate desired. Strong leadership with staff and community involvement are also necessary. The single-building rural school district is the epitome of school-based decisionmaking that could serve as a model for urban schools. On the other hand, rural schools are not noted for strong professional leadership, high expectations for their students, and careful monitoring of academic progress. Despite their success in teaching the basic skills to poor white populations, their record with poor African-American and Hispanic populations is abysmal. In these respects, rural schools can learn much from effective urban schools.

All schools require support services that they cannot provide themselves in a cost-effective manner. In rural areas, such services are increasingly being provided through intermediate districts. This trend needs to be greatly accelerated if rural schools are to keep up with modern demands. In enlarging the domain of decisionmaking at the building level and in reducing the domain of decisionmaking at the district level, central-city districts may begin to take on the characteristics of intermediate districts.

In this respect, it is interesting that Illinois has made radical changes in the governance of education in Chicago. By the fall of 1989, much of control of schools would be in the hands of local school councils consisting of six parents, two local residents, and two teachers. Day-to-day authority would be in the hands of principals, who would be selected by the councils. The councils would also have the authority to set the budget and to dismiss incompetent teachers on 45 days notice (Fiske, 1988). We see this as a precursor of things to come.

School building administrators will be responsible for many of the functions formally associated with central offices, such as budgeting, community relations, and personnel selection. Traditional responsibilities of building principals will continue although they may be shared to a greater extent with teachers. Discretion over curriculum and program will increase at the building level. The type of shared decisionmaking envisioned will require a substantially different orientation from the authoritarian, bureaucratic style characteristic of administrators in most urban and many other schools today.

The role of the principal of the future is likely to be cast in terms similar to that of today's rural school superintendent. The role of the big-city superintendent is likely to focus on strategic planning and policy development.

Programs preparing teachers and school administrators will have to adjust their curricula to prepare professionals appropriately for these newly defined roles. Teachers will require some orientation toward traditional administrative concerns such as group decisionmaking and organizational development. Principals will continue to need to be expert in curriculum development, but they will also need a fundamental understanding of school business functions and community relations. Superintendents will have to master skills and concepts related to strategic planning, policymaking, and negotiations, relying heavily on the disciplines of political science and policy studies.

REFERENCES

Barker, B. (1986). *The advantages of small schools.* Las Cruces, NM: New Mexico State University, ERIC Clearinghouse on Rural Education and Small Schools. (ERIC Document Reproduction Service No. ED 265988)

Barker, R., & Gump, P. (1964). *Big school, small school.* Stanford, CA: Stanford University Press.

Bidwell, C., & Kasarda, J. (1975). School district organization and student achievement. *American Sociological Review, 40,* 55-70.

Boyer, E. (1983). *High school: A report on secondary education in America.* New York: Harper & Row.

Brookover, W., & Lezotte, L. (1979). *Changes in school characteristics coincident with changes in student achievement.* East Lansing: Michigan State University, College of Urban Development.

Carnegie Foundation for the Advancement of Teaching. (1988). *An imperiled generation: Saving urban schools.* Princeton, NJ: Princeton University Press.

Coleman, P. (1986). The good school: A critical examination of the adequacy of student achievement and per pupil expenditures as measures of school district effectiveness. *Journal of Education Finance, 12*(1), 71-96.

Conant, J. (1959). *The American high school today.* New York: McGraw-Hill.

Corcoran, T., Walker, L., & White, J. (1988). *Working in urban schools.* Washington, DC: Institute for Educational Leadership.

Council of the Great City Schools (1987). *Challenges to urban education: Results in the making.* Washington, DC: Council of the Great City Schools.

Cusick, P. (1983). *The egalitarian ideal and the American high school: Studies of three schools.* White Plains, NY: Longman.

DeYoung, A. (1987). The status of American rural education research: An integrated review and commentary. *Review of Educational Research, 57*(2), 123-148.

Edmonds, R. (1979). Effective schools for the urban poor. *Educational Leadership, 37,* 15-24.

Fiske, E. (1988, July 20). Chicago braces for a battle over control of the public schools. *New York Times.*

Fratoe, F. (1980). *The education of nonmetro blacks.* Washington, DC: Department of Agriculture, Economics, Statistics, and Cooperatives Service. (ERIC Document Reproduction Service No. ED193399)

Fratoe, F. (1981). *The education of nonmetro Hispanics.* Washington, DC: Department of Agriculture, Economic Research Service, Economic Development Division. (ERIC Document Reproduction Service No. ED207735)

Goodlad, J. (1984). *A place called school: Prospects for the future.* New York: McGraw-Hill.

Jackson, S., Logsdon, D., & Taylor, N. (1983). Instructional leadership behaviors: Differentiating effective from ineffective low-income urban schools. *Urban Education, 18,* 59–70.

Jacobson, S. (1988). Effective superintendents of small, rural school districts. *Journal of Rural and Small Schools, 2* (2), 17–21.

Lomotey, K. (1987). Black principals for black students: Some preliminary observations. *Urban Education, 22* (2), 173–181.

Lomotey, K. (1989). *African-American principals: School leadership and success.* Westport, CT: Greenwood.

Lomotey, K. (in press). Cultural diversity in the urban school: Implications for principals. *National Association of Secondary School Principals Bulletin.*

Lou Harris and Associates, Inc. (1988). *Strengthening the relationship between teachers and students.* New York: Lou Harris and Associates.

Monk, D. (1984). Differences in the curricular offerings of large compared to small school districts. In J. Bail, W. Deming, & D. Monk (Eds.), *Improving the quality of small rural schools.* Ithaca, NY: Cornell University, Department of Education.

Monk, D., & Haller, E. (1986). *Organizational alternatives for small rural schools.* Ithaca, NY: Cornell University, Department of Education.

National Commission on Excellence in Education (1983). *A nation at risk: The imperative for educational reform.* Washington, DC: Government Printing Office.

Newman, F. (1981). Reducing student alienation in high schools: Implications of theory. *Harvard Education Review, 51,* 546–564.

New York State Education Department (1967). *Test results of the 1966 Pupil Evaluation Program in New York State.* Albany, NY: State Education Department.

New York State Education Department, Division of Educational Testing (1986). *State tests and high school graduation reference group summaries, 1985–86 school year.* Albany, NY: State Education Department.

Powell, A., Farrar, E., & Cohen, D. (1985). *The shopping mall high school: Winners and losers in the educational marketplace.* Boston: Houghton Mifflin.

Reed, L. (1985). *An inquiry into the specific school-based practices involving principals that distinguish unusually effective elementary schools from effective elementary schools.* Unpublished doctoral dissertation, State University of New York at Buffalo.

Rist, R. (1970). Student social class and teacher expectations: The self-fulfilling prophecy in ghetto education. *Harvard Educational Review, 40,* 411–451.

Rosenholtz, S. (1985). Effective schools: Interpreting the evidence. *American Journal of Education, 93* (3), 352–388.

Rutter, M., Maugham, B., Moritmore, P., Ouston, J., & Smith, A. (1979). *Fifteen thousand hours.* Cambridge, MA: Harvard University Press.

Sher, J., & Tompkins, R. (1976). The myths of rural school and district consolidation: part I. *Educational Forum, 41,* 95–107.

Sher, J., & Tompkins, R. (1977). The myths of rural school and district consolidation: part II. *Educational Forum, 41,* 137–153.

Skelly, M. (1988). Rural schools at the crossroads. *School and College,* August, 51–56.

Turner, C., & Thrasher, J. (1970). *School size does make a difference.* San Diego, CA: Institute for Educational Management.

U.S. Commerce Department, Bureau of Census (1984a). *Current population reports: Population characteristics,* Series P-20, No. 415, p. 83. Washington, DC: U.S. Government Printing Office.

U.S. Commerce Department, Bureau of Census (1984b). *Current population reports: Consumer income,* Series P-60, No. 145, p. 5. Washington, DC: U.S. Government Printing Office.

Venezsky, R., & Winfield, L. (1980). Schools that succeed beyond expectations in teaching reading. Newark, DE: University of Delaware Studies on Education, Technical Report #1.

Ward, J. (1988). *City schools, rural schools.* Unpublished manuscript. University of Illinois at Urbana-Champaign, College of Education, Champaign, IL.

Weber, G. (1971). *Inner city children can be taught to read: Four successful schools.* Washington, DC: Council for Basic Education.

Wellisch, J., MacQueen, A., Carriere, R., & Duck, G. (1978). School management and organization in successful schools. *Sociology of Education, 51,* 211–226.

CHAPTER 6

The Language of Politics, Education, and the Disadvantaged

Frank Brown
The University of North Carolina at Chapel Hill

Jerome Bruner (1967), a noted educational reformer of the 1950s and 1960s, stated that school people must justify over and over the purpose of education for their own generation. We need change in our educational leadership of elementary and secondary schools if we are to reduce disparities in educational opportunities and outcomes for racial and ethnic minorities in America. That is the central theme of this chapter. Education is, in fact, a handmaiden of our democracy, and as such, it is tightly interwoven with the political fabric.

This chapter calls specifically for a change in the language of those leaders in a position to influence the direction of financial and moral support for public elementary and secondary education. It calls for a new language of discourse on education by public officials and school administrators that is based on the hypothesis proposed by Edelman (1980) that views the political process as being highly symbolic. Political leaders, according to Edelman, use a political language, verbal and nonverbal, that is communicated through symbols to their constituents. Although this symbolic language is frequently used in state and national politics and on most issues of importance to the states and to the nation, education is perceived as being exempt from this political language. There is, however, increasing evidence that political leaders view education as just another item on their agenda and use the most effective symbolic language to improve or not improve education. Leaders who continue to cite the "facts" about education and view education as being exempt from the regular political process will continue to meet with failure in getting the resources necessary to make major improvements in our schools.

This chapter reviews the education of disadvantaged learners and recommends that our leaders adopt a policy that uses the full spectrum of the political process, including the use of verbal and nonverbal symbolism, to gain more support for education. There is no attempt in this chapter to develop the appropriate symbolic (political) language needed by leaders to gain increased support for education.

To understand how to bring about change in our educational system, and more specifically in our educational leadership, we must first take a quick look back in time. Change in a major social institution such as education is never easy, and we are reminded by Hoffer (1963) and Machiavelli (1952) about the difficulty of bringing about such a change. Machiavelli observed such difficulty over 400 years ago and concluded:

> There is nothing more difficult to carry out, nor more doubtful of success, nor more dangerous to handle, than to initiate a new order of things. For the reformer has enemies in all those who profit by the old order, and only lukewarm defenders in all those who would profit by the new order. . . . Thus, it arises that on every opportunity for attacking the reformer, his opponents do so with zeal of partisans; the others only defend him halfheartedly, so that between them he runs a great danger. (p. 49)

Hundreds of years after Machiavelli advised us about the difficulty of change, Burns (1978) stated that political leadership is still necessary to bring about real social change by transformation in attitudes and behaviors in the daily lives of people. In Burns's analysis of leadership, political leadership is separated into several components:

- Transformation leadership that involves intellectual leadership and moral persuasion.
- Reform leadership that involves incremental social change.
- Revolutionary leadership that requires catastrophic change.
- Transactional leadership that involves group leadership such as political party leadership, legislative leadership, and executive leadership.

Varying degrees of these political leadership qualities may be found in each social setting, and therefore specific goals and situations may determine the particular leadership that will dominate in seeking to bring about a particular change.

The political process in America involves so many actors that Summerfield (1974), before beginning his analysis of the impact of the federal government on the formulation of federal educational policy, was informed by members of the federal government that such an analysis would be almost impossible. Summerfield (1974, pp. 3–5) proceeded, however, and defined the process of political leadership at the federal level as a "pattern of events leading to a governmental decision." All change processes differ from one another. Within the same federal system, the process can be relied on to change because the substantive content of decisions changes, and with the change comes a partially new constellation of actors and structures. Furthermore, the process can change remarkably over time on the same substantive area, because many actors, bureaucrats, committees, and individuals hold partial authority over each decision. Fragmentation further characterizes the federal educational policy process because of a separation of powers between the states and the federal government.

In education matters, as opposed to other areas where the federal government is involved, the vision is particularly crucial because the delivery of elementary and secondary education is a function of the state governments. The same complex policymaking process involving education occurs at the state and local levels of government. Because the topic of educational leadership is so broad, it is necessary to limit it and thus facilitate understanding. This discussion will focus exclusively on desired changes in our urban educational systems. Change, it will be understood, is in this case intended as a way to better educate poor and disadvantaged minority students within our society.

THE SHAPING OF THE UNITED STATES

Before we proceed, it would be advisable to look at a little history of the shaping of the United States. This country was settled in the early sixteenth century by groups emigrating from Europe, seeking political and religious freedom. From the beginning, approximately 350 years ago, there were contradictions in the goals of political and religious freedom. Even before the first settlers from Europe had landed in this country, it became known that religious freedom meant freedom from persecution; religious freedom was based on specific religious sects and did not apply to all forms of religion. Political freedom for the first American settlers meant freedom for wealthy landowners, merchants, and the church (Schlesinger, 1983). The original Constitution of this country granted certain rights only to white male landowners; even the right to vote was extended only to white, male landowners. This same Constitution co-existed with slavery and the lack of enfranchisement of free African Americans, women of all racial and ethnic groups, and Native Americans. The American attitude toward equality for all has changed over the past 300-plus years, but those changes have been slow and we are still not providing the children of poor Americans equality of opportunity for a good basic education.

American Education: An Overview

In education, there is evidence that the middle and upper socioeconomic classes are well provided for (Gaines, 1972). Services exist in excellent quantities in elite public *and* private schools that provide quality education to students from these upper socioeconomic groups (Gaines, 1972). These students receive a superior education; their teachers, their facilities, and their curricula are similar. The problem for political educational leadership remains one of securing an equally high-quality education for children from lower socioeconomic backgrounds.

Strong political leadership is necessary to bring about real changes that will result in improving education for children from lower socioeconomic backgrounds. These changes must be made in the attitudes, norms, and behaviors of individuals from the upper socioeconomic groups who hold the power to prevent or to bring about significant changes in the way we educate children from minority racial and white ethnic disadvantaged groups.

Racial and social class prejudice in education against minorities and other economically disadvantaged groups are difficult to ascertain. Most Americans intellectually support the concept of equal educational opportunity, but in reality their behaviors, including financial contributions for the education of disadvantaged minorities, do not support the concept. Racial discrimination in education that results in inequality of educational opportunities appears to be a "clandestine affair" (Allport, 1958, pp. 50–53).

Lewis (1978) and Tesconi and Hurwitz (1974) reviewed the literature on equal educational opportunities and desegregation in the United States and concluded that there still exists a dichotomy between what most Americans say intellectually about equal opportunities and what they are willing to support. This is true of both liberals and conservatives. Political conservatives base their justifications for this differentiated educational system on individual initiatives and consider the environment to be benign, whereas political liberals justify this stratification system on the basis of individual differences. But the results are the same. Children from higher socioeconomic groups are well educated, and most children from lower socioeconomic groups are not.

Research also confirms the close relationship between race, poverty, and educational opportunities (Kain, 1969; Persell, 1977). Some social scientists (Fox-Piven & Cloward, 1971; Lewis, 1978) believe that the American welfare system and other devices used by society are means of regulating and controlling the poor and producing an atmosphere in which the poor exist psychologically with this inequality.

This country was stratified along socioeconomic lines long before blacks were freed from slavery, and much of that stratification continues to this day. Most children, both black and white, from families from the lower end of the spectrum in society do not stray far economically from their beginnings (Thurow, 1980). For black Americans, unemployment has been exactly twice that of whites in every decade since World War II (Thurow, 1980, p. 185), and there is nothing to suggest or predict improvements in the unemployment rates of black Americans in the near future. Comparatively, West Germans enjoy 30 percent less economic inequality than Americans, and the Japanese enjoy 50 percent less economic inequality among all workers than in America (Thurow, 1980, pp. 7–8).

Economically and educationally, blacks (Ogbu, 1978; Persell, 1977), Native Americans (Fuchs & Havighurst, 1973), and Hispanics (Brown, 1976) generally have not enjoyed the same economic and educational opportunities as white Americans. Wilson (1987) refers to the poor among those groups of Americans as a permanent underclass. It will take strong political leadership to convince Americans not in this category to share more of their resources with this group and to change their attitudes toward providing greater opportunities for children from these lower socioeconomic groups. According to Chrisman and Pifer (1987) this country's political leaders have an obligation to provide the leadership necessary to produce a consensus among Americans to help youngsters from this population. It is in our economic best interest to provide children from the lower socioeconomic groups with a good education. As already indicated, however, although Americans have always dealt fairly on an intellectual level with the concept of equality, in practice they are not willing to provide the resources and the commitment to achieve it.

Some social scientists believe that children of racial minorities in this country may represent more of a caste system than a socioeconomic system (Allport, 1958; Ogbu, 1978). Minority children (Allport, 1958; Ogbu, 1978; Myrdal, 1962) quickly learn their caste-like status and adopt social habits in order to survive socially and psychologically. In his study in the late 1940s, Myrdal (1962) suggested that this caste system had a negative impact on the social behavior, aspirations, and expectations of black children. Ogbu (1978), in his study of minorities across different international cultures, drew the same conclusions. The schools complement other societal caste-like barriers in producing minority academic failure (Ogbu, 1978, pp. 40–41). Because minorities perceive their future chances for good jobs and a good education as limited, many are not motivated to persevere in their school work. The perception by minority children that schooling is not related to future job opportunities may be largely unconscious, but it results in a lack of serious attitudes and efforts in school. These caste barriers promote the development of different types of school-related skills among minorities. Other researchers (Bell, 1986; Litwack, 1980; Marden & Meyers, 1968; Weinberg, 1977) have analyzed the relationship of minority group membership and school achievement and have drawn conclusions similar to the one proposed by Ogbu (1978). Although positive changes have been made and are continuing to be made in providing better opportunities for minorities, disparities in educational attainment between minorities and white Americans continue to exist.

EDUCATIONAL POLICY AND POLITICS

When we talk about the educational policymaking process in the United States, we are talking about the federal government and all the agencies within the federal government that have impacts on education, particularly the U.S. Department of Education and the National Science Foundation; we are talking about the President of the United States in the executive branch of government; we are talking about the Congress in the legislative branch; and we are talking about the federal courts in the judicial branch. In state governments we have a corresponding level of offices and agencies influencing educational policymaking. In addition, there are state boards of education and departments of education; below these, education is answerable to local boards of education, mayors, and city councils, to teacher and parent-teacher organizations. In addition, we have professional associations such as the National School Boards Association, the National Education Association, the American Federation of Teachers, the National Association for School Counselors, school administration, vocational programs, and a whole host of other special-interest groups seeking to have an impact on educational decision making.

Other groups likely to influence the educational process are academicians, professional associations, foundations, the programs they support in the name of educational reform, and noneducational entities such as industry and businesses that support educational reform to promote economic growth. All these groups interact on almost every major educational change, whether it is a law passed by the U.S. Congress, by state legislatures, or policy made by local school boards. All these actors are involved in the process. For example, to racially integrate the schools, the process may start with a law enacted by Congress; the courts then determine whether or not local units are violating the law passed by Congress; other groups get involved to have the law repealed or to invalidate an affirmative or negative decision rendered by a state or federal court of law. All these actors are involved in political leadership. *Political leaders are all the people concerned with the policymaking or decisionmaking process.*

Education and Political Leadership from the 1930s

Political leadership has influenced education from the founding of this country to the present. Most states in America began state-supported public elementary and secondary schooling by operating racially segregated schools

(Myrdal, 1962; Ravitch, 1985; Tyack, 1974; Tyack, Lowe, & Hansot, 1984; Weinberg, 1977) both in the North and in the South. The northern and border states ended racially segregated schooling between 1930 and 1960; most southern states ended this practice after 1963. Limiting this study of American education to the period from the 1930s to the present is designed to focus attention on current problems of inequality of opportunity and achievement. Within that time, problems concerning inequality of educational opportunities in this country have existed and have become paramount for the lower socioeconomic classes and members of racial minority groups. It is assumed throughout this chapter that increased opportunities may lead to increased academic achievement by students.

The National Association for the Advancement of Colored People (NAACP) (Kluger, 1975) undertook in the 1930s to deal with racial segregation, primarily in higher education institutions. This in turn led to later efforts to desegregate public elementary and secondary schools through the courts, culminating in the 1954 U.S. Supreme Court decision in *Brown* v. *Board of Education*. Before the *Brown* decision, which declared separate schools in America unconstitutional, the civil rights groups had sought through the courts and won efforts to equalize teacher salaries in both black and white schools, to equalize facilities between black and white schools, and to admit black students to graduate professional programs in white universities in the South. These hard-won decisions by the NAACP set the stage for arguments before the U.S. Supreme Court that segregation of black and white students in elementary and public schools was also unconstitutional. However, education is affected by the three layers of government—federal, state, and local.

The Three Levels of Government

Historically, the federal government's involvement with public schools remained fairly constant until the Great Depression years of the 1930s. It remained constant in that education was largely a state function, and the federal government did little to intervene in the educational process. However, as a result of the economic circumstances in the 1930s, the administration of President Franklin D. Roosevelt, through its New Deal programs, developed ways to assist those on the bottom of society by creating alternative educational agencies to help the underprivileged (Tyack, Lowe, & Hansot, 1984, pp. 104–108). Roosevelt's administration gave some assistance to regular public school programs by paying rural teachers and providing building funds, but the primary effort was in helping the underprivileged. President Roosevelt's New Deal programs included nursery schools for the poor, programs for adult education, and vocational training and work programs, as well as works programs in the arts, theater, music, and other educational programs.

The end of World War II brought an end to these New Deal educational programs, and the country returned to the pre-1930 era until 1954 when another American landmark was established. The U.S. Supreme Court in *Brown* v. *Board of Education* held that separate schooling was unconstitutional and unequal.

After the 1954 *Brown* decision, the federal courts, the federal government, and state governments all became bigger players in the game of educational policymaking. Members of Congress sought to pass laws to overrule the decision of the U.S. Supreme Court, and state governments passed laws designed to overrule or neutralize any future impact of the Supreme Court's decision that declared separate schools by race unconstitutional. Members of both the executive and legislative branches of government at the national level made political moves to appoint new judges to the U.S. Supreme Court who opposed the school desegregation ruling. A decade passed before the political leadership, involving actors at all levels of government, moved in to dismantle segregated school districts in this country and fought to put an end to *de facto* segregated school districts found mainly in the northern states (Kirp, 1982; LaMorte, 1987; Ravitch, 1985; Weinberg, 1977). In the late 1950s and the early 1960s, the federal courts were used to dismantle all *de jure* segregated schooling in the United States for racial minorities (Tyack, 1974), but in our large urban cities, schools were becoming *de facto* segregated and increasingly poor (Cross, 1987; Wilson, 1987).

The 1960s witnessed efforts to equalize educational opportunities by reducing fiscal disparities among school districts (Benson, 1978; Garms, Guthrie, & Pierce, 1978) and by funding special programs for disadvantaged students. The federal government, by passage of the 1964 Civil Rights Act, authorized the Justice Department to seek desegregation through the courts of public schools in the South, which also reduced fiscal inequalities among schools. Over a period of several years, *de jure* segregated school districts were eliminated throughout the country. Concurrent with efforts by the federal government to eliminate *de jure* segregated public schooling, the government enacted, as a part of President Johnson's Great Society program, measures that supported special programs aimed at helping underprivileged children.

The passage in 1965 of the Elementary and Secondary Educational Act sought to reduce educational inequality by providing special funds to support programs for disadvantaged students. The major component of the act was Title I, now relabeled Chapter I, which allocated special funds to educationally disadvantaged students (Brown, 1976). Other titles were designed to assist local educational agencies, state departments of education, and other related agencies. Later in the 1960s, Title VII assisted children whose first language was not English. Great Society programs, which most have termed *compensatory education*, continue to this day, with mixed reviews of success and promise.

In addition to federal help with the education of disadvantaged children, many states are now providing similar aid. However, the most troublesome component of the compensatory education programs involves their allocation formula, which eliminates that portion of a teacher's salary relating to seniority (Brown, 1976). By eliminating that portion, the program fails to reduce fiscal inequality among schools. A second negative component of the program is created by tying compensatory education funding to the test scores of pupils in need of help, which creates a negative incentive for improving the test scores of students. For example, if the test scores of targeted disadvantaged students are increased by services provided by these programs, funding will be correspondingly reduced. Furthermore, there is little evidence that people who are employed in these programs are trying to work their way out of employment. This negative incentive is true for compensatory education programs under Chapter I and for bilingual education programs under Chapter VII.

Political leadership at all levels should be credited with attempts to improve the education of disadvantaged learners. However, one could argue that a rich country like ours should have done more and should be expected to do more to erase disparities between the academic achievement of youngsters from lower socioeconomic status and those from higher socioeconomic backgrounds. Given the continuous stratification in this society by class and caste, most measures generated to eliminate those differences are largely symbolic (Edelman, 1980; Thurow, 1980) and not designed to bring about real changes in the status of the underclass. Cohen and Neufeld (1982, p. 69) state this conclusion about education another way:

> Public schools are one of the few American institutions that try to take equality seriously. In the schools, America seeks to foster equality—an individual American seeks to realize it. But in the market, Americans seek to maintain their economic and social position, thereby contributing to inequality even if they individually wish the reverse.

In reality, for many Americans, education has not served as a means of upward mobility. Most Americans remain close to their socioeconomic origins despite rhetoric about equal opportunities, and most Americans who end up with great financial fortunes get them through luck or the accident of birth (Thurow, 1980) and not because of major changes in our social systems. This use of the political process that pretends to aid disadvantaged populations was somewhat confirmed by U.S. Secretary of Health, Education, and Welfare, Joseph A. Califano, Jr., in describing the goals of education under the presidency of Jimmy Carter. Edelman (1980) refers to this process as the symbolic use of politics. Califano (1981) asserted that President Carter made symbolic use of education for political ammunition for getting reelected, and that the president had no great interest in using education to improve the lot of the disadvantaged. This is not to suggest that President Carter was not concerned about the disadvantaged, but budgeting for education was not at the top of his agenda. This symbolic use of politics was also used in a small way in the view of Daniel P. Moynihan (1970). Moynihan, now a U.S. Senator from New York, was special adviser to President Lyndon Johnson in the efforts to improve the welfare of the poor under Johnson's Great Society programs. President Johnson made strong efforts to improve the life circumstances of the disadvantaged in housing and welfare in hopes that these programs would also help improve the educational chances of children from those homes. However, even with President Johnson's strong support, certain portions of the Great Society program were "symbolic" (Moynihan, 1970), in that these programs were never intended to provide the poor with maximum involvement in solving their poverty status. Analyses of federal educational policymaking by Califano (1981), Summerfield (1974), and Spring (1976) seem to confirm the hypothesis (Edelman, 1980) that leadership is often symbolic.

Most researchers in education for the disadvantaged agree that school desegregation-integration will help students from disadvantaged homes academically and socially (Allport, 1958; Clark, 1963; Coleman, 1987; Lewis, 1978; Ogbu, 1978) and will not harm the academic growth of students from advantaged homes. However, integrated schools do not always produce quality education as defined by increased scores on achievement tests. Therefore, efforts must be continued to provide equal educational opportunity that improves equality of educational outcomes for disadvantaged pupils. However, to promote quality integrated education, it is generally agreed that schools must also have adequate financial and human resources (Benson, 1978; Garms et al., 1978), and schools must not track pupils from disadvantaged backgrounds into inferior academic curricula (Brown, 1976; Levin, 1987; Ogbu, 1978; Ravitch, 1985; Slavin, 1987; Spring, 1976).

Political Leadership and Change for Equal Education

Burns (1978) stated that in order for political leaders to bring about major changes, they must develop and implement strategies that will overcome resistance to the changes. He suggests several such strategies:

> Coercive strategies, normative strategies (achieving compliance by invoking values that have been internalized), utilitarian strategies (control over allocation and deprivation of rewards and punishments), empirical-rational

strategies (rational justification for change), power-coercive strategies (application of moral, economic and political resources to achieve change), and reduced reeducative strategies (exerting influence through feeling and thought). (p. 417)

Coercive strategies are ruled out in modern societies, leaving the other strategies as possible avenues for bringing about major changes in society. Effective leadership is the art of bringing about major changes in our social systems consistent with our needs, norms, and values (Burns, 1978).

The policymaking process within the federal educational establishment may be characterized as one of fragmentation (Summerfield, 1974) and one that is in perpetual conflict (Cross, 1987; Spring, 1976). This was true across several federal administrations beginning in the 1930s and ending with President Reagan's administration; it was also true regardless of whether or not the incumbent in the White House was a Democrat or a Republican.

At the federal level, as we have noted, all government processes are channeled three ways: legislative (the Congress), executive (the President), and judicial (the courts). Congress, the *first component*, assumes an important role in the shaping of educational policies for the disadvantaged. It was Congress during the depression years of the 1930s that supported and promoted the New Deal legislation of President Roosevelt's educational programs. And it was Congress that supported the Great Society's legislation involving public education, of which the most important were compensatory education and bilingual education funneled from the Elementary and Secondary Educational Act of 1965. Over the past two decades, Congress has allocated billions of dollars to support compensatory education for disadvantaged learners. President Johnson was a strong supporter of these measures, but it did not necessarily follow that successive presidents would be strong supporters of funding for compensatory education for disadvantaged learners. For example, Presidents Ford and Reagan did not support these programs at the same levels as did Presidents Johnson and Carter.

Within the House of Representatives, the 435 members are required to reach a collective agreement on a wide variety of bills. Most legislation on education is handled by the Committee on Education and Labor. Within this committee, elementary and secondary education matters are allocated to the Education Subcommittee, the chairperson of which wields an inordinate amount of power in determining what legislation will be considered and eventually passed by the House of Representatives.

In addition to committee work, members of Congress often hold oversight hearings designed to test the implementation of specific education legislation. It is possible for members of Congress to highlight areas of need, thus gaining political power (Summerfield, 1974). Education committees are made up of representatives from both parties, and ideology often plays a role in determining support by congressmen for legislation. Because equal educational opportunities are so important to the black and Hispanic communities, in the House of Representatives those two groups, or caucuses, put extra efforts into education legislation. Special racial interest groups seem not to exist in the U.S. Senate, where there are no black or Hispanic members.

In the United States Senate there are only 100 members who must cover the same legislative territory as the 435 members of the House, and therefore, there is a greater demand on the time and energy of members of the Senate. There are several subcommittees on education in the House of Representatives, but there is only one Subcommittee on Education in the Senate. The Senate Subcommittee on Education also holds hearings, and often only the chairperson of that committee is in attendance (Summerfield, 1974, p. 91–92).

The Senate generally gives little personal attention to education, and much of the work that does take place is performed by staff members. Perhaps this environment exists because there is not an identifiable special interest group in the Senate similar to the black and Hispanic caucuses of the House. In each session of Congress, the House passes a number of education bills, whereas the Senate typically drafts one omnibus bill made up of all the bills passed by the House.

After an education bill is passed by the House and the Senate, it is sent to a conference committee to review differences between the two versions of the bill. Conferees have a responsibility to work out differences between the bills passed by the two bodies and to report out a single agreed-on version that Congress as a whole can approve. The major educational leadership functions of the President and the Secretary of Education (the *second component*) are to set priorities for the administration. In addition, the president has a number of policy-level units under his control, such as the Council of Economic Advisers and the Office of Management and Budget (OMB), which has a small education staff that reviews proposals coming from the Department of Education and issues presidential directives to that department.

In compensatory education, Presidents Johnson, Nixon, Ford, and Carter were considered supporters of compensatory education programs designed to improve the educational opportunities of disadvantaged learners. President Johnson was the strongest supporter of such programs. On the other side, President Reagan and his Secretary of Education, William Bennett (1988) came out in opposition to strong federal involvement in education and promised to eliminate the U.S. Department of Education newly established under President Carter.

The federal judiciary is the *third component* of the federal policymaking system. The federal courts assured racial integration of our public schools, equal salaries of employees within school districts, improved rights for students, teachers, and parents, and improved allocations of educational resources between and within our public schools. In one particular instance (Robbins, 1988), a district federal court ordered the residents of Kansas City to increase the amount of taxes paid in order to improve educational facilities for the public schools. Numerous improvements by school districts for the disadvantaged are directly traceable to decrees issued by federal courts (LaMorte, 1987; McCarthy & Cambron, 1985).

Our fifty states contain more than 16,000 separate school districts. It is difficult to produce a model of political leadership at the state level because of the vast differences among the states—their histories, their racial compositions, their economic capabilities, and their levels of support for education. The state governor, the legislature, and the state department of education play a role at the state level similar to that performed by Congress, the Executive Branch, and the U.S. Department of Education at the federal level. And the state judicial system plays a role similar to that performed by the federal judicial system. Even though education is a state function, in practice the state leaves the administration and governance of education to the many local school districts within the state. For political reasons, state governments rarely intervene in local educational matters, either directly or indirectly. The state takeover of education in certain New Jersey cities is a rare exception.

It is also difficult to generalize about political leadership (Cronin, 1973) because of diversity of statutes regulating local school districts. For example, Cronin (1973, pp. 25–28) finds that in New York City, school board members are appointed by the mayor of the city, funding for education is approved by a separate unit called the Board of Estimate, another separate unit approves school construction funds, and the superintendent is elected by the Board of Education. For teachers to be nominated for positions in the New York City public schools, they must be reviewed by still another separate, independent unit, the Board of Examiners, whose members are appointed for life. Compare this with Detroit, where board members are elected at large by the voters of the district, funds for education are approved by the city council and their Board of Estimates, school construction is approved by the popularly elected Board of Education, the superintendent is elected by the Board of Education, and the superintendent selects teachers to work in the school district. In other cities, the Board of Education may be elected by districts, or subdistricts, funds for the schools are approved by popular vote, and construction for the schools is voted by popular votes through bond issues. Some states have county school districts. In other states there are numerous school districts even within single city boundaries and dozens of districts within one county. And in Hawaii there is one school district for the entire state.

As might be expected with 16,000 separate educational units enjoying varying degrees of freedom, there is great diversion in the provision of an equal educational opportunity for all students, including racial minorities and white members of the underclass. Under the guise of local folklore and local customs, school people have been allowed to discriminate against racial minorities and whites from the underclass in the allocation of teachers to different academic tracks and ability levels according to race and socioeconomic status. In those districts that practice the "neighborhood school" concept, it is often a common practice for school districts to provide superior resources to those schools serving middle- and upper-class children.

All too frequently, we find that merely integrating schools by race and class does not automatically produce equality of educational opportunity. Experience has shown that those blacks, Hispanics, and poor whites who have moved into middle-class neighborhoods have found equal education opportunity as elusive in this setting as in the setting they left. Typically, when blacks and lower-class whites move into a middle-class school, they are tested by the "experts" and immediately placed in lower academic tracks and ability groups. Thus, even though they are all in the same school building with their middle-class counterparts, they rarely come together in an academic classroom. These transferees may see their middle-class classmates only in gym classes, in homeroom, and during the lunch hour. Because they generally leave school heading home in different directions, they are not even apt to ride on the same buses.

Local school boards are not likely to interfere with this academic sorting process (Spring, 1976). Cronin (1973), who reviewed urban school boards, found that local school boards were not likely to change this sorting system of the schools by race and socioeconomic status. Lewis (1978) reviewed the political leadership of a middle-sized school district in the Midwest and found that the school board in this community consisting primarily of whites and blacks was content to allow the schools to serve as a sorting mechanism for properly educating white students and undereducating black students and white students from disadvantaged backgrounds.

Evidence (Persell, 1977; Spring, 1976; Weinberg, 1977) compiled over the past 100 years suggests that the superintendent and the professional staff most often will carry out this implicit inequality of educational opportunity policy as they interpret it to be supported by their local board of education. Employees are generally hired because they believe in the policies of the organization and are willing to implement those policies (Edelman, 1980), and they are encouraged to quit the system when they no longer agree to enforce organizational policies. Edelman (1980) believes that most administrative systems serve as symbols and rituals to legitimate elite objectives and that administrators, not the laws, determine what people get from public agencies.

The professional staff usually justifies its position in this academic sorting system by referring to academic concepts such as individual differences (Ogbu, 1978; Ravitch, 1985). From an ideological perspective, we feel that liberals and conservatives on this issue may be surprised to find that they had both reached the same conclusion—that this sorting mechanism is justifiable. Liberals justify the sorting system on the basis of testing, the concept of individual differences, and the cultural deficit model that victimizes children from poor circumstances. Conservatives typically justify this sorting mechanism on the assumption that minorities are intellectually inferior to whites, and that poor whites, having been victimized by their lower-class status, would thus hold back the academic achievement of those who are not impoverished.

The practice of sorting is pervasive throughout this country, despite years of substantial evidence that heterogeneous grouping by academic achievement does not place a burden on the students of higher academic achievement. (I am assuming that intelligence throughout the population is randomly distributed; therefore, I have consciously used the term *academic achievement* instead of *intelligence*).

This sorting process is further enhanced by the practice of assigning less qualified teachers to teach students in the lower academic tracks and ability levels. You will have noticed that I have not discussed money extensively in analyzing inequality of educational opportunity because most funds in education are used to pay for salaries for teachers, and poor teachers are paid the same salaries as excellent teachers. Thus, salary differences cannot be used to distinguish between students getting a good education within a school building and those getting a poor education within the same school building. I am not comparing school districts, across districts, or even between schools. I am comparing the opportunities for a quality education within an individual school building.

To eliminate inequality of educational opportunities for disadvantaged racial and ethnic minorities and whites, we need strong political leadership at the federal, state, and local levels. Most social scientists who have reviewed political leadership suggest that it is difficult to define a single definitive political style that would be successful for the 50 states, 16,000 school districts, and the myriad of political interests at the federal level and across all issues related to improving equal educational opportunities for all children. Burns (1978) suggests that when power in an organization is decentralized, it is very difficult to collectively bring about real changes in attitudes, values, and norms in people.

Even though governmental leadership is often fragmented and difficult to predict and evaluate from one issue to the next and from one governmental unit to the next (Dror, 1968; Dye, 1978), governmental leadership is still an important avenue for improving educational opportunities for children from disadvantaged backgrounds. I do not agree with Lewis's (1978,

p. 51) hypothesis that advantaged Americans need the poor in America in order to achieve psychological success. Without the poor, Lewis contends, most Americans could not muster the psychic energy to feel good about themselves. Although political leadership may be largely symbolic (Edelman, 1980) with its unique language, this language could be used to improve educational opportunities for the poor in America. Successful leaders must learn to use these political symbols in order to bring about needed changes. Edelman (1980, pp. 11, 13, 172) feels that: "Political analysts must examine how . . . [t]he . . . mass public responds to currently conspicuous political symbols: not to "facts," and not to moral codes embedded in the character of the soul but to the gestures and speeches that make up the drama."

A good leader must be able to communicate with constituents through a common shared language in such a manner that they will follow his or her vision for fairness and equality. For example, information that exceeds an individual's information-processing capacities is useless (Bruner, 1967). If this nation is to carry out its creed of equality and justice for all, then our political leaders must convey to their constituents (in the proper language) that equal educational opportunity is good for everyone. These educational leaders must convince the public that educational opportunities will reduce illiteracy, improve human capital, improve our economic vitality in the world, reduce crime and make our communities healthier and happier places to live, and make democracy work. To achieve these goals, we need political leaders who can provide the symbolic language needed to convince the advantaged members of society that equal education opportunity is in their best interest and the interest of the country.

To produce that needed language, we need social scientists, educators, and public relations people working together to produce a language pool that leaders from diverse situations may use to promote equality. We must produce a language that all major actors in the policy process may use to promote equality. The political process is difficult for many persons fully to understand, even for many of those involved in the process, but they must recognize that the process has worked only for some and not for others. Social scientists and educators have an obligation to inform our leaders about the political language needed to improve the life chances of the underclass. We do not have a national educational system (Spring, 1976, pp. 259-266), but we do have a national goal to reduce educational inequalities, a goal that is justified by the concept of equal educational opportunity. Now we seek to make this goal a reality for all Americans. Our leaders must use the language that brings our educational system closer in line with the concept of equality. Education ought not be exempt from the full political process in seeking scarce resources, and our political language should reflect that reality.

REFERENCES

Allport, G. (1958). *The nature of prejudice.* Garden City, NY: Doubleday.

Bell, D. (1986). *And we are not saved: The elusive quest for racial justice.* New York: Basic Books.

Bennett, W. (1988). *James Madison Elementary School: A curriculum that works.* Washington, DC: U.S. Printing Office.

Benson, C. (1978). *The economics of public education.* Boston: Houghton Mifflin.

Brown, F. (1976). Title I: Is it compensatory or just a partial equalizer? *Emergent Leadership,* 1(1), 10–14.

Bruner, J. (1967). *Toward a theory of instruction.* Cambridge, MA: Harvard University Press.

Burns, J. (1978). *Leadership.* New York: Harper & Row.

Califano, J. (1981). *Governing America: An insider's report from the White House and the Cabinet.* New York: Simon & Schuster.

Chrisman, F., & Pifer, A. (1987). *Government for the people.* New York: Norton.

Clark, K. (1963). *Prejudice and your child.* Boston: Beacon Press.

Cohen, D., & Neufeld, B. (1982, Summer). The failure of high schools and the progress of education. *Daedalus, 110,* 69.

Coleman, D. (1987, August 31). Feeling of inferiority reported common in Black children. *New York Times.*

Cronin, K. (1973). *The control of urban schools.* New York: Free Press.

Cross, T. (1987). *The black power imperative.* New York: Faulkner Books.

Dror, Y. (1968). *Public policy making re-examined.* San Francisco: Chandler.

Dye, T. (1978). *Understanding public policy.* Englewood Cliffs, NJ: Prentice Hall.

Edelman, M. (1980). *The symbolic uses of politics.* Urbana: University of Illinois Press.

Fox-Piven, F., & Cloward, R. (1971). *Regulating the poor.* New York: Vintage Books.

Fuchs, E., & Havighurst, R. (1973). *To live on this earth: American Indian education.* New York: Anchor Press.

Gaines, R. (1972). *The finest education money can buy.* New York: Simon & Schuster.

Garms, W., Guthrie, J., & Pierce, L. (1978). *School finance.* Englewood Cliffs, NJ: Prentice Hall.

Hoffer, E. (1963). *The ordeal of change.* New York: Harper & Row.

Kain, J. (1969). *Race and poverty.* Englewood Cliffs, NJ: Prentice-Hall.

Kirp, D. (1982). *Just schools: The idea of racial equality in American education.* Berkeley: University of California Press.

Kluger, R. (1975). *Simple justice.* New York: Vintage Books.

LaMorte, M. (1987). *School law.* Englewood Cliffs, NJ: Prentice-Hall.

Levin, H. (1987, June). *Towards accelerated schools.* Stanford, CA: Stanford University. Unpublished manuscript.

Lewis, M. (1978). *The culture of inequality.* New York: New American Library.

Litwack, L. (1980). *Been in the storm so long.* New York: Vintage Books.

Machievelli, N. (1952). *The Prince.* New York: Mentor Books.

Marden, C., & Meyer, G. (1968). *Minorities in America* (3rd ed.). New York: Van Nostrand Reinhold.

McCarthy, M., & Cambron, N. (1985). The status of historical research of Chicago education. *Review of Educational Research,* 57(4), 467–480.

Moynihan, D. (1970). *Maximum feasible misunderstanding.* New York: Free Press.

Myrdal, G. (1962). *The American dilemma: The Negro problem and modern democracy* (Vols. 1 & 2). New York: Harper & Row.

Ogbu, J. (1978). *Minority education and caste.* New York: Academic Press.

Persell, C. (1977). *Education and inequality: The roots and results of stratification in America's schools.* New York: Free Press.

Ravitch, D. (1985). *The schools we deserve: Reflections on the educational crisis of our times.* New York: Basic Books.

Robbins, W. (1988, August 20). Tax for school desegregation upheld. *New York Times.*

Schlesinger, Jr., A. (1983). *The almanac of American history.* New York: A Pedigree Book, Putnam Publishing Group.

Slavin, R. (1987). Ability grouping and student achievement in elementary schools: A best-evidence synthesis. *Review of Educational Research, 57*(3), 293–336.

Spring, J. (1976). *The sorting machine.* New York: McKay.

Summerfield, H. (1974). *Power and process.* Berkeley, CA: McCutchan.

Tesconi, C., & Hurwitz, E. (1974). *Education for whom? The question of equal educational opportunity.* New York: Dodd, Mead.

Thurow, L. (1980). *The zero sum society.* New York: Penguin Books.

Tyack, D. (1974). *The one best system: A history of American urban education.* Cambridge, MA: Harvard University Press.

Tyack, D., Lowe, R., & Hansot, E. (1984). *Public schools in hard times: The Great Depression and recent years.* Cambridge, MA: Harvard University Press.

Weinberg, M. (1977). *A chance to learn: A history of race and education in the United States.* Cambridge, England: Cambridge University Press.

Wilson, W. (1987). *The truly disadvantaged: The inner city, the underclass, and public policy.* Chicago: University of Chicago Press.

CHAPTER 7

The Impact of New Technologies on Schools

Austin D. Swanson
State University of New York at Buffalo

Technology is the application of science to control the material environment for human benefit through the use of tools and intellect.* Educational technology is the application of scientific knowledge, including learning theory, to the solution of problems in education. When used prudently, technological advance, by improving productive efficiency, allows society to produce more and better goods and services from a fixed amount of resources. Advances in technology have permitted mankind to live longer and more comfortably, but they have also led to undesirable results, including environmental exploitation and the capacity for total human annihilation.

Education and technology are at the same time cause and effect with each other. Technological developments continually make curricula and instructional methods obsolete. At the same time, an educated populace is essential to the generation and implementation of new technology, and schools are a primary instrument for assimilating new technology into standard practice. Whereas social enterprise in general has tended toward enhanced technological sophistication and increased capital intensity, the education sector has retained a traditional, labor-intensive, craft-oriented technology. Vaizey, Norris, and Sheehan (1972, p. 228) refer to education as "the part of the economy where time has stood still." This "standing still" creates both

---

*The author acknowledges with appreciation the thoughtful criticisms made to earlier drafts of this chapter by Professor Taher Razik, State University of New York at Buffalo. Although the criticisms were influential in shaping subsequent revisions, the author assumes full responsibility for the content of the chapter.

sociological and economic problems. From an economic standpoint, labor-intensive education is unnecessarily expensive, and it does not produce a workforce with prerequisite attitudes and skills applicable to the workplace. From a sociological standpoint, technologically unsophisticated schools are losing their credibility and thereby their effectivenes with pupils because they are no longer congruent with the larger context of society.

This chapter examines the relationships between technological change and education. It begins by focusing on the current global shifts in techno-logical paradigms and the implications for schooling in general. Through considering three questions, the chapter then addresses the specific implications for schools if they are to become fully involved with these shifts:

1. What is the impact of technology on the role of educational systems in preparing individuals for participation in society?
2. What is the impact of technology on the way in which schooling is organized?
3. What is the impact of technology on the methodology of education?

The chapter concludes with a discussion of the politics of educational change and implications for school administrators.

TECHNOLOGICAL CHANGE AND EDUCATION

The view taken in this chapter is that technological change occurs as an interdependent phenomenon with scientific, political, economic, and social change. It is not the primary determinant of social change in a one-way causal manner but, instead, has a mutually causal—or recursive—and di-alectical relationship with other forces (Mesthene, 1981; Boyle, Wheale & Surgess, 1984). Major shifts in technological paradigms occur in periods when there is economic selection from the range of technologically feasi-ble combinations of labor and capital within the context of an interplay of scientific, social, and political factors (Freeman, 1984).

Large-scale changes in technology systems that have a major impact over the entire economy have been referred to by Schumpeter (in Freeman, 1988, p. 100) as "creative gales of destruction" in that they radically modify how things are done in almost every sector and extensively affect the rela-tionships among all factors of production and distribution, as well as social conditions. Toffler (1980) has described the current gale sweeping away the industrial society. He has identified six principles of both the capital-ist and socialist wings of industrial society—standardization, specialization, synchronization, concentration, maximization, and centralization.

These principles in turn, each reinforcing the other, led relentlessly to the rise of bureaucracy. They produced some of the biggest, most rigid, most powerful bureaucratic organizations the world had ever seen, leaving the individual to wander in a Kafka-like world of looming megaorganizations. . . . Today, every one of these fundamental principles is under attack. (pp. 59–60)

Today's schools are products of that industrial era. They are unabashedly called "mass schools" designed to prepare people to live in a mass culture and work in facilities of mass production producing goods for a mass market. The emerging information society appears to be quite different (Masuda, 1981; Naisbitt, 1982; Toffler, 1980), being more decentralized, more personalized, with more networking and fewer hierarchical structures, and with more participation and less delegation.

Technological advances in electronics, communications, and computers are transforming all social institutions. Ironically, among the slowest to adjust are educational institutions. The gap between educational and other social institutions has become so great that pervasive dissatisfaction over schooling as presently constituted has developed. As a result, major reforms can be expected in the near future; many are already underway.

The National Governors' Association (1986) report on education, *Time for Results*, notes:

. . . despite extensive purchase and high expectations, most American schools have not become significantly more cost-effective or more efficient because of technology. The structure of most schools has not changed significantly because technology is available. (p. 123)

A 1987 report by the National School Boards Association (Perelman, 1987) criticizes the school reform movement because it fails to address the issue of increasing efficiency in education. It sees a technological transformation of teaching and learning as being inevitable in the United States and elsewhere in the world.

The term *increasing efficiency* is anathema to many persons in education, teacher and learner alike. But from a policy perspective, it is an inescapable issue. Today, the United States spends over $300 billion a year on formal education, more than 7 percent of its gross national product. It is estimated that another $100 billion is spent each year for corporate and military training (Eurich, 1985). Expenditures for education and training represent one of the largest categories of national public spending. Even after accounting for the effects of inflation, per-pupil expenditures for education at the primary and secondary levels have increased more than 500 percent over the last 50 years (Guthrie, Garms, & Pierce, 1988, pp. 20–21).

The social demand for education continues to mount because the most desirable jobs in modern manufacturing, communications and information industries, and in the professions require high levels of education. Furthermore, the rhetoric of the educational reform movement has linked knowledge and skill resources of the population to the economic well-being of the country and its security in a troubled world. Critics of the status quo call for higher standards, more years of schooling, and better teachers. Given the existing structure of education and a limited amount of total resources, educational improvement means taking from other areas of need that may be equally important and reallocating them to education, a tactic the nation may be unwilling to pursue. The alternative is to restructure the schooling enterprise, integrating human and nonhuman resources into a more efficient educational enterprise.

Traditionally, the education sector has been highly resistant to the integration of technology into its operations. Levin and Meister (1985) comment that educational technologies have been characterized by promise rather than realization of that promise. During this century, the educational potential of new inventions such as radio, motion pictures, television, video cassettes and disks, and now computers has been touted, only to be followed by disappointment as the invention remains ancillary to traditional instructional procedures. Levin and Meister diagnosed the generic failure of educational technologies as being due largely "to a misplaced obsession with the hardware and neglect of software, other resources, and instructional setting that are necessary to successful implementation" (p. 9). They point out that equipment purchase represents only about 10 percent of total costs of an innovation.

To improve the situation, Levin and Meister (1985, p. 38, 43) propose three initiatives: (1) more coordinated market information; (2) improved decision mechanisms in schools; and (3) large-scale institutional approaches to software development and funding. The decision mechanism they propose provides for districtwide coordination of the purchase and installation of technology, integration of software in relation to district curricular objectives and materials, and training of professional and support staff in the use of hardware and software.

Similarly, a 1982 report by the Office of Technology Assessment of the United States Congress pointed to the desirability of integrating technology into the instructional system. After presenting a series of case studies of the use of information technology in education, the report concluded:

> The most important of these observations is that information technologies can be most effectively applied to tasks when they are well integrated in their institutional environments. (p. 9)

This is not the way technology has been used in schools, however. The purpose of technology is to make labor go further by replacing it with mechanical devices and more efficient organization in order to produce a better product or service and/or to reduce the costs of production (Benson, 1961). Yet, even with the increasing availability and sophistication of technological devices in today's schools, pupil-teacher ratios have declined by over 20 percent since 1971, and pupil-adult ratios have dropped even more. Although public school enrollment is currently more than 6 million pupils fewer than in 1970, the number of teachers employed is nearly 1 million more. During the same period, the support staff has increased by 600,000 (National Center for Education Statistics, 1988). Labor-intensive strategies to program improvements have been the norm. The adoption of Public Law 94–142, Education of All Handicapped Children Act, in 1976 may account for part of these increases.

These increases are not a recent phenomenon. In a 1972 study, Vaizey et al. noted that teacher costs accounted for half of all school costs and that unless increases in pupil-teacher ratios took place as a result of the use of new technologies, then the new technologies necessarily added to total costs:

> . . . it seems unlikely that any teacher substitution will occur—certainly none has yet taken place. Thus for new methods to be used on a wider scale, the decision will have to be taken that the educational benefits are worth the resulting increases in costs. (p. 234)

In assessing the educational potential of the microcomputer, Becker (1982) concluded that "disappointment and poorly utilized resources" will result without forethought about the integration of technology with traditional classroom instruction. He sees as the biggest problem overcoming the contrast between the computer's profitable interaction with a single student and the group-based organizational structure of schools. In the remainder of this chapter, we will discuss some of the technological design and implementation that schools must consider *if* they are to take full advantage of the instructional potential of information and communication technologies.

IMPACT OF TECHNOLOGICAL CHANGE ON EDUCATIONAL ORGANIZATIONS

What is the impact of technology on the role of educational systems in preparing individuals for participation in society?

The forces leading to educational reform in the United States are not unique to education or to the United States. Rather, they reflect worldwide changes in social, economic, political, and technological relationships. Their amalgam has been referred to as both the postindustrial society and the information society. Whatever it is called, the present age is quite different from that which preceded it. The magnitude of the shift has been likened to that from feudalism to capitalism or from an agricultural economy to an industrial one. All social institutions must make appropriate adjustments; educational institutions are not exempt.

Both optimistic, almost euphoric, predictions of the future as well as highly pessimistic scenarios may be considered. One of the most promising pictures is offered by Masuda (1981), who developed his ideas as early as 1971 as author of the Japanese *Plan for an Information Society: A National Goal for the Year 2000*. In his vision of the future, which he refers to as "Computopia," the production of information values, not material values, is the driving force. Computer technology substitutes for and amplifies mental labor. Manual labor for production purposes is almost entirely replaced by such nonhuman systems as numerically controlled automation and robots. Relationships based on exchange are replaced by synergetic principles and shared forward-looking goals for social benefit. Realization of time value (i.e., the planning for and realization of future goals) characterizes individual aims within the context of mutual and synergetic goals.

Toffler (1980) elaborated on the differences in the use of information in the industrial age and in the information age. According to Toffler, the sources of information of the industrial age were few and the imagery used was standardized. Now, however, our stimuli are becoming increasingly more complex and diverse because of the greater number and sophistication of potential sources. Communication is now discontinuous.

> Instead of merely receiving our mental model of reality, we are now compelled to invent it. This places an enormous burden on us. But it also leads toward greater individuality, a demassification of personality as well as culture. (p. 2)

The thinking pattern that was most valued during the industrial age was analytical. Things, ideas, and concepts had to be taken apart in order to learn their essence. Educators responded by dividing the curriculum into discrete disciplines and programs. The strategy was successful in producing the information-rich society of today. However, society is finding that all its social and ecological systems and problems are interrelated and that its experts specialize only in fragments of those systems and tend to work in isolation one from another. This fragmentation has led to the phenomenon of information overload because sufficient paradigms for piecing knowledge together into integrated wholes (i.e., synthesis) have not been developed. While analysis continues to be important in the information age, synthesis, according to Toffler (1980), will be the *most* valued thought process.

Since early in this century, industrial concepts of standardization and economies of scale have dominated thinking about the organization and administration of schools (Callahan, 1962). These concepts have led to increasingly larger schools so that a greater variety of course offerings and specialists would be available to students. This same trend, however, has made the system so rigid that it cannot adequately respond to individual differences of students or changing conditions in the environment. We have refused to recognize that learning is primarily a function of the interest, motivation, and hard work of the student. It is assumed that learning takes place best in the physical presence of a teacher to guide and supervise learning activities from moment to moment. The practical effect of this assumption has been to claim that in order for a child to learn, a course has to be established. More critically, that course requires a certified teacher, and cost considerations require approximately 20 or more pupils per class. In a mass school, individualization requires many individuals.

Contemporary schooling has become rigidified and standardized in ways that actually thwart learning and fail to educate young people for productive lives in a society now facing accelerating change and diversity. Rather than create self-directed continuing learners who can function independently and interpret change, the mass school continues to create teacher-dependent role players. In an increasingly literate and sophisticated society, ways must be found to meet the unique needs of individual students. School regimen and instructional methods need to be more flexible to provide students with programs and content that are individualized according to student learning abilities and personal interests. School curricula must become more interrelated across subject boundaries in order to promote thinking skills that require the synthesis of various ideas and individual decisionmaking.

What is the impact of technology on the way in which schooling is organized?

A dynamic period in education is emerging, and institutional governance structures must be flexible enough to respond. Typically, for public schooling, this structure has four service levels with authority for making policy concentrated at two of these levels. The primary level of authority is the state as represented by legislators, governors, state boards of education and superintendents, and state education departments. This level is charged with establishing basic policy for the system and overseeing and coordinating its components. The second level of authority is local school districts, which establish operating policies. The basic operating unit is the school, however little discretion is allowed school-based personnel. The most recent school governance invention has been the intermediate district, which provides support and instructional services to school districts in a region.

If the four-layered structure is viewed as a network of educational resources available to highly diverse communities, it is perfectly reasonable for states to delegate or decentralize those functions that can more effectively and more efficiently be handled at the regional, district, or school levels. It is also reasonable for schools and school districts to do cooperatively that which they cannot do well independently. The procedures for assigning functions should permit flexibility because an optimal allocation will vary among regions according to demographic and geographic characteristics and over time according to changing definitions of standards and new technological developments.

Advances in information and communication technologies have neutralized the traditional arguments for large schools and consolidation of school districts. Goodlad (1984, p. 309), for example, in his influential study, *A Place Called School*, asks: "What are the defensible reasons for operating an elementary school of more than a dozen teachers and 300 boys and girls?" He answers his own question by saying, "I can think of none." With reference to secondary schools, Goodlad concludes that none should have more than 500 or 600 students. Others have come to similar conclusions (Barker & Gump, 1964; Coleman, 1986; Monk & Haller, 1986; Sher, 1976).

The time is at hand for state education departments and the U. S. Department of Education to redirect their efforts from forcing school district consolidation to providing information and communication infrastructures including a national educational satellite network, microwave and cable transmission networks, and the funding and coordinating of software development. Such infrastructures will improve educational quality for all children regardless of the size or location of the school in which they are enrolled. These are things that small districts cannot do, but the cost is so great that neither can large districts do them. These tasks require state and even national cooperation.

What is the impact of technology on the methodology of education?

In an information-rich society, the teacher as a primary source of information is rapidly becoming obsolete. Libraries, textbooks, television, video discs and cassettes, audio tapes, computers, CD-ROM data bases, computer software and information systems provide the means whereby any student, once she or he learns how to read and to use these resources, can obtain most information needed. This capability portends new roles for educational professionals. They need to become experts in managing information resources and in designing learning experiences for individual students relevant to their needs, growth, and development; for the most part, they need not be purveyors of information. Teachers—if we continue to call them that—need to be involved primarily in diagnosis of learning needs, prescription of learning experiences (i.e., curriculum design), motivation of students, and evaluation of the results (Nelson, 1978). In carrying out these functions, the primary interaction with students is of necessity on a one-to-one basis, in essence eliminating the classroom as we know it.

The new focus needs to be on learning rather than teaching. With the nearly unlimited accounting capabilities of the mainframe computer, emphasis can be placed on *continuous* rather than discontinuous learning. Continuous learning is *individualized* to capitalize on student strengths and to remedy student weaknesses as these are diagnosed. The learning experience can be a function of all life experiences, not just those in a school. This makes community resources much more useful because time in school is no longer a prime objective. Student-teacher ratios are relevant only when they can be shown to contribute to greater efficiency in the learning process. A multimedia approach to learning does not eliminate traditional teaching; however, it becomes only *one* of many methods. Others include books, drill, computer-assisted instruction (CAI), video disc enhanced by computer, audio tape, lecture (large group), discussion (small group), drama, chorus, band, athletic teams, tutoring (by teacher, aide, volunteer, or other student), laboratory, and field experiences. Since the passage of Public Law 94-142, children with learning disabilities and other handicaps must receive individual diagnoses and individualized education prescriptions. All children, not only the handicapped, should be so treated in the near future.

The combining of teacher assessments of individual student needs and a multimedia approach to instruction makes possible the development of an individualized education plan for each student. Simultaneously, the individualization of instruction increases the problems of scheduling and control. Means need to be devised to build into the accounting software a capability for handling far greater complexities of scheduling resulting from the use of a variety of resources on an individual basis.

The difficulty of the task is not to be understated. It is of such magnitude that general systems and material need to be developed at the state and national levels with adaptations made at the district and "learning center" (i.e., school) levels. Some good software packages do exist (even comprehensive systems such as PLATO for CAI), but they need to be adapted and others need to be developed. For example, it is doubtful that having a plethora of media resources available will of itself stimulate the type of synthetic thinking skills described earlier. Focusing existing multimedia learning on such goals would require extensive review of each media package, listing the objectives obtainable with each package, cross-referencing, and so on. The curriculum development effort would be substantial. The existence of complex, computerized military defense systems, inventory and financial control systems in business, and on-line reservation systems for airlines, hotels, and entertainment events suggests that the problem is not insurmountable. They are tasks best handled at the state or national levels of government, however.

To take full advantage of available technology, planned reliance needs to be placed on the machine for its complete range of capabilities but subject to human direction, planning, and control. Teachers are still essential, but their roles are changed from director, leader, final authority, to diagnostician, prescriber, motivator, facilitator, and evaluator. Teachers, students, and aides are seen as multidimensional human resources leading to specialization and division of labor, breaking the self-contained classroom mold of today's schools. Tasks requiring professional judgment are separated from those that are routine. Expensive, professionally trained persons are assigned to the former and lower-cost paraprofessionals are assigned to the latter. The pupil-teacher ratio is likely to increase, but the adult-pupil ratio is likely to remain the same or decline from current levels. Teachers would be perceived as managers of instruction supervising students and paraprofessionals.

In using existing technology to enhance the educational productivity and effectiveness of humans and in dividing control tasks into those that require professional training and those that do not, an overall design is permitted that is not only capable of meeting the schooling needs of an information society, but that, using the most conservative estimates, is no more expensive than the labor-intensive mass school. Willett, Swanson, and Nelson (1979) argue that the cost would be much less. On the basis of studies by McCusker-Sorensen (1966), they determined that learning centers can be operated with an adult-pupil ratio of only 30 to 1,000. This compares to a nationally prevailing professional-pupil ratio of over 60 to 1,000. Even allowing a generous provision for support equipment, the estimated cost of an integrated man-machine schooling system averaged less than 60 percent of its contemporary counterpart.

Levin, Glass, and Meister (1984) made cost-effective analyses of four commonly proposed reform interventions: reducing class size, lengthening the school day, CAI, and cross-age tutoring. The interventions were treated as modifications of current practice and not as complete redesigns of the instructional system. They found the interventions of CAI and cross-age tutoring to be cost-effective in reading instruction. As an add-on, CAI was not cost-effective in improving achievement in mathematics although cross-age tutoring was. Reducing class size and extending the school day are not relevant concepts to the design of learning centers as set forth previously. CAI and cross-age tutoring could prove to be even more cost-effective when they are made part of a total redesign package that reduces reliance on expensive labor.

Intelligent direction for learning centers of the future will depend on the professional educators associated with them; school-based decisionmaking is likely to be the norm. Teachers will need to be experts in learning theory, curriculum design, motivational techniques, and developmental procedures. They must have highly specialized skills in diagnosing the strengths and weaknesses of individual students with respect to the students' various intellectual skills and backgrounds.

Student assistants and paraprofessional adults will be essential staff in learning centers. The roles of both will be arranged to complement and supplement the roles of the highly trained professionals who have the prime responsibility for individualizing student instruction. The use of these two ancillary groups results in distinct advantages to the professional personnel: Each professional can specialize in the areas of expertise to which that individual is best suited by personality and training, and the required omniscience in the classroom that is assumed under the present system as necessary for the professional can be relaxed.

Graduate study at the doctoral level could easily be justified for training teachers to function as just described. Different staffing and the extensive use of less expensive paraprofessionals would release resources sufficient to enable teacher salaries to be raised to a level competitive with those of other professions, thereby attracting more capable persons into the teaching profession.

THE POLITICS OF EDUCATIONAL CHANGE AND IMPLICATIONS FOR ADMINISTRATORS

Our arguments in support of restructuring elementary and secondary schooling through the use of available technology are derived from economic and pedagogical considerations. The decision to modernize or not to modernize, however, is political in that 90 percent of elementary and secondary schooling is provided through the public sector. Because of the highly decentralized structure for policymaking in education and because of the incremental nature of democratic policy development, modernization will come about as a series of decisions made over an extended period in a variety of legislative forums.

Any strategy for change will have to take into account two factors that tend to perpetuate the status quo. The first is the strong articulate constituency of professional and auxiliary employees of public schools who have a vested interest in maintaining things much as they are. The second is that, even with their recognized shortcomings, elementary and secondary schools as presently constituted are familiar; the proposed is unknown. A new system could be better, but then it could be worse. Under such circumstances, the prudent person is likely to opt for the known until there is convincing evidence of the merit of the proposed.

Reforms will be accomplished most quickly if they can be done in collaboration with professional organizations. To obtain collaboration will require a recognition on the part of state and local officials that the innovations pose threats to the psychological and economic security of professional employees and their associations. Fear of change appears to be functionally related to uncertainty, which is often associated with lack of knowledge concerning the reality of the change proposed and the effects that will result. An incremental strategy of implementation allows time for building a base of experience to alleviate fear.

The costs and benefits to the present members of the teaching profession are mixed. For teachers of the future, the benefits should far exceed the cost. For persons currently teaching, significant changes in their professional duties would be required, and some might face the possibility of losing their positions. Both possibilities can cause an inordinate amount of trauma. Movements of labor are essential if society is to improve its productivity through technological change, but it does not follow that it needs to be a financial burden to those directly concerned. Start-up costs must be borne by the public to offset economic losses to individuals caused by early retirement and to cover costs of retraining and relocating younger educational personnel. On the positive side, there would be substantially higher salaries for those remaining in teaching, the possibility of more interesting job definitions that would be wholly professional in nature, and the possibility of career advancement without leaving the field of teaching. Providing fair guarantees of economic security to current teachers would be a major challenge to teacher organizations, local school leadership, and the state and federal governments.

The implications for administrators at both the district and school levels are significant. The changes will require professional leadership, which at the initial stages is most likely to come from professionally alert principals and central office administrators.

At the central office level, a strategic plan needs to be developed and implemented for moving from the status quo to the desired future state. The board of education, the professional staff, and the community need to be convinced of the merits of the objectives of the plan and its strategy. Tough negotiations can be expected with the district unions, especially if there are to be cutbacks in personnel and redefinitions of duties. Extensive staff development programs will have to be initiated. Political action and strategic planning at the state and federal levels will be necessary to secure the necessary technological infrastructure, human support systems, and financing.

The most dramatic change in administrative roles is likely to be at the school level. High-caliber and highly trained teachers will be largely responsible for curricular and instructional decisions made at the school. The building administrator will be more concerned with providing a sound environment and properly functioning support systems. Administrative responsibilities will include general supervision, personnel functions, technical support systems, public relations, and district liaison. In many respects, the principal's role will be quite similar to that of today's superintendents of small rural districts (Jacobson, 1988).

First and foremost, administrators of the future must be visionaries. They also need to be politically astute, diplomats, planners, negotiators, and trainers. These traits are desirable in today's administrators but not always found.

SUMMARY

There is a recursive relationship between education and technological innovation. Technological innovations place social and economic pressures on educational institutions to change. Educational institutions are the means by which scientists, engineers, planners, and designers are developed to create technological innovations, and they are primary institutions through which society assimilates innovations.

The world is currently going through a basic shift in its technoeconomic paradigm that is affecting the very structure and conditions of production and distribution for almost all sectors of the economy. This paradigm shift is manifest in educational institutions in what has been called the "educational reform movement." An educational system designed for an industrial age is slowly adapting to the requirements of an information society.

This chapter has described the interdependent relationships between technological change and social change with particular emphasis on the probable impact of technological changes on schools. Schools need to efficiently integrate information and communication technologies into instructional systems, making schooling compatible with a technologically sophisticated world. This will transform the role of elementary and secondary teachers from purveyors of information to managers of instruction. School administrators need to be visionaries, planners, coordinators, and negotiators and need to provide liaison with the community and other levels of government.

REFERENCES

Barker, R., & Gump, P. (1964). *Big school, small school.* Stanford, CA: Stanford University Press.

Becker, H. (1982). *Microcomputers in the classroom: Dreams and realities* (Report No. 319). Baltimore, MD: Johns Hopkins University, Center for the Social Organization of Schools.

Benson, C. (1961). *The economics of public education.* Boston: Houghton Mifflin.

Boyle, C., Wheale, P., & Surgess, B. (1984). *People, science and technology.* Brighton, England: Harvester Press.

Callahan, R. (1962). *Education and the cult of efficiency: A study of the social forces that have shaped the administration of the public schools.* Chicago: University of Chicago Press.

Coleman, P. (1986). The good school: A critical examination of the adequacy of student achievement and per pupil expenditures as measures of school district effectiveness. *Journal of Education Finance, 12,* 71-96.

Eurich, N. (1985). *Corporate classrooms: the learning business.* Princeton, NJ: Princeton University Press.

Freeman, C. (1984). Keynes or Kondratiev? How can we get back to full employment? In P. Marstarand (ed.), *New technology and the future of work and skills:* Proceedings of a symposium organized by Section X at the annual meeting of the British Association for the Adevancement of Science. August 1983 (pp. 103-123). Dover, NH: Frances Pinter.

Freeman, C. (1988). *Induced innovation: Diffusion of innovations in business cycles.* In B. Elliott (ed.), *Technology and social process.* Edinburgh, Scotland: Edinburgh University Press.

Goodlad, J. (1984). *A place called school: Prospects for the future.* New York: McGraw-Hill.

Guthrie, J., Garms, W., and Pierce, L. (1988). *School finance and educational policy: Enhancing educational efficiency, equality, and choice.* Englewood Cliffs, NJ: Prentice-Hall.

Jacobson, S. (1988). The rural superintendency: Reconsidering the administrative farm system. *Research in Rural Education, 5,* (2), 37-42.

Levin, H., Glass, G., & Meister, G. (1984). *Costeffectiveness of four educational interventions* (Project Report No. 84-A11). Stanford, CA: Stanford University, Stanford Education Policy Institute.

Levin, H., & Meister, G. (1985). *Educational technology and computers: Promises, promises, always promises* (Project Report No. 85-A13). Stanford, CA: Stanford University, Stanford Education Policy Institute.

Masuda, Y. (1981). Parameters of the post-industrial society: Computopia. In World Future Society, *The information society as post-industrial society* (pp. 57-59). Bethesda, MD: World Future Society.

McCusker, H., & Sorensen, P. (1966). The economics of education. In P. H. Rossi & B. J. Biddle (Eds.), *The new media and education: Their impact on society.* Garden City, NY: Aldine.

Mesthene, E. (1981). How technology will shape the future. In T. J. Kuehn & A. L. Porter (Eds.), *Science, technology and national policy* (pp. 57-79). Ithaca, NY: Cornell University Press.

Monk, D., & Haller, E. (1986). *Organizational alternatives for small rural schools.* Ithaca, NY: Cornell University Department of Education.

Naisbitt, J. (1982). *Megatrends: Ten new directions transforming our lives.* New York: Warner Books.

National Center for Education Statistics. (1988). *The condition of education: Elementary and secondary education.* Washington, DC: U. S. Department of Education.

National Governors' Association, Center for Policy Research and Analysis (1986). *Time for results: The governors' 1991 report on education.* Washington, DC: Author.

Nelson, E. (1978). *Occupational education in New York State: The transition from vocational to career education* (Occasional Paper No. 28). Albany, NY: Unpublished monograph, New York State Education Department, School Finance Law Study Project.

Office of Technology Assessment, Congress of the United States. (1982). *Informational technology and its impact on American education.* Washington, DC: U.S. Government Printing Office.

Perelman, L. (1987). *Technology and the transformation of schools.* Alexandria, VA: National School Boards Association.

Sher, J., & Tompkins, R. (1976). The myths of rural school and district consolidation: Parts I & II. *Educational Forum, 41,* pp. 95-107, 137-153.

Toffler, A. (1980). *The third wave.* New York: Morrow.

Vaizey, J., Norris, K., & Sheehan, J. (1972). *The political economy of education.* New York: Wiley.

Willett, E., Swanson, A., and Nelson, E. (1979). *Modernizing the little red schoolhouse: The economics of improved schooling.* Englewood Cliffs, NJ: Educational Technology Publications.

PART III

Administrator Preparation and Educational Reform

Part III takes the background of the waves of reform (Part I) as they are influenced by the selected undercurrents (Part II) and focuses them on the specifics of administrator preparation. The five chapters that comprise Part III examine these diverse forces in terms of role expectations of future educational leaders and the strategies for recruiting and preparing them.

In Chapter 8, "Rethinking the Clinical Aspects of Preparation Programs: From Theory to Practice," Mike Milstein considers the diverse ways that clinical content is integrated into programs of administrator preparation. He focuses specifically on the purposes of a clinical sequence and the relationships between theory and practice within a clinical sequence. Milstein then elaborates on a six-phase program designed to create a more meaningful clinical training experience.

In Chapter 9, "The Administrator of the Future: Combining Instructional and Managerial Leadership," Robert Heller and Albert Pautler consider the principalship as a key position in schooling and in the tensions created by the undercurrents of teacher empowerment and effective schools research. These educational undercurrents and the movement to reform have lent currency to some old questions: Can educational administrators be both instructional and managerial leaders? And should administrator preparation become more specialized or generalized? The authors examine these polarized tensions and then argue for a compromise position.

In Chapter 10, "Normative Roles and Administrator Preparation: Examining Three Sports Metaphors of Organizations," James Conway takes three sport metaphors (baseball, football, and basketball) and looks at them in terms of organizational structures and leadership. Although this approach may be viewed by some as another example of the male-oriented perspective that dominates educational administration, Conway's intention is to use the metaphoric argument to describe decision-making and leadership roles in traditional and empowered educational organizations.

He foreshadows the next chapter as he considers the need for considering alternative intelligence measures for those entering this profession.

In Chapter 11, "Future Educational Leaders: From Where Will They Come?" Stephen Jacobson develops a supply-and-demand analysis of positional needs in educational administration. He argues that a restructured teaching profession that offers teachers increased compensation, more administrative responsibility, and a greater role in educational decisionmaking may severely affect this traditionally self-selecting profession. Jacobson addresses such questions as: Who will enter educational administration in the future? Will alternative career paths be made available for individuals without educational backgrounds? And, finally, how should preparation programs respond to representational equity—specifically, the marked underrepresentation of women and minorities in the field?

In Chapter 12, "An Epilogue: Where Is Educational Leadership Going?" Conway and Jacobson summarize and integrate the issues developed in the previous chapters. The authors then raise additional questions as they extend the diverse challenges raised by the other contributors to this book. Implicit in the chapter is an agenda for future research and development in administrator preparation that should provide much room for faculty and student discussion. For students the critical questions are: What roles in educational administration, if any, do I want to pursue? Am I intellectually and emotionally suited for these career challenges? For faculty and students together the questions are: What should our program goals be? Do we have the intellectual and human resources necessary? And, most important of all, do we have the desire to restructure the experiences we can control to achieve them?

CHAPTER 8

Rethinking the Clinical Aspects of Preparation Programs: From Theory to Practice

Mike M. Milstein
University of New Mexico

There is a major debate going on concerning the appropriate role, content, and instructional format of university-based programs for the preparation of educational administrators. In fact, the focus on required changes in preparatory programs has become a national pastime among those responsible for these programs. For example, beginning in 1987, the University Council on Educational Administration (UCEA) instituted an annual meeting to bring its 50 member institutions, as well as nonmember institutions, together with the specific purpose of sharing programmatic changes that are being explored in response to environmental demands.*

During the first half of the twentieth century, the preparation of administrators was dominated by retired practitioners who tended to be fond of telling old war stories (National Society for the Study of Education [NSSE], 1964). It may be argued that this hardly constituted adequate training, but at least those entering the field were socialized by practitioners. That is, preparation programs were concerned with the world of practice.

During the 1950s, major changes in administrator preparation began to take shape, at least in part at the prodding and resource support of influential organizations such as the Kellogg Foundation (NSSE, 1964). An effort was made to raise the caliber of training with a particular emphasis on the

---

*The UCEA also sponsored efforts of the National Commission on Excellence in Educational Administration, and the Commission's findings (see *Leaders for America's Schools, 1987*) take university preparation programs to task, particularly concerning their minimal provision of clinical experiences.

development of a "science" of administration. The number of preparatory programs expanded rapidly. Increasingly, the faculty members in these programs were highly trained in the behavioral sciences, but as compared to their predecessors, few had prior experience as administrators. As the theory movement gained more adherents, these trends continued through the 1960s and 1970s, moving training programs ever further away from hands-on approaches.

Not surprisingly, practitioners began to doubt the usefulness of university-based training programs. In fact, recent surveys (Griffiths, 1988; Heller, Conway, & Jacobson, 1988) report that practitioners feel negative about the utility of the training they receive in university preparation programs. As Murphy and Hallinger (1987) note:

> Practitioners have become disillusioned by the failure of university programs to ground training procedures in the realities of the workplace and by their reluctance to treat content viewed as useful by administrators. This disenchantment, in turn, is partially fueling the demand for changes in methods of training school administrators. (p. 252)

During the 1980s the American Association of School Administrators, in cooperation with the UCEA, felt it necessary to publish a set of guidelines (1964) that detailed the necessary elements to be included in the clinical aspect of preparation programs. They stated in their Foreword:

> In some instances learning opportunities for interns have been limited to observation with no chance to assume responsibility for administrative tasks. . . . Professors . . . must accept new functions and responsibilities . . . that take them out of familiar fields of operation. They have little precedent to guide them in negotiating financial agreements, in cooperatively planning learning experiences for interns, or in evaluating those experiences.

Twenty-three years later the National Commission on Excellence in Educational Administration (UCEA, 1987) came to the same basic set of conclusions. In its final report the commission stated that the practitioner-related aspects of preparation programs were marked by "lack of a definition of good educational leadership . . . lack of collaboration between school districts and universities . . . lack of systematic professional development for school administrators . . . lack of sequence, modern content, and clinical experiences in preparation programs" (pp. xvi, xvii).

In short, although the clinical aspect of training should be a central program component, it more frequently is treated as an afterthought. Most professors trained to emulate the arts and sciences model of academic preparation are not enthused about devoting energies to extensive field-based activities. Nor, given their lack of administrative experience, are they typically capable of providing adequate supervision for clinical efforts.

As a result, clinical experiences in educational administration preparation programs are often optional (unless required by state policy), infrequently preplanned as integral program experiences, and rarely well coordinated. Instead, the norm is that clinical aspects of preparation programs are often supervised by retired administrators or passed around among faculty members as an obligation, or worse yet, assigned to the newest faculty member in the program.

Too often field sites are chosen haphazardly and/or are not closely monitored. The potential for interns being constrained to passive observation, being placed in roles that do not fit closely with their career goals, or being used as "go-fers" is great when clear and agreed-on expectations are not developed. Likewise, campus-based practicums and seminars on a regular basis are rarely available or required, and clinical experiences are often isolated from the rest of a student's program flow. Finally, the connecting linkages between on-campus experiences and field-based experiences are rarely adequately developed.

In short, more than 30 years after the preparation of educational administrators came under close scrutiny, we are still searching for more viable ways of organizing and managing training programs. In fact, several major bibliographies have been developed about the growing literature on clinical aspects of administrator training (Daresh, Gallagher, & Balmores, 1987; Grady, Layton, & Bohling-Phillipi, 1988).

It is relevant for us to get on with clarifying what we mean by *clinical experiences* so that we can set our houses in order. This is true not only because of the need for coherence but because, if we refuse to come to grips with the development of meaningful clinical efforts, these experiences will be defined and required by state legislatures and state departments of education. In fact, since the mid-1970s the number of states requiring one form or another of field experience has increased from 10 to 25 (Gousha, Lopresti, & Jones, 1986).

PURPOSES OF CLINICAL EXPERIENCES

The first step in improving our capacity to provide high-quality clinical experiences is to establish purposes. Basically, although intellectual competence is a must, it has to be linked to outstanding performance if we are to promote distinguished leadership for our schools. It stands to reason that learning takes place most effectively when meaningful application is part of the process. In professional fields such as law, medicine, and business, as well as education, internship experiences, when thoughtfully planned and carried out in stimulating settings, have proven useful for sharpening minds and for developing and refining performance skills.

The purposes of clinical experiences are to enable students to be exposed to reality-based programs that permit a balance between *learning about* and *learning how* and that are rooted in a solid foundation of *learning why*. In the process, students should have multiple opportunities to demonstrate mastery of those skills and knowledge traditionally required of administrative positions as well as those that have not yet been clearly identified but that may be required in the future.

Most important is the opportunity to pursue "professional formation wherein administrative candidates put together learning acquired in the field and in the classroom and also their own values and priorities to form more wholistic and personal understandings of educational leadership" (Daresh, 1988a, p. 14). Donald Schön (1984) refers to this as "knowing-in-practice" or "reflection-in-action," that is, "on-the-spot surfacing, criticizing, restructuring, and testing of intuitive understandings of experienced phenomena." (p. 42).

Based on this approach, the Danforth Foundation's Program for the Preparation of Principals is supporting innovative clinical program developments at such institutions as Georgia State University, the University of Alabama, and Ohio State University. Basic purposes for intern development at these institutions include the following (Daresh, 1988b):

> *Personal Reflection:* Aspiring administrators need to not only gain skill learning *how to* do things on the job; they also need to think about *what* they learned from their experience, and generalize to future practice.
>
> *Educational Platform Development:* Following from a recommended practice of Sergiovanni and Starrat (1988) future (and present) administrators would do well to state formally their personal educational philosophies, beliefs, and values, and share these statements with others in their organizations.
>
> *Understanding of Interpersonal Styles:* Future administrators need to develop an appreciation of different styles in others, and how those differences relate to their own styles.
>
> *Personal Professional Development:* The candidate is expected to articulate a formal statement of future career goals, identified strengths and weaknesses, and strategies for avoiding weaknesses and capitalizing on strengths in the pursuit of the goals. (p. 16)

These purposes could become the foundational cornerstones of *what* clinical experiences in university-based training programs are all about. The *how*, or the ways, these management programs are organized could be tested against the litmus of purposes, such as those noted here.

Specific, locally relevant purposes can be inferred from these general guidelines. However, to accomplish these purposes, designers of preparation programs will first have to place greater emphasis on the relationship of the world of practice and the world of thought—that is, on the importance of partnerships between educational administrators and university training departments. As Griffiths (1988) concludes, "We should be proud to become the professional backbone of the schools. . . . We must, in educational administration, make the preparation of administrators our first priority and focus our research on achieving excellence in that endeavor" (p. 10).

THE CLINICAL SEQUENCE

The first step in rethinking our approach to clinical experiences is to develop a set of programmatic building blocks from which students can develop maximum skills and confidence. There are alternative ways of conceptualizing the sequence. For example, it could be organized as follows:

- *Linear.* In the linear approach, learning experiences are sequenced so that theory and concepts are learned first, with application opportunities following.
- *Dialectic.* In this approach theory and learning are woven together tightly so that the learner has numerous opportunities to test practice against a knowledge base.
- *Reflective Practice.* In reflective practice, as Schön argues, theory is learned on the job. Thus, practice comes first and theory building becomes relevant only as experience is accumulated.
- *Developmental.* This approach focuses on development of a foundation of theoretical orientations, with expanding opportunities to apply and test these theories in reality-based settings.

There is no one best model. However, to clarify the importance of planning and sequencing, it is useful to select one for discussion. The developmental approach will be explored because the author is most familiar with that approach. Figure 8.1 visualizes the flow that is suggested.

Figure 8.1 illustrates a proposed six-phase sequence of clinical activities as a student proceeds through a preparation program. The notion of phased experiences that build on one another over time is central to the schema. The logic, as visualized, is to focus most of the initial activities on campus and then gradually to move toward field-based sites that introduce students to the world of administration in ways that enhance learning and internalization. Of course, individual modifications will have to be taken into consideration

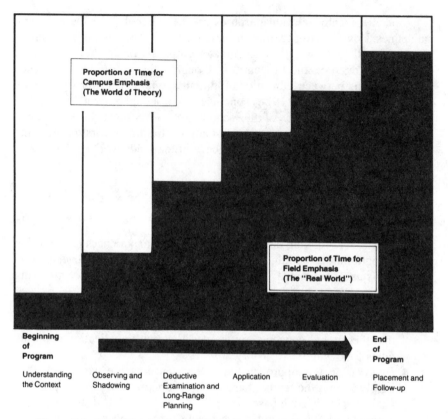

Figure 8.1. Time Distributions of Field-Based and Campus-Based Learnings in the Developmental Model

to account for differences in prior academic background, experience in administration, and career orientations.

Phase One: Understanding the Context

The first phase, understanding the context, focuses on initial map building (formal diagramming of the work situation) for the novice student. The emphasis is on identifying and subsequently interrelating the critical functions, skills, and behaviors that are integral parts of administrators' work situations. To the extent possible, students should encounter these contextual learnings early in their studies to enhance subsequent observations and applications.

The content for this phase constitutes the diverse role responsibilities administrators conduct. There are multiple ways that this set of responsibilities can be defined. The approach at the University of New Mexico (UNM), which is similar to the approach at the State University of New York (SUNY) at Buffalo, is to categorize them within four functional areas:

1. *Program Management.* The management of the educational program, including purpose setting, curriculum change and development, and evaluation.
2. *Human Resource Management.* The management of those activities that have to do with identifying resource needs and the hiring, supervision, development, and evaluation of personnel.
3. *Operations Management.* Acquiring, managing, and maintaining the fiscal and plant resources required to support the educational program.
4. *Organizations.* Institutional management, including a focus on organizational theory, behavior, and analysis.

At UNM we also require all students to take a beginning level course, "Problem Solving in Educational Organizations." The purpose of the course is to introduce the four functional areas to our students by having students work in teams to diagnose the status quo of a simulated school and to prescribe appropriate changes for that setting. The information base they use for this exercise, which is an adaptation of materials originally developed at Teachers College, Columbia University, includes data concerning personnel, students, program, resources, and community. Using this seminar-lab experience as a foundation, students then take discrete courses that deal with particular elements of the four functional areas previously listed.

Organizing diverse knowledge bases into logical categories is a useful exercise that leaders of preparatory programs should go through, both to increase self-understanding of their curriculum and to help them understand the larger context of the field they intend to enter.

Phase Two: Observing and Shadowing

The second phase, observing and shadowing (literally following the role model as a "shadow"), focuses on learning by watching seasoned administrators conduct their role activities. These activities take place in various settings, including classrooms, throughout the school, community settings, and the central office.

Armed with skills in ethnographic observation, students should have opportunities to observe interactions that take place in the daily lives of administrators. In particular, they should have opportunities to shadow administrators who are perceived to be excellent, so they can begin to form role images that they will strive to emulate once they have an opportunity to become administrators. Preferably, they should shadow two or more administrators so they can gain a sense of the impact of diverse roles and different leadership styles.

To enhance learning potential, students should be encouraged to maintain daily logs that document their observations. Working with a faculty-based supervisor, students can meet on a regular basis to share their observations and the meanings they have derived from these observations. This format not only enhances learning from observations but provides faculty members with further opportunities to particularize and personalize information that has been shared with students during the first phase of the program.

Phase Three: Deductive Examination and Long-Range Planning

Phase Three is an important turning point in the program; for the first time, it moves students into a proactive role. At this point, students are introduced to a major problem-solving situation. During this phase students work, preferably in teams, to clarify a problematic situation in an educational setting, diagnose the problem, develop alternative prescriptions, and to the extent possible assist with implementation of prescriptions and evaluation of outcomes.

Phase Three focuses on several objectives. First, it provides opportunities to apply learnings and observations to real-life situations. Second, it emphasizes to the students that problem solving, long-range planning, and visioning are as important to the success of an educational organization as effective daily management of routines. Third, it encourages students to work in team situations. Although this is often a reality of administrative life, it may be foreign to students who have spent their professional lives as teachers working in splendid isolation from other adults in their school settings.

At SUNY/Buffalo, school districts are invited to volunteer problematic situations for which they would like to find solutions. These situations, which vary according to district interests, have included business management and technology modifications, morale issues, structural reorganizations, and development of policy manuals. Teams of students working in conjunction with faculty members contract for one or two semesters to help school districts clarify and resolve their concerns. At UNM students work individually on problems identified at their internship sites but share their analyses and proposed prescriptions in regularly scheduled seminar sessions with fellow interns.

Phase Four: Application

In the fourth phase students move into a concentrated focus on field experiences with an attendant reduced presence on campus. It is the time when neophytes begin to put it all together and test their abilities to practice what they have been learning. It is the moment of truth when learnings garnered from readings and seminars, which are enhanced through extensive case analyses, simulations, role playing and observation, are brought to bear on application in leadership roles in educational organizations. It also provides opportunities to modify expectations that are tested against the hard rock of reality. Finally, it is clearly a major rite of passage from teaching into administration that is achieved through first-hand experience, preferably under the guidance and supervision of campus-based and field-based tutors.

To enhance the probability of maximum positive outcomes for students, several criteria should guide development of the activities. First, the internship should come late in the course of studies. Preferably, it should be a culminating program experience, reserved until the student has had opportunities to learn about the content of the role, has had numerous occasions to shadow good administrators, has worked with others to help organizational leaders confront problem situations that emphasize long-range planning and visioning.

Second, the site for the experience should be chosen very carefully. Specifically, the site and the role should relate directly to candidates' career aspirations, and field supervisors should have reputations as excellent administrators who are willing to give time and energy to the students assigned to their sites.

Third, if at all possible, the application phase of the clinical experience should be a full-time effort. This criterion may be difficult to operationalize, especially if sufficient resources are not available, but the intent should be to move as far in this direction as is feasible. Half days or one or more full days per week may be the best that can be attained, but certainly anything less (e.g., during teachers' preparation periods or before or after school hours) is not the kind of experience that will achieve the intended purposes of clinical efforts.

Fourth, the experience should encompass a complete cycle of activities, from start-up events through closure. In most cases, this means involvement as an intern from the beginning of school in the fall to the completion of the academic year in the late spring. There is no substitute for clinical involvement through the entire cycle.

Fifth, a task-specific contract should be arranged that reflects the student's career aspirations and assures experience with a wide variety of administrative responsibilities. Generally, contracts can be designed along the lines of competencies identified by such major organizations as the American Association of School Administrators or the National Association of Secondary School Principals, but they should also encompass the specific career orientations and growth needs of the candidate. The importance of the contract is that it outlines expectations for all parties involved and provides the basis for supervision and evaluation.

Sixth, campus-based supervisors should have experiential background and field legitimacy. It is preferable for them to have been administrators and be viewed by their field colleagues as capable of providing direction for the clinical program. Identifying such practitioner-scholars is vitally important for meaningful guidance of interns' activities. It is not sufficient, as noted earlier, to pass this responsibility around among faculty who either do not desire to be involved or, worse yet, are not able to provide adequate supervision.

Seventh, site visits should be made regularly by campus-based supervisors. At least three visits per semester should be made: one to be sure that start-up activities get rolling positively; another to observe the intern in action and talk to the field-site supervisor to be sure activities are going well and, if necessary, to revise and modify the contract; and a third visit to confer with the intern and the field supervisor to evaluate outcomes and make plans for the second half of the experience.

Eighth, as during the shadowing phase, interns should be required to keep a log of their experiences and, at appropriate intervals, to review and analyze the high and low points of the experience. Through writing and review, the accumulation of events and episodes begins to take on patterns that may not otherwise be discernible.

Ninth, a campus-based seminar should be instituted to bring all interns onto campus on a regular basis (preferably weekly). This seminar can extend interns' learnings as they share experiences and help one another to discover alternative perceptions of administration.

Phase Five: Evaluation

The fifth phase focuses on evaluation for program modifications as well as for student feedback. Formative evaluations should be conducted throughout the program to allow corrective actions as necessary. Summative evaluation is required to help students assess the entire experience, to develop a synthesis of the learnings they have attained, and to identify those that they should continue to explore and master. It is a time when students, preparation program leaders, and field-based supervisors and sponsors can independently and in unison step back and reflect on the experience. It is a time for examination of perceptions as they relate to experience in the real world of administration and a time to develop corrective behaviors when such is deemed appropriate.

Everybody can benefit from the effort. Students' reflective evaluations should help them to comprehend the totality of the experience and to pinpoint areas of growth need. Graduate training programs can profit from such evaluations in the sense that they provide continuous feedback about the relevance of program content and design, which in turn can serve as the basis for keeping program modifications relevant as the environment inevitably changes. School district and school-level leaders also benefit from summative evaluations that help keep field-based managers current on evolving administrative trends and that sharpen their abilities to supervise clinical aspects of students' programs. Summative evaluation also can bring the three parties—students, campus-based supervisors, and field supervisors, together and thus develop close linkages among them.

Phase Six: Placement and Follow-Up

The culminating phase of the clinical sequence is too often honored in the breach. Directors of preparation programs, whether because of an attempt to be impartial or because of a lack of a sense of responsibility, often disregard their responsibilities to students in the areas of placement and follow-up.

Placement activities focus on helping students learn how to get the jobs they want. The activities include obtaining state certification, career planning, appropriate dress, preparation of résumés, and handling interview situations. They also include assisting with the search for positions that might be appropriate to the needs of specific students. Using their networks of relationships with educational leaders, campus-based supervisors can help students find placement in positions that will be challenging to them. Similarly, school district leaders who supervise and sponsor interns should be encouraged to give special selection consideration to students who perform well in these situations.

Follow-up activities are also important. They are intended to help former students make career moves. Through follow-up activities, former students can also become part of the sponsorship system for the clinical needs of preparatory programs. That is, they can become sources of sites for clinical experience as well as sources of placement for students who have completed their preparation programs.

IN CLOSING

With attention to placement and follow-up, the clinical sequence is completed. This full circle of activities should provide the basis for designing and maintaining a clinical capacity that meets the needs of our schools and those who seek to lead them.

Examples of the phases of the clinical sequence that we have proposed can be found in preparatory programs at universities around the country. Unfortunately, there are few examples of university programs that encompass *all six* of them. A commitment to such a coherent, sequenced approach is vital if we intend to meet the increasing demands for meaningful clinical experiences that are coming from within the profession as well as from leaders of educational reform.

Responding effectively to these demands requires human and fiscal resources. Most important, it requires the will to change our ways. Given environmental pressures, change is likely to occur anyway, but it is clearly to our advantage to take the leadership in this effort. Becoming part of the solution will make it more likely that the clinical programs that are developed will serve *our* purposes.

REFERENCES

American Association of School Administrators and the University Council for Educational Administration. (1964). *The Internship in administrative preparation: Some action guides.* (Mimeo)

Daresh, J. (1988a). *The role of mentors in preparing future principals.* Paper presented at the annual meeting of the American Educational Research Association, New Orleans, April.

Daresh, J. (1988b). *Are "field-based" programs the answer to the reform of administrator preparation programs?* Paper presented at the annual meeting of the American Educational Research Association, New Orleans, April.

Daresh, J., Gallagher, K., & Balmores, N. (1987). *Annotated bibliography on the use of field experience to train educational leaders.* A Project Paper of the UCEA Center on Field Relations in Educational Administration Training Programs. (Mimeo)

Gousha, R., LoPresti, P., & Jones, A. (1986). *Mapping of a dynamic field: Results from the second annual survey of certification and employment standards for educational administrators.* Paper presented at the annual meeting of the Midwestern Educational Research Association, Chicago.

Grady, M., Layton, J., & Bohling-Philipi, V. (1988). *Clinical experiences in educational administration, 1960–1987.* A UCEA Resource Document, Tempe, AZ: UCEA.

Griffiths, D. (1988). *Educational administration: Reform PDQ or RIP.* A UCEA Occasional Paper. Tempe, AZ: UCEA.

Heller, R., Conway, J., & Jacobson, S. (1988, September). Executive Educator Survey. *The Executive Educator,* pp. 18–22.

Murphy, J., & Hallinger, P. (1987). *Approaches to administrative training in education.* Albany: State University of New York Press.

National Society for the Study of Education. (1964). *Behavioral science and educational administration.* Chicago: University of Chicago Press.

Schön, D. (1984). Leadership as reflection-in-action. In T. Sergiovanni, & J. Corbally, *Leadership and organizational culture.* Urbana: University of Illinois Press.

Sergiovanni, T., & Starratt, R. (1988). *Supervision: Human perspectives.* New York: McGraw-Hill.

CHAPTER 9

The Administrator of the Future: Combining Instructional and Managerial Leadership

Robert W. Heller and Albert J. Pautler
State University of New York at Buffalo

This chapter discusses and clarifies the differences between the principal as instructional leader and the principal as managerial leader as influenced by two of the undercurrents of the current reform movement. These two undercurrents, teacher empowerment and the effective schools research, were described in earlier chapters of the book. In this chapter, we focus our discussion on the administrator serving at the building level as principal or assistant principal. We see the position of building-level administrator as one of the most critical, demanding, challenging, stressful, and time-consuming in the educational profession. At the same time, it is also one of the most satisfying and rewarding.

This chapter is organized around three unifying questions:

- What are the dilemmas of the field as administrators and teachers try to sort out their own expectations about principals as leaders and managers?
- What are the characteristics of instructional and managerial leaders as viewed from various conceptual focuses?
- What are the implications for administrative preparation programs as their directors seek ways to help prepare future administrators?

THE PROBLEM OF PREPARATION

University and college programs preparing school administrators are frequently accused of preparing managerial rather than instructional leaders.

Future principals are, for the most part, present or former classroom teachers who, for one reason or another, want to become school administrators. These aspiring administrators may have been excellent, good, fair, or even poor teachers. Some may very well be seeking an escape from the day-to-day trials of teaching. Others are perhaps motivated by the financial rewards usually associated with the position. Still others, because they have been recognized for their outstanding teaching skills, have been encouraged to move into administration.

Although some of these aspiring administrators may have developed leadership skills through military, church, civic, or athletic participation, in many cases they have not had the opportunity to test their educational leadership skills other than in the classroom. Their first real opportunity to test themselves in educational administration may occur during the course of their preparation for administration in some form of clinical experience, such as a paid or unpaid internship experience. This clinical experience, much like a student teaching experience, most often occurs at the end of their course of study. One problem, as we see it, is that those managing administration preparation programs make the assumption that entering teachers are already instructional leaders within their own classrooms. Although some teachers are instructional leaders, others have been only followers or imitators. Therefore, attention must begin at this entry level to develop instructional as well as managerial skills in the aspiring administrator. How is this best accomplished? Faculty members of the programs for administrator preparation must first agree as to whether or not these future administrators need to be *and can be* both instructional and managerial leaders.

THE PROBLEM OF PLACEMENT

Once an individual completes a program of administrator preparation and becomes certified for the role of principal, the job search begins. Boards of education appoint principals on the basis of the recommendations of school officials. In some school systems, the hiring and placement of principals is almost entirely in the hands of the board of education. In many urban centers, there is a tendency to assign principals to schools without regard to their particular training. For example, we followed the brief career of an experienced male teacher when he was appointed principal of a rather troubled city high school. This was his *first* appointment as principal, and the assignment was to a school with serious problems that needed immediate attention. Unfortunately, this novice principal lasted but two years, and because he was so ineffective he was reassigned as an *assistant* principal in another school. What personal harm was done to this good teacher but unproven principal by thrusting him into a difficult school that demanded a proven administrator skilled both as a manager and instructional leader? What harm was done to the students and teachers in the school? Why did this board of education assign an untested administrator to such a troubled school? Troubled schools need the most talented, proven administrators and teachers, the proven pros, yet these same individuals may have opted out long ago and requested transfers based on seniority to the "good" schools with the "good" kids.

Other examples of placement problems occurred in Rochester and Buffalo, where women secondary school principals have been assigned to vocational schools with programs that have been traditionally male dominated. Their lack of experience with the technical knowledge in the trade areas taught in these schools had a negative impact on the *instructional* leadership these women could make available to their faculties, thereby undermining opportunities for these administrators to demonstrate their full range of leadership skills.

While some argue the importance of the principal as instructional leader, others might argue that the best leadership is provided by those principals who simply let their teachers teach. For example, when asked about how good her principal was, a teacher in a suburban school district indicated that he was a good principal because he left her alone and let her do whatever she wanted to. One might ask whether a "good" principal would leave teachers alone to do their thing. Perhaps the principal trusted her instructional judgment and respected her teaching ability. It is also possible that he knew little or nothing about her subject area.

It is our opinion that the instructional leadership ability of a principal *is critical* to teachers and students within a school. We feel that principals need to be *both* competent managers *and* creative instructional leaders if schools are to fulfill their mission in American society. But is it possible for principals to be both managerial and instructional leaders? What can administrative preparation programs do to help aspiring administrators develop the skills essential for managerial as well as instructional leadership?

SCHOOL LEADERSHIP

Scores of books have been written on leadership in general as well as leadership directly related to schools and the role of the principal within them. Persons responsible for appointing principals must know what skills are needed, how to recognize an individual's leadership skills on the basis of his or her past experience, as well as the individual's potential for leadership in situations not yet imagined.

Ideally, the best preparation for the role of principal would seem to be several years as a classroom teacher, followed by experiences as a team leader or department chairperson. After sufficient academic preparation, including a meaningful full-time supervised administrative internship, the candidate would move to an assistant principalship.

As a member of the administrative team of a school, the person could gain desirable experiences while preparing for a career move to principal. During those years as teacher, team leader, and/or chairperson, the individual would by necessity be working toward certification as a school administrator. Theory from graduate studies mixed with experience working in schools and through an administrative internship would help to add balance to the career preparation of aspiring principals. Unfortunately, far too few preparation programs are adequately balanced between theory and appropriate clinical experiences. In our program at the State University of New York (SUNY) at Buffalo, we attempt this balance by providing students with three levels of clinical experiences: an aideship, an associateship, and an administrative internship, which are built into the beginning, midpoint, and culminating points of the program respectively.

The *aideship* allows the student to work at least eight hours a week with a practicing administrator while shadowing and studying the role of that person. The aideship allows the student an early opportunity to see if this is the appropriate career of choice.

The *associateship* occurs at about the midpoint of the graduate program. Students work in small groups on a school improvement project within a local educational agency. A university professor monitors and guides the students, assisted by a representative from the local educational agency. The associateship is a team effort among the students, local educational agency, and the university. The thrust is toward a cognitive-based socialization.

The *administrative internship* is the final phase of the administrator certification program. The expectation is that students will spend one year full time as an administrative intern in a local school district or other educational agency. Ideally, this is a paid experience in a position similar to that which the candidate hopes to obtain after gaining administrative certification. This clinical experience, which is carefully monitored by the university and school district, provides the student with opportunities to perform the three roles that Cuban (1988) has argued the administrator's domain can be divided into: instructional, political, and managerial. Our program at SUNY/Buffalo tries to develop all three of these areas for students preparing for careers in administration through a continuous mix of theory and clinical practice. Yet, depending on the personal interests of the student, the result is not necessarily an equal balance among the three. Indeed, this imbalance need not be detrimental, for as Duke (1987) indicates, there is little agreement on the best way to describe the role of the principal. The principal is often seen as a manager, leader, or administrator. Keidel (1986), for example, in *Game Plans: Sports Strategies for Business,* compared the management aspect of various professional sports to business organizations. In another chapter of this book, Conway expands this analogy to education. Conway's analogy suggests that the principal may be compared to the manager or coach of a team, such as in baseball or football. In baseball each member of the team is a specialist at a certain position, not unlike in an elementary school where ideally you have the best first-grade teachers teaching first grade and the best third-grade teachers teaching third grade. At the secondary level, the principal is more like a football coach, using a different mix of skills to lead the team.

Why mention this? To encourage you to think about the management of schools and the ways various school administrators manage or coach the school team. We know what happens to managers and coaches of professional and college teams when the teams do not perform well for several years. However, the "report cards" for professional and college sports teams are easy to read. The grades for these cards are read in the won and lost columns. It is much more difficult to attempt to read the report card of various schools and those who manage them. This leads us to continue our discussion based on the three areas as mentioned in Cuban (1988).

INSTRUCTIONAL LEADERSHIP

The effective schools movement calls for principals to be or to become strong instructional leaders. At the same time, the current reform movement urges teachers to seek a strong decisionmaking role, leading to the idea of teacher empowerment. Teachers are seeking more say in controlling their profession. The dual desires for principals to be instructional leaders and teachers to have more of a say in educational decisions have created a tension that must be dealt with. Cuban (1988) sees the principal as a teacher's teacher and yet does not feel that principals in general are prepared to teach adults. Most principals are selected for their position on the basis of their prior teaching performance with children rather than their ability for managing other adults. This presents the principal, who frequently is already spread too thin in dealing with the day-to-day operation of a school, with an additional role dimension. Many principals, however, have developed the necessary skills and abilities to work with both teachers and students. With over 16,000 school districts in the United States, you would expect to find wide variations in the competencies, motivation, interests, and instructional leadership skills of principals. These differences can be demonstrated through a variety of rating scales.

For example, Hallinger and Murphy (1987) describe an instructional leadership framework on which they have developed the Principal Instructional Management Rating Scale (PIMRS). The PIMRS can be used by school districts to rate the instructional leadership of principals. Hallinger and Murphy's framework uses three dimensions: defines the mission; manages curriculum and instruction; and promotes school climate. The three dimensions are further broken down into 10 functions. The PIMRS can be used by teachers to rate the instructional leadership of principals. The results can then be used as the bases for staff development programs for principals.

Andrews (1987) reports on the Self-Assessment Study conducted at the University of Washington on the Dimensions of Instructional Leadership of Principals. On this instrument, teachers are asked to rate principals on 18 statements. The statements are divided into four categories: resource provider, instructional resource, communicator, and visible presence. Andrews reports that the three most important factors selected by the teachers from the list of 18 were: visible presence, vision for the school, and making resources available for the teachers to provide quality instruction. How might these perceptions correlate with the perceptions by the superintendents of the principals within their districts? Reliable measures are needed to rate the instructional leadership skills of principals. Research efforts such as that of Andrews provide us with the necessary tools to undertake this task in an objective and efficient fashion.

Persons concerned with instructional leadership must first be able to clearly define what they mean by instructional leadership. The Hallinger and Murphy (1987) principal rating may serve as a starting point for anyone interested in this subject. It would be useful to have a similar rating scale to evaluate the instructional leadership potential of teachers seeking a more active decisionmaking role vis-à-vis the teacher empowerment movement.

MANAGER VS. INSTRUCTIONAL LEADER

Rallis and Highsmith (1986) offer a different view of the "great principal," suggesting that school management and instructional leadership are two different tasks. They question whether one person can perform both tasks simultaneously and well. They go on to attempt to define what a "great principal" is and then to define the role of an instructional leader. We may have to settle for principals with demonstrated management and leadership skills but also accept that the balance between both will not necessarily be equal.

What is at issue? According to the U.S. Department of Education, (1988), ". . . we do not know enough about how and why school leadership affects the quality and quantity of school work, especially the basic work of schools: teaching and learning" (p. 5). It seems that the entire reform movement and the effective schools effort center on school improvement rather than on teacher improvement. Given the present organizational structure of schools, teacher improvement might be more significant. This would also appear to have a direct relationship to the empowerment of teachers (Blumberg & Greenfield, 1986; Edmonds, 1982). But what role should teachers have in instructional leadership?

Teachers have the opportunity within their classrooms to improve their skills as instructional managers and classroom leaders. We are not sure how many teachers realize that they have control over the basic teaching-learning environment each and every year that they teach. The empowerment issue has encouraged teachers to be more active in instructional leadership when dealing with both the entire school and their own professional development. Teacher empowerment should begin in one's classroom and be demonstrated clearly there before taking on an entire school program. Since teachers are usually held equally accountable with the principal for the success or failure of students, you can understand the empowerment issue from the teachers' viewpoint. If teachers are going to be held accountable for the instructional aspects of schools, they want to be actively involved in those decisions that have an impact on the instructional program.

In a Request for Proposals (RFP) from the United States Department of Education (1988), there is a call for more extensive research on the issues of leadership and management that has a direct relationship to instructional leadership. It states:

> The links between school leadership and the work of teaching and learning, for the most part, remain hidden in one of those black boxes that are ubiquitous in education. Moreover, whether the things that those in school leadership positions do to improve teaching actually constitute leadership—as distinct from management—is still an open question. We need studies, therefore, that can conceptually and empirically distinguish school management from leadership and that can identify and trace the effects of each on teaching and learning. (p. 5)

MANAGERIAL LEADERSHIP

Cuban (1988) refers to managerial leadership as "crowd control" and "instructional order" for both the teachers and principals. The teacher is concerned with control and order within a single classroom, shop, or laboratory. The principal is responsible for control and order within the entire building. The principal also serves as the leader or, as Cuban has stated, the teachers' teacher.

The principal as manager means dealing with all the administrative tasks associated with carrying out the policies of the school district as well as the school. One need only look at the job description for a principal in almost any district to gain a respect for the totality of the position. Compounding the complexity of the role of principal is that most school districts are so lean in administrative staff that they may in fact be poorly administered. In Rochester, New York, the department chairs supervise and evaluate and are classified as administrators. An hour west in Buffalo, New York, the department leaders are called coordinators, *not* administrators, and do not do teacher evaluations.

In some cases, principals have one or more assistant principals that make up the administrative staff. In many other schools, such assistance is not available. In these cases, all the managerial and instructional responsibilities rest with the principal.

The principal's job is not routine. The principal must often change plans because of a crisis situation that must be dealt with immediately. The principal may have blocked some time to work on short- or long-range planning but because of some pressing emergency must put planning on hold.

The principal as manager must deal with carrying out district and school policies as well as day-to-day operating procedures. In large schools, where support staff is available, some of this work may be delegated to others. In small schools or large schools with too few administrators, the principal must be more involved in the day-to-day operation of the school. Managerial tasks that need to be dealt with include the following:

- Personnel selection, including administrators, teachers, aides, secretaries, custodians, cafeteria staff, and so on
- Completing state or board-requested reports
- Budgeting
- Scheduling
- Student matters
- Contact with parents
- Transportation
- Building maintenance
- Conflict resolution
- Curriculum development
- Supervision and evaluation.

The list obviously can be greatly expanded. As a veteran principal of an area vocational center related: "The Board of Education promised me a full-time job and they meant it. I am free between midnight and 1:00 A.M."

The workday of a principal can be unpredictable and spent dealing with many tasks requiring constant shifting of emphasis. Planning and the development of a vision for the school may have to be left to nonschool hours or put indefinitely on hold even though such planning is essential for effective schools. But can others be delegated the concerns of the day-to-day operations of the school? Principal visibility, sometimes considered as management by walking around (MBWA), is an important element in developing school climate. How can principals do both effectively? Although we support the notion of the principal of the future being both the managerial and instructional leader of the school, if it were necessary to select one role over the other, our choice would be the principal as the leader of teachers, the instructional leader.

After visits to several small school districts in Illinois, Indiana, and Ohio, Cole (1988), reported that ". . . staying alive is labor enough for many small schools" (p. 144). Visits with principals in these small districts clearly shows that most principals see their roles as managers rather than instructional leaders. On the other hand, teachers in these small schools see the principal as the person in charge of their staff development. Some principals appear not to be adequately prepared to handle both of these demanding roles.

Rallis and Highsmith (1986) suggest that managerial principals may empower outstanding teachers within their schools to assume more active roles in instructional improvement. This type of principal, operating in the effective schools mode, can attempt to create an environment for school and instructional improvement by empowering selected teaching staff to take on significant aspects of instructional responsibility. This *may be* a plausible solution to the complex issue of teacher empowerment, but it certainly warrants more research before universal implementation.

POLITICAL LEADERSHIP

In addition to instructional and managerial leadership, Cuban (1988) also identifies a political role for both principals and teachers within the educational system of the community. He sees this as political leadership for principals in the sense that they observe and sense public desires for the schools and then try to transform those desires into school practices and policies.

The role may be considered political in another sense according to Cuban (1988). In this sense, the principal is in a position of being forced to respond to pressures from an increasing number of individuals or groups including the superintendent; national, state and local policymakers; parents with their expectations; teacher demands; and the desires and demands of students.

How the principal responds to these pressure groups may indeed be considered critical to the aims of education in a democratic society. These are significant factors to which principals must respond, about which they must exercise moral judgments, and over which they must assume political leadership.

Perhaps it would make sense to include this political activity as a part of the managerial leadership role of the principal rather than place it in a separate category as Cuban does. Whatever the choice, the fact remains, the political aspects of the job must be dealt with.

TEACHER EMPOWERMENT

As mentioned earlier in this discussion, a concept popular with teachers in the current reform movement is that of teacher empowerment. Although there has been some hesitancy to come out directly and say so among the leadership of teacher organizations, there appears to be a national agenda on their part to gain power for teachers. The nation's two most influential teacher organizations, the National Education Association (NEA) and the American Federation of Teachers (AFT), are both aggressively advancing the empowerment of teachers in the decisionmaking process. At the state level, there is also activity in this direction. Nowhere is this better exemplified than in New York State. The recently appointed State Commissioner of Education, Thomas Sobol, appointed a Task Force on the Teaching Profession (1988). The final report of the task force resulted in a document entitled, "New York Report: A Blueprint for Learning and Teaching," which called for a regulatory restructuring of schools in New York State along with the *collectively bargained* empowerment of teachers. Membership of the task force was composed predominantly of members of teacher unions. The chairperson of the task force was the president of the largest teacher union in New York State. The basic premise of the report (along with similar calls for teacher empowerment), is, we believe, flawed and unsupported by research findings. No one knowledgeable of our public educational system would deny that there are shortcomings and issues that demand attention. However, the successes are many and outweigh the flaws. We believe learners today are receiving a better, more sophisticated education than learners have in any period of history. Much of the success and strength of our public educational system has been attributed to the leadership of lay boards of education. The states have entrusted citizens at the local level with the authority and responsibility of providing the best quality education. On the other hand, there have not been any research findings to date documenting that restructuring schools or empowering teachers will result in increased learning or achievement gains for students. Another concern addressed in the argument by advocates of empowerment is the erroneous impression that teachers are not actively involved in significant educational decisions. Teachers always have been, most likely always will be involved in the management of their classrooms. Teachers make important decisions on grading, grouping of learners, curriculum content, lesson planning, instructional methodology, textbook selection, parent conferencing, curriculum development, goal development, space use, and staff development. If empowerment of teachers means ensuring that teachers keep control of these curriculum and learner concerns, that is supportable. When appropriate and necessary, teachers should have an expanded role in educational decisionmaking. Every effort should be extended to teachers to ensure greater time with students. Time on task and quality time spent with students are important to student learning. To better use their educational expertise as the facilitators of learning, teachers should be pressing for removal of clerical and administrative tasks from their job descriptions instead of seeking an expansion of these responsibilities.

The wave to bring about the empowerment of teachers has already begun to crest, yet several major issues must be addressed before the force becomes a tidal wave and we pass the point of no return. One issue is the need for a clearer understanding of what an effective restructuring of our schools might look like in order to assure quality instruction for learners. The public will most likely not be enthusiastic about restructuring our schools to empower teachers until they have some notion of what resources would be necessary and what instructional gains for students would result.

One final thought on teacher empowerment. Although efforts are under way in many states to strengthen and tighten up requirements for the certification of school administrators, those who support the notion of empowerment feel that it is okay to turn over to teachers, many of whom have had no training in administration, the responsibility for managing our schools. Is this governance by those most naïve about the system?

Instead, what is needed before massive efforts are initiated to empower teachers is further dialogue on the concept. We must experiment, perhaps over several years, with a variety of participatory decisionmaking approaches in an effort to identify those that will both significantly improve the achievement outcomes of our schools and promote the greater professionalization of the teaching workforce.

There exists a pressing need to attract quality candidates to the teaching profession. One of the conditions necessary to attract talented bright persons to education is a guarantee that they will be entering a true profession. They also need assurance that teaching commands the respect, rewards, and conditions of employment afforded to other professions.

IMPLICATIONS FOR THE PREPARATION OF EDUCATIONAL LEADERS

If principals are going to develop the leadership skills necessary to operate in the three areas suggested by Cuban (i.e., instructional, managerial, and political leadership), changes in administrative preparation programs will have to be made. Administrators will have to develop the skills essential to these areas either in pre-service or in-service programs. It would be difficult to envision administrators learning new roles while simultaneously trying to cope with the conflux of problems and forces that engulf their schools daily. A detailed task analysis would have to be developed first and then suitable content and methods attached to instruct in these tasks. Certainly the case study method would be one of the ingredients suitable to this goal.

Deal (1987) cautions that principals choosing to become instructional leaders may actually jeopardize their managerial and political leadership. Deal's concern is that a good managerial principal choosing to become an instructional leader may lose some effectiveness in school management, as might well be the case. Rallis and Highsmith (1986) suggest a conservative solution by encouraging principals to empower experienced master teachers to assume a larger role in instructional improvement. Another way to deal with the issue might be to appoint additional assistant principals and delegate some of the managerial and instructional responsibilities to them.

Based on the research of Cole (1988) in small districts and schools, teacher empowerment seems to be a viable method that could lead to instructional improvement but only if the principal feels comfortable with this use of empowerment. Additionally, the principal needs to be perceived as the instructional leader using empowerment in a teamwork fashion.

These factors all have implications for those charged with the responsibility of preparing future school administrators. University-based programs of administrative preparation will have to structure experiences that include the use of teacher empowerment as a means to improve instruction and schools. Additionally, preparation programs will need to encourage research that addresses the question of how principals can be instructional leaders, yet empower teachers to assist in school improvement.

Those institutions responsible for preparing future school administrators, particularly the principalship, will have to look carefully at issues dealing with instructional and managerial leadership. The task is not easy, nor is it clearly spelled out. However, if our schools are to meet the educational and social needs of America's youth, then those responsible for leading our schools must be skilled as both instructional and managerial leaders.

REFERENCES

Andrews, R. (1987). On leadership and student achievement: A conversation with Richard Andrews. *Educational Leadership, 45* (1), 9–16.

Blumberg, A., & Greenfield, A. (1986). *The effective school principal.* Boston: Allyn & Bacon.

Cole, B. (1988). Teaching in a time machine: The "make-do" mentality in small-town schools. *Phi Delta Kappan, 70*(2), 139–144.

Cuban, L. (1988). *The managerial imperative and the practice of leadership in schools.* Albany: State University of New York Press.

Deal, T. (1987). Effective school principal: Counselors, engineers, pawnbrokers, poets . . . or instructional leaders? In W. Greenfield (Ed.), *Instructional leadership: Concepts, issues, and controversies.* Boston: Allyn & Bacon.

Duke, D. (1987). *School leadership and instructional improvement.* New York: Random House.

Edmonds, R. (1982). Programs for school improvement. *Educational Leadership, 40*(3), 4-11.

Hallinger, P., & Murphy, J. (1987). Assessing and developing principal instructional leadership. *Educational Leadership, 45*(1), 54-61.

Keidel, R. (1986). *Game plans: Sports strategies for business.* New York: Berkley Books.

Rallis, S., & Highsmith, M. (1986). The myth of the "great principal": Questions of school management and instructional leadership. *Phi Delta Kappan, 68*(4), 300-304.

Task Force on the Teaching Profession. (March, 1988). *New York report: A blueprint for learning and teaching.* Albany, NY: State Education Department.

U.S. Department of Education (1988). *Application for educational research and development centers program.* Washington, D.C.: U.S. Department of Education. (CCFDA #84.117 C 2).

CHAPTER 10

Normative Roles and Administrator Preparation: Examining Three Sports Metaphors of Organizations

James A. Conway
State University of New York at Buffalo

The language that administrators use often betrays their underlying metaphors and predicts their biases for action (Hanson, 1984). Over the past few decades, the language of school administrators has gone through a number of transitions. In the early part of this century, school leaders tended to use the language of the military to convey meaning for their school or school system. They took pride in "running a tight ship," expected teachers and other staff to "shape up or ship out," and promoted a cult-like concern for efficiency. Other examples of the military metaphor included:

> Welcome aboard; line and staff; march to a different drummer; get in step; unity of command; chain of command; span of control; subordinates; superordinates; standard operating procedures; disciplinary measures; lead into battle; hierarchical control; supply lines; situation rooms; fail-safe mechanisms; all out attacks; communication lines; let's get the troops out; did you lose anyone?; battle fatigue; R & R; combat pay; the old man; best line of defense; . . .

In the past two decades or so, schools and school work have been described with the language of the professions. Administrators were more likely to refer to themselves and their teachers as "professionals" rather than as "good soldiers," and we heard the sorts of terms often associated with the legal, economic, and medical professions:

> Welcome to the firm; diagnostic teaching; malpractice; legal concerns; labor intensive; prescriptive teaching; observation and diagnosis; PPBS;

PERT networks; entrepreneurs; autonomy; schedule the tests; indicators of the marketplace; strategic planning; informed consent; interns; residency; doctors of education; clients; conferencing; networking; feedback; file a brief; . . .

Another metaphor that has been used intermittently but with increasing frequency of late is that of the professional athlete with its particular sports-world lexicon. Some sociologists, for example, have described the management of schools as akin to a *soccer* game with its constant flow of evolving action, and school administrators have grown accustomed to the vernacular of "*team* management," while "peer *coaching*" has become the catchphrase of the 1980s. Nor is it surprising that sports should be a popular metaphor among school people. It was long a belief that the high school coach was the training ground for the principalship, then we denied that as more myth than reality. However, in the course of conducting our recent *University of Buffalo/Executive Educator Poll* (Heller, Conway, & Jacobson, 1988), we found that 65 percent of the male and 20 percent of the female school administrators who responded have had some coaching experience (35 percent having more than five years of experience) so that the phenomenon may be more substance than myth.

In this Chapter I will capitalize on the sports metaphor in order to accomplish three goals: (1) to identify and describe three dominant sport-to-school analogies; (2) to clarify the implications of these descriptions for school leadership and in the process to identify some skills or knowledge that the administrators of the 1990s might find helpful (if not necessary) to preserve their positions in the organization as instructional and empowering leaders; (3) to consider the implications for preparation of educational leaders. Robert W. Keidel's *Game Plans: Sports Strategies for Business* (1986) will be used to build the argument. Keidel, a Senior Fellow at the Wharton Applied Research Center of the University of Pennsylvania, has explored theoretical configurations of three sports as useful models for understanding and analyzing business organizations. The models, it is argued here, are also appropriate for viewing schools.* The notion is that schools, as organizations, are structurally similar to certain types of athletic teams—that is, they have some analogous relationships to the *sport and the play of that sport.* I recognize that there are real and significant differences between schools and sports; the analogies provide extreme examples of organization types and, therefore, are useful for developing insights about schools and their leaders.

---

*It would be easy to see this metaphor as another example of the male-dominant factor in society. I acknowledge that reality but follow the lead of Mangan and Park (1987) who give equal recognition to the role of sport as a factor in the socialization of women.

THREE MODELS OF SPORTS AS ORGANIZATIONS

One of the main reasons for using sports as a metaphor for analysis is that in team games, more so than in other types of work systems, clear and distinct examples of certain critical attributes can be identified. One such important attribute is *interdependence*. Thompson (1967) defines interdependence as the degree to which an individual is dependent on and supports others in task accomplishment. Interdependence is also an attribute of organizations that is related to the "loose-coupling" concept that Weick and others have made so much of for educational organizations. For example, Weick (1976) says:

> It may be the case that the counselor's office is loosely coupled to the principal's office. The image is that the principal and the counselor are somehow attached, but that each retains some identity and separateness and that their attachment may be circumscribed, infrequent, weak in its mutual affects, unimportant, and/or slow to respond. (p. 3)

The Baseball Model

Baseball is a sport with a relatively low level of player interdependence. The players are highly dispersed over a large field with relatively little opportunity for sustained interaction while on the field. For the most part, the players pursue *individual* goals such as maximizing their number of hits, hitting for power (extra-base hits), demonstrating speed on the bases as indicated by the numbers of stolen bases, increasing reliability in hitting with men on the base (runs batted in), speed in pitching (strike outs), and so forth. Although these individual goals *may* contribute to team success, such an outcome is only loosely predictable from the individual attributes of the players.

The flow of a baseball game is also loosely configured. Each person takes a turn in coming to bat with the next move indeterminate till the last move is completed. There is little opportunity to plan ahead and "strategize." What strategy there is is mainly in terms of the individualistic qualities of the players. "Do I want a left-handed pitcher or not?" "Should we maximize speed or our power?" "Shall we sacrifice the runner along? Who is on deck?"

The organization has a leader (manager) assisted by coaches who relay signals while the game is in progress. The major responsibilities of the manager and coaches takes place *before* the season begins when they condition the team, review the essential elements of the game, and practice hitting, fielding, throwing, and on-the-field tactics. Once the season starts, the manager can be seen walking back and forth in the dugout with arms folded or staring expressionless at the players on the field. At this time, the apparent role of the manager is mainly to worry for the players. Only occasionally does the manager-coach enter into an on-the-field decision. When that happens, it is mainly centered around replacing one player for another (hitter for hitter, pitcher for pitcher).

In many ways the key to success in the baseball organization is the same as in the professional organization. Dan Gamache of Innotech (Keidel, 1986) characterizes the successful formula as: "Pick the right people, give them broadstroke performance goals and *leave them alone*" (p. 28) (emphasis added).

The Football Model

Football is a high, or moderately high, interdependent form of sport. It is a game with rigidly controlled players performing highly structured, choreographed activities in short bursts. Each person on the team knows exactly what to do and when. Plays are often sent to the quarterback by direct signals from the sidelines or by a courier (a lineman); the quarterback acts the role of field general by "calling the play" (relaying the play to the players). At a signal from the quarterback, the players act out their assignments, then await the next decision from the coaching staff.

Over time football has increasingly become a sport of specialization. Whereas at one time players performed in both offense and defense positions, today they rarely play in more than one position on either the offensive or defensive team. The offense has its linemen, pass receivers, blockers, downfield blockers; the backfield has wide or short receivers, running backs, fullbacks, passers. Defense has another set of persons with another catalog of skills and knowledge; inside and outside linebackers, pass rushers, tackles, and so on. Special teams have other highly differentiated players: kickers (field goal and kickoff), ball holder, center, punters, downfield rushers, blockers, kickoff returners. Offensive and defensive players practice apart from one another and are expected to develop cooperative relations *within* their own teams.

Keidel (1986) indicates that football as a game belongs to the coaches, and there are many of them. The organizational arrangement is for a head coach, offense and defensive coordinators, and specialized coaches for the major positions. The head coach bears heavy responsibility for the final outcome of the season. "Football is designed to reward comprehensive planning, co-ordination, and execution. It is what might be called a 'business textbook' sport" (p. 37). Its organization is a classic example of a bureaucracy, of top-down management. It is hierarchical, *tightly* controlled or linked, and its rewards come from *long-term planning*.

The Basketball Model

The third model that Keidel describes is that of basketball. This game is characterized by highly fluid, patterned yet spontaneous teamwork (high reciprocal interdependence). Keidel (1986) quotes one of the sport's greats, Bill Russell, as he describes the game:

> In each split second a basketball game changes as fast as ten rapidly moving objects can create new angles and positions on the floor. Your game plan may be wiped out by what happens in the first minute of play. The coach can't be out there; the player has to see what's going on. More, he has to predict where a pattern of action will lead, and then act to change that pattern to the advantage of his team. Teams that can do this under the greatest pressure will win most of the time. (p. 53)

Basketball relies on *team relations* for success. Cooperation is more important here than in the other sports. "Players continually face situations in which they can either go it alone or work cooperatively with other players" (Keidel, 1986, p. 55). As with the related sports of hockey and soccer, the player may win glory or disgrace as an individualist, but the sacrifice that comes from "passing off," from having the assist rather than the shot, will more often than not lead to team success. Although a player begins the game in a certain position (guard, center, or forward), there is often a rotation to a different post as a set of actions unfold and evolve. A small forward may be forced to switch to defending against a taller center, then suddenly need to rebound when ordinarily that player would be on the outside waiting for the fast-break pass. In other words, specialization is evident but not rigidly enforced.

The basketball team is usually light on administrative personnel with a head coach and one or two assistants.* The coach in this sport has preseason responsibilities similar to those of both baseball and football coaches. Conditioning and the essentials are the areas of focus, plus learning the coach's system: full court press, high and low posts, passing drills, zone and man-to-man defenses, and the like. Unlike baseball, when the basketball game begins, the role of the coach does not diminish—in fact, if anything the coach has a more important role now than before. During the flow of the game, constant reminders are called to the players to "drop off the guard," "freeze the ball," "play for one shot," "call time-out," "give it to Smith," and so on. The coach's calls are not limited to instructions; they may also include

---

*The number of coaches might be a function of the size of the team so that the overall ratios could be similar, although it does not seem that such is necessarily the case. In fact, fewer administrators (coaches) may be behind the favorable differences that James Coleman reports relative to private versus public schools (Fiske, 1988).

words of encouragement or reinforcement: "Good shot!" "That's the way to do it," and so on.

The nature of the game requires particular skills from the coach. The coach in baseball is skilled in player selection but *laissez faire* in the flow of the game. The football coach must be authoritative as to strategy if not actually authoritarian in actions. In basketball, the role of coach is as an involved leader of the key participants, equally knowledgeable in human nature and the game itself.

THE MODELS APPLIED TO SCHOOLS AS ORGANIZATIONS

What, if anything, can we learn from the sport models relative to schools? Although this is a matter of personal analysis, experience would tend to label *most* elementary schools as having many similarities to baseball organizations, school districts to football teams, and secondary schools to a hybrid of football and baseball. I shall argue later that the basketball team is the model that could apply at any level and that many readers would find most appropriate for empowered schools and school systems. Some discussion may help to justify these classifications.

Elementary Schools: The Baseball Organization

The typical elementary school has each teacher performing the teaching act in a private cubicle, called classroom, hidden from most other adults. The teachers are physically dispersed throughout a building and rarely interact with one another, save in the lunchroom or after school. As with the baseball team participant, interdependence is low and the players are loosely coupled. The principal is often viewed as a "nice person" who does his or her job by leaving the teachers alone and by keeping the "administrivia" away from the teachers so that they can do their very best in teaching at their particular grade level. Specialization is minimal because "regular" teachers teach all the major subjects; only visual and music arts and physical education have special teachers. *Articulation is a necessary condition in the elementary school, but teamwork is only optional.* When coordination is necessary, it occurs more by standardization of outputs (results on standardized tests) than by interactive decisionmaking. As Maeroff stresses in his 1988 work, *empowerment in this organization is primarily a function of the individual's status (usually length of service in the school); this in turn relates to how well that teacher knows the system and how to get things done (political knowledge).*

School Districts and Secondary Schools:
The Football (or Hybrid) Organization

As with football teams, secondary schools and school districts tend to have *specialization* as a key design feature. The specializations for school districts are the levels or types of schools (elementary, middle, senior, vocational, special, etc.). Districts and secondary schools are also specialized in terms of departments. Typical department arrangements are the subject areas and such special fields as art, music, physical or vocational education, special education, remediation, and the like, each with a head administrator who acts not unlike an assistant coach. Among the responsibilities of the department head are (1) ensuring some level of quality in that instructional area; (2) communicating the state's expectations for comparability of coverage within similar courses; and (3) communicating and monitoring to assure appropriate subject coverage across the grade levels.* The school principals are expected to have particularized knowledge and skills for the level of school they manage, and often within schools the assistant principals are specialized in terms of who handles which grade levels.

As organizations, both the school district and the secondary school tend toward the bureaucratic, chain-of-command structure of the football model. Secondary schools are typically larger than elementary schools and require a hierarchy of positions for pupil control more than for instructional improvement. I view the secondary school as a hybrid organization since its teachers, as in the elementary schools, tend to work in relatively isolated cubicles, performing their solitary acts of instructing without the knowledge, assistance, or interference of other adults. Although the departmental structure of high schools fosters an apparent interdependent of "linked" structure, the teachers within the departments have the protection of a closed door and the privacy of the classroom as a way of ensuring independence, autonomy, or at worst, a professional indifference to one another.

Because of the size and complexity of school systems, and to a lesser extent secondary schools, the chief administrator often behaves authoritatively, issuing commands (policies) about the conduct of the schools and tightly controlling the distribution of resources. Within the school, he or she allocates teachers to their cubicles, signals when to begin teaching and when to stop, when to be in the halls and when not. The principal assigns special duties such as "hall monitor," "bathroom monitor," or "bus supervisor," as well as the more rewarding posts dealing with plays, yearbooks, games, and so on. Secondary school principals, particularly in urban areas, are less likely to be rewarded for being "nice" than for being "tough." The

---

*These functions are often the responsibility of a central office coordinator, supervisor, or director for elementary schools.

Vince Lombardi image is one that many have in mind when thinking of a "successful" secondary principal.* Joe Clark, a principal in Patterson, New Jersey, is a prime example of an individual who has recently received nation-wide attention for his tough, Lombardi-like stand on controlling the climate of a difficult, inner-city high school. My intent is not to endorse the behaviors of tough principals but simply to recognize that they do persist—among women as well as men.

Empowered Schools: The Basketball Model Organization

Examples of the third type of organization have always existed in elementary and secondary schools as well as school systems, but they are more rare than usual. Such schools are often made up of teams of teachers who interact frequently in controlling the flow of instruction in the school. Albert Shanker, president of the AFT, describes one of the more extreme examples of this type, the Holweide Comprehensive School in the Federal Republic of Germany (*New York Times,* 1988).

> Holweide has a mixture of students with different abilities. But it's the school structure that's radically different.
>
> Students are not assigned to a given teacher or class. Instead, 85 to 90 students are assigned to a team of 6 or 8 teachers. This team then makes important decisions. How will the students be grouped? Which teachers will be assigned to which students? Which teachers will teach German, math, history? Should students be taught 7 or 8 different subjects each day? Or should they concentrate on a few subjects this month and other subjects next month?

In the same issue of the *New York Times* (1988), there was a description of a major experiment in school structure occurring at selected Dade County Public Schools, in Miami, Florida. Thirty-two of the Miami public schools have been granted waivers to allow them to restructure themselves under the leadership of management teams of teachers, parents, and administrators. A third-grade teacher at North Miami Elementary School has noticed significant changes in the work relationships that have occurred. She points out, as an example, that in the fall it became necessary to move about half of the teachers into new classrooms, an event that would traumatize almost any organization.

---

*As a longtime and very successful coach of the Green Bay Packers football team, Lombardi built a reputation for motivating his players but not with monetary incentives. "Vince Lombardi never paid his Packers very well. He terrorized them." (Zimmerman, 1984: p. 238)

The *order to move normally would be issued by a principal.* But this time the management team asked teachers in each department to design a solution that would satisfy not only their own needs but those of the whole school. (p. 18) (Emphasis added.)

"Before, you would have gone to a faculty meeting and be given the decision as if it came down from heaven above," she said. "In this case we all had some input. We were treated as professionals. What more could you ask for?" (p. 18)

The role of the administrator in the empowered school is one that requires:

- High interaction with the teachers.
- Skill in managing across teams to assure coordination while at the same time encouraging autonomy for innovation.
- Skills in working with people to create the relationships necessary for working as a team.

In short, the role of this sort of principal is aptly characterized in Keidel's (1986) description of a basketball coach:

The discretionary character of teamwork in basketball makes special demands on a coach's human relations skills. He must be able to induce his players to *want to cooperate, as well as to show them how to.* That is, he must integrate the interpersonal and the technical. (p. 56) (Emphasis added.)

THE SPORTS METAPHORS AND ADMINISTRATIVE LEADERSHIP

Now we are ready to look at some of the expectations for administrator knowledge and skills if these leaders are to function in empowered organizations. The descriptions of the three models indicate that different behaviors are appropriate, and even expected, for the different sports. Keidel (1986, p. 15) has identified some tasks that are necessary to all organizations but that are reconfigured in emphasis in relation to specific sports and their organizations:

To succeed, whatever its game, a team must effectively carry out three related sets of tasks: staffing, planning, and operating. *Staffing* is deciding which players will be on the team and in the game; *planning* is specifying in advance how the game should be played; and *operating* has to do with influencing the process or flow of the game. The dominant challenges, however are not identical for each sport. They are as follows:

• Baseball: Get the *players* right;
• Football: Get the *plan* right;
• Basketball: Get the *process* right.

Making our metaphoric translation, this suggests that the skills that *have been necessary* in the past for leading effective elementary schools were those that assured the availability of the best teachers for the level and type of children to be taught ("get the *teachers* right"). For the school district and its secondary schools, the emphasis has been on setting a common mission and coordinating the efforts of the diverse teachers and curricula ("get the *plan* right"). Now, we are entering an era in which a new set of skills are needed, skills having to do with faciliating the involvement of teachers in "self-managed" teams. Thus, it is argued, the leadership skills for this new era are similar to those of the basketball model where the emphasis is to "get the *process* right." However, it is also the case that the model is too simple for the realities of schools. The empowering school administrator is working with a complex system that I shall term a "Multi-Basketball Model." To envision this system takes a bit of imagination.

The multi-model would place the coach in the center of a dozen or so overlapping and concurrent basketball games. The role of this multi-game coach is to maneuver the players into well-suited teams and to encourage them to manage themselves as they manufacture their plays.* Thus, the dominant skills of this leader are twofold: (1) having knowledge about structuring multi-teams and staffing them with the best combination of players, and (2) teaching, developing, and encouraging player leadership.

The first set of skills requires a knowledge of the intracies of matrix organizations, how to form them and how to operate within them. The matrix is one of three general structures for organizing personnel for goal accomplishment. The three are variously named in the literature, often being labeled *functional* (specialization by function as in secondary schools, business offices, etc.); *product* (organized according to outputs as in elementary schools, vocational schools, magnet schools, etc.); and *matrix* (a combination product and function into a dual-focused design, as with a school-within-a-school design). Duncan (1979) has described the strengths and weaknesses of the three types and the environmental conditions that might cause one to take

---

* This might also be viewed as similar to a 3-dimensional chess game where the same piece has "powers" on at least three levels. A playing piece may join with others to attack on one level (team 1) but at the same time work with another group to defend in a different dimension (team 2).

precedence over another. Principals will need to know *what* these strengths are, as well as *when*, and *how* to move from one structure into another.

A second set of skills requires knowledge of how to motivate and develop *intra*-team leadership. These skills were the focus of a study by Manz and Sims (1987) when they examined the leader behaviors that facilitated worker self-management.

Skills of the External Leader of Self-Managing Teams

> According to an ancient Chinese saying, "The best of all leaders is the one who helps people so that, eventually, they don't need him" (Lao Tzu).
> . . . This statement seems to capture the idealistic essence of what external leadership *should be* like in contemporary self-managing work teams. Yet, some evidence seems to suggest that reality often falls short of the ideal (Manz & Sims, 1987).

Manz and Sims (1987) conducted intensive studies of a medium-sized manufacturing plant that had been structured for several years with semi-autonomous workteams ranging in size from three to 19 members. Within each team there was an elected team leader who had leader responsibilities that differentiated him or her in role and pay from the other group members.* Their central question was: What were the behaviors of the *external* leaders responsible for teams (coordinators†) that were most facilitative for self-management of group members? The underlying expectation that the head administrators held for coordinators was that they influence the team and team members to be able to do for themselves rather than that the coordinators exercise direct control or be the primary doers (Manz & Sims, 1987, p. 114).

From direct observations, surveys, and stimulations, the investigators observed some fundamental differences in the role of external leaders of self-managing teams from traditional leadership roles. The most important of these self-management leader behaviors were the following:

1. *"To encourage self-reinforcement:"* Workers indicated that they were encouraged to praise each other and give praise for a job well done and encouraged to feel positive about themselves and about a job he or she did well.

---

*The "election" of the leader may place this study closer to the master teacher concept that the traditional administrator roles. On the other hand, department chairs are quasi-administrators and often elected from the department membership.

†Coordinators is the Manz-Sims term; we might label these persons as principals or central office administrators in a school organization.

2. *"To encourage self-observation/evaluation:"* Workers were encouraged to be more aware of their own level of performance and encouraged to know and judge how well he or she was performing that job.

IMPLICATIONS OF THE METAPHORS
FOR PREPARATION OF ADMINISTRATORS

The critical question for schools or school systems is how to achieve the behaviors associated with empowering leadership. But why is this a problem? After all, if we know that the keys are in the processes, then what is holding us from action?

Despite the compilation and dissemination of extensive work on effective leadership as empowering leadership (Duttweiler & Hord, 1987) and despite the development and publication of extensive models for when and how to involve workers in decisionmaking (Vroom & Jago, 1988), and despite the eloquent pleas for "allowing teachers access to the lofty towers of power" and exhortations for a connecting of "teachers with principals, building a kind of collegiality that has been all too unusual in elementary and secondary schools" (Maeroff, 1988, p. 7)—we find uncertain successes in the sharing of decisionmaking power and involvement of teachers in the processes of self-management (Conway, 1984). It is rare to see a matrix form of organization in practice in schools. In addition, in our administration courses we find that students often have great difficulty in creating feasible, hypothetical examples, even after a unit exposing them to the intricacies of the matrix. Why are the *processes for this model of governance so difficult to implement?* For insights here we turn to another source with possible relevance: Howard Gardner's 1983 *Frames of Mind.*

Gardner theorizes that humans possess multiple intelligences. He postulates that there are five basic intelligences and a sixth that is derived or of a higher nature, as follows:

1. *Linguistic intelligence:* included are (a) the rhetorical aspect of language—"the ability to use language to convince other individuals of a course of action"; (b) the mnemonic potential—"the capacity to use this tool to help one remember information"; (c) the role of language in explanation, teaching, and so on; and (d) the "ability to use language to reflect upon language" (metalinguistic analysis) (Gardner, 1985, p. 78).

2. *Musical intelligence:* made up of pattern recognition and composition, using the cores of pitch, rhythm, and timbre with a totality not unlike linguistic intelligence (as analogy). "Bamberger has called attention to two contrasting ways of processing music which correspond roughly to 'know-how' versus 'know-that'" (Gardner, 1985, p. 110). *Know-that* is essentially propositional knowledge or theory of the subject; *know-how* is the intuitive

knowledge derived from experience ("figural approach"). Gardner contends that the theoretical (know-that) knowledge may *inhibit* one from gaining musical competence, at least initially:

> Certain important aspects of music that are "naturally" perceived accord ing to the initial "figural" mode of processing may be at least temporarily obscured ("wiped out") as an individual attempts to assess and clarify ev- erything according to a formal mode of analysis—to superimpose propo- sitional knowledge upon figural intuitions. (Gardner, 1985, p. 111)

3. *Logical-Mathematical Intelligence:*

> [T]he competence that I am terming "logical-mathematical intelligence" does not have its origins in the auditory-oral sphere. Instead, this form of thought can be traced to confrontation with the world of objects. For it is in confronting objects, in ordering and reordering them, and in assessing their quantity, that the young child gains his or her initial and most fundamental knowledge about the logical-mathematical realm. (Gardner, 1985, p. 129)

This is essentially the intelligence of the scientist who "must come up with statements, models, and theories which, in addition to being logically consistent and susceptible to mathematical treatment, must also bear a justifiable and continuing relationship to facts which have been (and will be) discovered about the world" (Gardner, 1985, p. 136). As Jacobson indicated earlier, these theoretical behaviors are the philosophical underpinnings of the "cult of efficiency" that has prevailed in educational administration.

4. *Spatial Intelligence:* the world of visual-spatial thinking. It involves the capacity "to perceive the visual world accurately, to perform transformations and modifications upon one's initial perceptions, and to be able to re-create aspects of one's visual experience, even in the absence of relevant physical stimuli" (Gardner, 1985, p. 173).

5. *Bodily-Kinesthetic Intelligence.* "Characteristic of such an intelligence is the ability to use one's body in highly differentiated and skilled ways, for expressive as well as goal-directed purposes. . . . Characteristic as well is the capacity to work skillfully with objects, both those that involve the fine motor movements of one's fingers and hands and those that exploit gross motor movements of the body" (Gardner, 1985, p. 206).

6. *Personal Intelligences:* Gardner (1985) presents two of these: the internal aspects of a person, which focuses on the ability to access one's own feelings of life (intrapersonal), and the outward aspect, which is the capacity "to notice and make distinctions among other individuals and, in particular, among their moods, temperaments, motivations, and intentions" (interpersonal) (p. 239).

The brief meanings given in the preceding paragraphs suggest that a combination of the six intelligences (but with critical emphasis on the *inter-personal* and kinesthetic intelligences) would be necessary for administrator performance in the multi-basketball model described earlier. In addition, the distinction between "know-that" and "know-how" knowledge acquisition also gains in importance. Since the so-called *theory movement* in educational administration, there has been a tendency among institutions to seek professors with particular competence in the logical-mathematical intelligence as we sought to make a science of this field. The result has been an emphasis on "know-that" knowledge. For example, we know-that "encouraging self-reinforcement" and "self-observations and evaluation" are essential behaviors for external leaders of self-managing teams, but that knowledge has *not* been useful for knowing *how to implement* such behaviors.

The multiple theories of intelligence also shed important light on the experiential (informal) forms of knowledge or skill acquisition for enhancing particular capacities such as the bodily-kinesthetic and interpersonal intelligences. Gardner (1985) suggests that the acquisition of expertise associated with these intelligences flourished in preliterate societies. The major forms of education in such societies were through initiation rites, bush schools, and apprenticeship systems. It is this last element that we must reconsider as a vehicle for fostering the "know-how" behaviors associated with empowerment. We need to create a new balance in the preparation programs that brings the experiential learning into an equal, sequential, interactive balance with the more science-oriented approach of knowing the principles (theory) of involvement, decisionmaking, and/or shared governance.

In addition to our argument for balance in program emphasis, we must also consider the possibility that we have been using the wrong measures for accepting students to our programs. The Miller Analogies and Graduate Record Exams may give us a reading on certain intelligences, but these may be secondary to the kinesthetic and personal intelligences that we have previously discussed. We need to uncover ways to distinguish these capacities. Perhaps through assessment centers, an initial screening could be conducted to uncover alternative intelligence strengths of applicants to administrator programs. On the other hand, it may even be that there are not large enough numbers of these alternative, highly developed, intelligences among teachers—in which case a new population for recruitment may need to be identified.

Finally, we should remember that different styles of leadership are demanded, or at least feasible, for the different sport models. It is a mistake to assume that *all* organizations require the basketball type of leadership. At some stages a team (or school) may need the tough-minded authoritative style; at another period a more participative, empowering style may be necessary. The leader must seek for a consistency between the model of the organization and the technical and human skills of leadership. If teachers behave as if they want to function as a baseball type of team, then a football or basketball style of management will create more chaos than success. This problem is compounded if teachers are the decisionmakers for organizational design and school leader selection. There is nothing more upsetting than a mismatch of a leader's style with an organization's structure. Nor should we expect that all teachers want to work in highly empowering (multi-basketball) organizations. We taught a summer class of 35 graduate students where we were each able to conduct a set of in-depth interviews with five teachers and/or administrators about the concept and meanings of empowerment. The results of the more than 150 interviews indicated that most teachers considered empowerment to be what the experts (legislators and union) thought that teachers should want. Empowerment (as outsiders have defined it) was not their overwhelming desire. And why should it be? After all, neither teachers nor administrators have had significant experience in performing in multi-basketball-model organizations. In our preparation programs, we must provide our students with opportunities to explore these models, function within them whether as interns or apprentices, then plan and practice for transforming organizations (should they wish to be changed) from one model to another. Indeed, *transformational leadership* (Tichy & Devanna, 1986; Levy & Merry, 1986; Conway, 1985) may well be the most difficult challenge of all.

REFERENCES

Conway, J. (1984). The myth, mystery and mastery of participative decision making in education. *Educational Administration Quarterly, 20*(3), 11–40.

Conway, J. (1985). A perspective on organizational cultures and organizational belief structure. *Educational Administration Quarterly, 21*(4), 7–25.

Duncan, R. (1979, Winter). What is the right organization structure?: Decision tree analysis provides the answer. *Organizational Dynamics,* pp. 59–79.

Duttweiler, P., & Hord, S. (1987). *Dimensions of effective leadership.* Research Triangle Park, NC: Southwest Educational Improvement Laboratory.

Fiske, E. (1988, August 31). Lessons: Are private schools better because they have fewer administrators? *New York Times.*

Gardner, H. (1985). *Frames of mind: The theory of multiple intelligences.* New York. Basic Books.

Hanson, M. (1984). Exploration of mixed metaphors in educational administration research. *Issues in Education, 11*(3), 167–185.

Heller, R., Conway, J., & Jacobson, S. (1988, September). Executive educator survey. *The Executive Educator,* pp. 18–22.

Keidel, R. (1986). *Game plans: Sports strategies for business.* New York: Berkley Books.

Levy, A., & Merry, U. (1986). *Organizational transformation.* New York: Praeger.

Maeroff, G. (1988). *The empowerment of teachers: Overcoming the crisis of confidence.* New York: Teachers College Press.

Mangan, J., & Park, R. (Eds.) (1987). *From "Fair sex to feminism:" Sport and the socialization of women in the industrial and post-industrial eras.* London: Frank Cass.

Manz, C., & Sims, Jr., H. (1987). Leading workers to lead themselves: The external leadership of self-managing work teams. *Administrative Science Quarterly, 32,* 106–128.

Thompson, J. (1967). *Organizations in action.* New York: McGraw-Hill.

Tichy, N., & Devanna, M. (1986). *The transformational leader.* New York: Wiley.

New York Times, January 10, 1988, p. 18.

Vroom, V., & Jago, A. (1988). *The new leadership: Managing participation in organizations.* Englewood Cliffs, NJ: Prentice-Hall.

Weick, K. (1976). Educational organizations as loosely coupled systems. *Administrative Science Quarterly, 21,* 1–19.

Zimmerman, P. (1984) *The new thinking man's guide to pro football.* New York: Simon & Schuster.

CHAPTER 11

Future Educational Leaders: From Where Will They Come?

Stephen L. Jacobson
State University of New York at Buffalo

Perhaps the most provocative and challenging of the recommendations to be found in *Leaders for America's Schools* (University Council for Educational Administration [UCEA], 1987) is the plaintive call for administrator preparation programs to prepare "fewer—better." This recommendation from the National Commission on Excellence in Educational Administration (NCEEA) accuses graduate training programs of not only having provided inadequate preparation but of having allowed far too many aspiring administrators to pass through their deficient programs. If implemented, the commission's proposal to close more than half of this nation's 505 administrator preparation programs would reduce drastically the flow of newly minted administrators into the pool of available administrative talent.

Concurrently, important changes are emerging in the field that could alter dramatically the way schools are presently configured and how they will be governed in the future. In Chapter 5 of this book, for example, Lomotey and Swanson point out that bigger is no longer considered to be necessarily better when it comes to determining the optimal size for units of educational governance. Instead, these authors suggest that smaller, site-based units of school governance may offer students and communities significant educational benefits that outweigh many of the advantages previously thought to be gained only through economies of scale. Swanson further contends in Chapter 7 that, as a result of recent advances in electronic technologies, specifically computerized instructional management systems, student learning outcomes may soon be independent of either school or district size.

What these field-based changes portend is that in order to improve, small school districts need no longer look only to consolidation, and large school districts should consider what Peters and Waterman (1982) have called "chunking" (i.e., decentralizing into smaller, more manageable units). In fact, a movement toward urban school decentralization has already begun. For example, as a result of legislation that took effect July 1989, considerable authority was shifted from Chicago's central school bureaucracy to local councils in each of that city's 592 schools (*New York Times*, 1988). These local councils, composed of parents, teachers, and community residents, will exercise control over such key areas as the hiring and firing of building principals, the development of school improvement plans, and some aspects of local school spending.

This newly emerging movement toward increasingly site-based, computer-rich forms of educational governance will arguably produce an increased demand for high-quality educational leaders adept at providing the necessary managerial, instructional, and political leadership described by Cuban (1988). Although some of this increased demand might be offset by increasing the administrative responsibilities of empowered teachers, particularly in the area of instructional leadership (as proposed by reformers of the second wave), supply-side reductions in administrator preparation (recommended by third-wave reformers) could produce serious shortfalls in the number of adequately prepared future educational leaders.

Indeed, field-based changes notwithstanding, some educators would argue that many of the problems currently faced by our nation's schools are more a consequence of *under* administration than *poor* administration. In their attempts to restrict the growth of school budgets and resultant property tax increases (perhaps the last arena over which many citizens feel any measure of political control), some communities have simply capped the size of their school districts' administration, thereby forcing incumbents to assume more responsibilities than time will allow them adequately to discharge. For example, in a small rural district that I examined (Jacobson, 1988), the school board attempted to make do by having the superintendent also serve as secondary school principal, school business manager, personnel director, staff development coordinator, athletic director, football and wrestling coach, and, on rare occasions, substitute bus driver. This superintendent's support staff included one assistant superintendent whose job titles included elementary school principal, curriculum coordinator, director of vocational education, chairman of the committee for special education, district representative for collective negotiations, clerk of the board, and girls' softball coach. Similar staffing patterns in neighboring districts in the region suggest that this district's administrative understaffing was not an anomaly. Therefore, even within existing educational governance structures, providing adequate administrative support could increase the demand for certified administrative personnel, just as third-wave reformers are seeking to reduce the supply.

The purpose of this chapter is to examine administrator supply and demand and to consider the implications of reform for the future of educational leadership. It begins with a look at current administrator supply and demand in the United States. As we shall see, simple supply-demand figures can seriously misrepresent both the availability and distribution of highly qualified administrators, even in jurisdictions that apparently have an oversupply of certified personnel. The chapter continues with a review of several key factors that influence administrator supply—specifically, teacher-administrator career patterns, selection processes, and occupational socialization. I will argue that traditional routes to school administration have served to impede the entrance of high-caliber women and minorities into positions of educational leadership. I will then discuss how proposed reforms in education might change these traditional factors and have an impact on the supply, demand, and composition of future educational leadership. New alternative employment opportunities outside the teaching profession notwithstanding, there presently exists a pool of talented minorities and women in the field of education who should be aggressively recruited to address the shortage of high-quality administrators this chapter predicts. The chapter concludes with an examination of the issue of whether future educational administrators should continue to come almost exclusively from the ranks of classroom teachers or whether alternative paths should be made available to talented individuals from other professions who exhibit leadership potential.

PUBLIC SCHOOL ADMINISTRATOR SUPPLY AND DEMAND

An Administrator Glut?

In a study commissioned for *Leaders for America's Schools,* James Bliss (1988) compared the number of individuals presently holding administrator certification with the current number of administrator positions by state. Bliss's examination of administrator supply and demand revealed considerable variation among the states, ranging from an apparent shortage of 1,622 certified administrators in Virginia to a surplus of 45,131 in New York. But, as Bliss himself cautions, his data overestimate the *actual* demand for administrators because many, if not most, administrative positions are currently filled. As a result, a reported administrator shortage in five states (Hawaii, Kansas, North Carolina, Utah, and Virginia) may be more a statistical artifact than a labor market reality.

In contrast, Bliss's findings revealed a mean oversupply of 5,758 certified individuals per state, which translates to roughly 1.34 school administrators available for every current administrative position. Taking the most extreme case, New York State's surplus of over 45,000 administrators yields a supply-demand ratio of 4.38 certified individuals for every administrative position. Washington, South Carolina, Florida, and Illinois were other states where supply-demand ratios exceed 3:1. In light of the fact that his methodology overestimated administrator demand, it is not surprising that Bliss concludes, "The oversupply is more than large enough to replace all incumbent school administrators" (p. 198).

One might argue from a simple labor-market perspective that an oversupply of this magnitude could only bode well for school districts seeking to fill administrative vacancies because the potential size of the pool of available candidates should allow districts greater selectivity in hiring. Yet many districts in New York, the state where this argument should be most applicable, have experienced difficulty in attracting and retaining educational leaders of the caliber they would most desire. The problem is perhaps most pronounced among New York's small and rural districts. For example, reflecting on the problems faced by the 18 school districts that comprise a predominantly rural region of central New York, one superintendent noted (Jacobson, 1988):

> They have had a very heavy turnover of superintendents. One of the reasons is that they were never willing to pay enough to attract decent candidates. Another one is, who wants to go to that size school, that isolated, where you run the risk of being buried professionally? How do you get out? If there's a decent superintendent and he gets the opportunity to move, he moves right away. (p. 21)

The Distribution of High-Quality Administrators

As the preceding quotation clearly suggests, problems of attracting and retaining high-caliber educational administrators are created not only by deficiencies in administrator preparation, as cited in *Leaders for America's Schools*, but by factors endogenous (such as low pay and school size) and exogenous (such as professional isolation) to the school districts themselves. It is important to add that administrative problems of poor quality and high turnover are not restricted to rural schools and that the phenomenon of inner-city schools "running" as opposed to "being run," as noted by Lomotey and Swanson, result from factors that may differ in specificity across the rural-urban continuum but are systemically identical. For example, the *Executive Educator/University at Buffalo* survey (Heller, Conway, & Jacobson, 1988) revealed that although urban administrators earn $11,000 more per year, on average, than do their rural counterparts ($52,000 to $41,000 respectively), the majority of respondents from *both groups* were dissatisfied with their pay (52 percent of urban administrators and 60 percent of rural administrators reported being dissatisfied with their compensation). And, although inner-city administrators may be in closer physical proximity to administrative colleagues, the size of the schools they run and the magnitude of the problems they face can often cause them to feel as professionally isolated as their peers in the countryside.

My point in raising these issues is to suggest that although some schools undoubtedly have been able to capitalize on what appears to be an administrator glut, an oversupply of certified administrators provides no assurance that all districts are able to recruit selectively. Even in New York, the state with the highest supply-demand ratio, there are schools that have few options when staffing administrative positions because high-quality administrators are either unavailable or unwilling to offer their services. The reasons that many talented individuals choose *not* to make themselves available when administrative openings arise are perhaps best understood by examining first the traditional routes that people follow to public school administration.

TRADITIONAL PATHS TO SCHOOL ADMINISTRATION

Who Enters Administration?

Throughout its history, public school administration has been a profession represented almost exclusively by former classroom teachers. During the first decade of the twentieth century, female participation in administration was more pronounced than it is today, with women holding 61.7 percent of elementary school principalships in 1905—a figure that declined to 19.6 percent by 1972–1973 (Tyack & Hansot, 1982, p. 183). During the intervening years, public school administration has become a predominantly white male bastion. The preponderance of majority males currently in administrative positions in education is illustrated by the *Executive Educator/University at Buffalo* study, in which men represented 85.2 percent of the more than 1,100 respondents, of whom 91.8 percent were white. Focusing on the superintendency exclusively, only 2.9 percent of the respondents were minority and only 4.8 percent were female. As Miklos (1988) observes, "Administrators come from traditional pools of candidates even when changing conditions support broader recruitment" (p. 55).

The fact that teachers would choose to self-select school administration is not at all surprising because administration represents the logical, if not the only, step upward in education's rather flat organizational hierarchy. The fact that others from outside the classroom so rarely find their way into administrative positions in education is perhaps more a function of state certification and licensure requirements than of individual interest or initiative. From their examination of the evolution of administrator preparation, Cooper and Boyd (1988) conclude that the present One Best Model of administrator training effectively closes entry to all nonteachers: "This path to the school administrator's office is so long and narrow that latecomers and outsiders are almost never welcome" (p. 252).

Although they defend the importance of state certification requirements, Cooperman and Klagholz (1987, p. 2) argue that there are two basic licensing errors that need to be recognized: (1) accepting someone who is likely not to possess entry-level competence, and (2) rejecting one whose basic competence is probable. The effective exclusion of all nonteachers from public school administration represents potential errors of the second type. The possibility of overcoming errors of exclusion through alternative routes to administrator preparation will be discussed later in the chapter, but first let us examine the path of educational administration's traditional pool of candidates: classroom teachers.

Teachers choose to become administrators, or at least begin administrator preparation programs, for a variety of personal reasons not the least of which is the fact that an administrative position provides the opportunity to increase one's overall package of compensatory benefits. Let me be clear in noting that my conception of compensatory benefits is not limited to pecuniary rewards only. The opportunity to have a greater voice in decisionmaking, as well as the potential recognition, respect, and authority that come with an administrative role, are intrinsic, nonpecuniary rewards that may play as important a role in career choice as salary. In a more callous vein, the chance to escape the classroom may be the most attractive reward that administration has to offer some teachers. In fact, in a study of New York City teachers, Griffiths, Goldman, & McFarland (1965) suggest that the desire to be promoted *out of the classroom* may be the primary reason that one in eight teachers spends considerable time "GASing" (i.e., Getting the Attention of Superiors).

The process of GASing, which appears to be more common among men than women (Gilbertson, 1981), involves taking on extra work responsibilities, affiliating with, and exhibiting attitudes similar to those of superiors (Ortiz & Marshall, 1988). Indeed, as a mechanism for entry into educational administration, GASing for the sponsorship of administrative incumbents appears to be more important than open competition based on merit (Ortiz & Marshall, 1988). Griffiths et al. (1965) underscore the importance of getting the attention of superiors when they observe that in New York City, "to climb in the system one must first GAS" (p. 23). Furthermore, these authors contend that a teacher who GASes does so, ". . . not to become a better educator, but rather to get promoted, since this promises greater reward in less time" (p. 29).

Focusing for a moment on monetary reward only, it's interesting that although administrator salaries still exceed teacher salaries in absolute terms, data from New York state suggest that since the first wave of the current reform movement in 1983, relative increases in teacher salaries have kept abreast and even exceeded increases in salaries paid some categories of administrators (see Table 11.1).

Table 11.1 reports changes in median salaries paid teachers and various levels of administrators in New York state between 1981/82, the year immediately before the release of *A Nation at Risk*, and 1986/87, five years later. Recall that one of the top priorities of the first wave of the reform movement was the improvement of salaries in teaching to attract more talented individuals to the workforce. Table 11.1 reveals that during this period, New York's median teacher salary grew more rapidly than median salaries paid elementary assistant principals and senior high principals. Continued calls by second-wave reformers to make teacher salaries more professionally competitive, coupled with nationwide attention to local efforts to reach that goal (such as the much-publicized Rochester City School District contract that will pay a top teacher salary of approximately $57,581 in 1989/90 and reward some "lead" teachers upward of $70,000), suggest that the once

TABLE 11.1 CHANGE IN MEDIAN SALARIES OF NEW YORK STATE SCHOOL PERSONNEL 1981/82 TO 1986/87

	1981/82	1986/87	Percentage Change
Teachers	$23,437	$32,000	36.5
Assistant Principals			
Elementary school	32,253	43,266	34.1
Middle school	32,128	44,633	38.9
Junior high school	32,253	45,370	40.7
Senior high school	32,627	44,633	36.8
Principals			
Elementary school	36,477	50,313	37.9
Middle school	36,257	51,000	40.2
Junior high school	39,500	55,088	39.5
Senior high school	39,041	53,000	35.8
Central Office			
Superintendent (independent)[a]	48,000	70,125	46.1
Superintendent (dependent)[b]	35,300	48,070	36.2
Assistant superintendent	39,137	53,659	37.1

[a] Superintendents of independent school districts including Community District Superintendents in New York City, BOCES Superintendents, Superintendents of City, City Central, Independent Union Free, and Independent Central School Districts.
[b] Superintendents of dependent school districts including Superintendents of Union Free, Central, Central High School, and Common School Districts. *(Source: State Education Department, "Public School Professional Personnel Report," Information Center on Education (1981/82 & 1986/87 reports, Albany: Author.)*

TABLE 11.2 MEAN SALARIES PAID PRINCIPALS AND ASSISTANT PRINCIPALS NATIONWIDE 1986/87 AND 1987/88

	1986/87	1987/88	Percentage Change
Assistant Principals			
Elementary school	$34,347	$36,364	5.9
Middle/junior high	37,958	40,093	5.6
Senior high school	39,758	41,839	5.0
Principals			
Elementary school	41,536	43,664	5.1
Middle/junior high	44,861	47,078	4.9
Senior high school	47,896	50,512	5.2

(*Source: National Association of Secondary School Principals [NASSP] and Educational Research Service [ERS], "Salaries Paid Principals and Assistant Principals, 1987–88 School Year" Administrative Information Report [February 1988], Reston, VA: Author.)*

potent monetary appeal of administration may begin to diminish. Comparing Rochester's top teacher salaries with mean salaries paid principals and assistant principals nationwide gives some idea of the extent to which salary differentials between teaching and administration have narrowed (see Table 11.2).

Notice that in 1987/88, the highest paid group of building-level administrators, senior high school principals, earned $50,512 on average, which was an increase of 5.2 percent over the previous year. Assuming similar increases for the next two years, the average salary paid senior high principals will be $55,902 in 1989/90, or almost $1,700 less than Rochester's projected top teacher salary that same year. Obviously, comparing top teacher salaries with mean administrator salaries across different educational jurisdictions exaggerates the extent to which teacher-administrator salary differentials are changing. But one must also consider that the number of administrator positions available within a teacher's home district are just a small subset of the total number of administrative opportunities that presently exist. For example, a veteran teacher in Rochester might do better financially by becoming a principal in Rochester but might also have to consider taking a pay cut if entering administration elsewhere. Therefore, although the salary comparison offered may be less than ideal, it does suggest that in the future money may play a lesser role in administrator career choice.

It should be noted also that although improved teacher salaries may make entry into *administrative positions* less financially attractive than in the past, there continue to exist monetary incentives in many teacher contracts that still make entry into *administrative preparation* attractive—specifically, salary differentials based on accumulation of graduate credits. Returning to

Rochester's contract, for example, the basic salary index for July 1, 1986 to June 30, 1987, reveals that the district offers teachers a 4 percent differential for each 15 hours of graduate credit accumulated beyond their bachelor's degree. In New York state, a master's degree is required for permanent teacher certification, whereas administrator certification is usually based on completion of an additional 30-hour preparation program beyond the master's. In Rochester in 1986/87, a classroom teacher who completed a 30-hour administrator preparation program earned from $1,508 to $1,696 per year more (based on years of teaching experience) than a teacher with similar experience but only a master's degree.

New York's present surplus of certified administrators undoubtedly includes a considerable number of teachers who are not especially interested in leaving the classroom but who enter administrator preparation anyway because the salary differentials provided by the district underwrite the cost of their education. If, at a later date, these teachers decide to enter administration, they then have the proper credentials; if they decide not to enter administration, they still have the additional income derived from the differentials that accrue over the course of their teaching career. The difficulty experienced by some districts in attracting high-caliber individuals into educational administration may be due in part to the fact that many entry-level administrator salaries are lower than salaries being paid to experienced teachers holding administrator certification. In other words, from a strictly financial perspective, there is a marked disincentive for an experienced teacher to assume administrative responsibilities in return for lower pay. The potential strength of this disincentive is further magnified if one also considers that administrators typically have a longer work year (11- or twelve-month contracts as compared to a standard ten-month teacher contract) *and* less job security than teachers (in many jurisdictions administrators cannot be tenured).

School Administration and Teacher Orientation

In addition to those teachers who GAS in order to be promoted out of the classroom, Griffiths et al. (1965) identified three other categories of teachers on the basis of what they value most in their work. This typology of orientations is helpful in understanding what motivates or inhibits teacher entry into administration:

1. *Pupil-oriented teachers:* teachers who are most interested in children, choosing, therefore, to stay in the classroom and avoid administrative positions. These are individuals Griffiths et al. (1965) call the "dedicated" teachers.
2. *Subject-oriented teachers:* teachers who are primarily interested in the subject they teach. Similar to pupil-oriented teachers, subject-

oriented teachers typically do not aspire to administrative positions because it would take them away from what they enjoy most. When subject-oriented teachers do leave the classroom, it is usually for industry or college teaching, not administration.

3. *Benefits-oriented teachers:* teachers who are interested primarily in the package of compensatory benefits that come with teaching. In addition to salary, these benefits include teaching's generous vacation schedule. Griffiths et al. (1965) note that benefits-oriented teachers are only mildly interested in career advancement and move horizontally "until they find a good deal" (p. 24). Some benefits-oriented teachers are simply former GASers who grew "weary of the chase" (p. 24).

On the basis of this typology, it becomes clear that if a teacher's primary orientation is toward instruction, (i.e., if the teacher is either a pupil- or subject-oriented teacher), then school administration as presently conceived offers little in the way of inducement. If, on the other hand, a teacher's primary orientation is toward escape from the classroom and enhanced benefits, particularly in terms of organizational control, then administration can be very attractive. Ortiz and Marshall (1988) contend that "a misreading of Taylor's scientific management turned schools into competitive bureaucracies, rather than collaborative service organizations, emphasizing control over instruction" (p. 123). As a result, educational administration has come to be viewed by teachers and aspiring administrators as a "technical practice focused on efficiency and hierarchical control" (p. 138).

One of the consequences of this perception is the "the long-standing bifurcation of education by gender [that] has routed women to instruction and men to administration (Ortiz & Marshall, 1988, p. 133)." Shakeshaft (1988), for example, asserts that women are concerned primarily with the administrator's function as master-teacher, whereas men view administrative positions from a managerial-industrial perspective. Shakeshaft contends that because women enter teaching in order to be near children, the more disassociated with learning they perceive administration to be, the more likely they are to avoid it. In other words, the prevailing perception of administration as being divorced from instruction makes the field less desirable to women than to men, who find it less traumatic to leave the classroom for an administrative position (Marshall, 1979).

Administrator Selection

Obviously, the desire for upward mobility is simply the first step necessary for entry into educational administration. Even for highly qualified individuals, desire alone provides no guarantee of entry into administration, because administrator selection, as noted earlier, appears to depend more on local sponsorship than personal merit. Miklos (1988), for example, contends that local candidates have a distinct advantage when competing for entry-level positions, such as assistant principal. In addition, Miklos reports that teachers who aspire most to administration place a significantly greater emphasis on deference to authority than teachers who do not. These findings suggest the existence of an informal promotion system that perpetuates traditional teacher-administrator hierarchical role relationships by rewarding loyalty to superiors with selection into entry-level administration positions.

This informal process of rewarding loyalty and reinforcing deference to authority is perhaps not surprising given the composition of education's present administrative leadership, for, as Achilles (1984) points out:

> When most of today's superintendents were still classroom teachers . . . they were quiescent, conservative, and respectful of authority. Those who didn't accept these norms dropped out.
>
> Surviving male teachers, then, tended to become politically conservative and to develop an unusually high need for respect, an exaggerated concern for authority, and a personal rigidity and fear of risk-taking behavior. (cited in Griffiths, Stout, & Forsyth, 1988, p. 285).

In contrast, Ortiz and Marshall (1988) argue that administrator selection based on loyalty is less a fear of taking risks than a simple desire by education's predominantly white male power structure to maintain control:

> The chiefs want to retain the power inherent in defining what is valuable, good, and proper. Different values and behaviors can simply be defined as deficient, devalued and wrong when they are displayed by people who appear to pose threats to those in control. (p. 136)

Regardless of which explanation one accepts, a selection preference in favor of known and loyal candidates has worked to the disadvantage of women and minorities. For example, Ortiz and Marshall (1988) report that this bias in administrator selection "manifests itself in less encouragement from superiors, less preparation and motivation" (p. 131). In fact, Valverde (1974) found that administrators in one urban district actually discouraged women and minorities from pursuing administrative preparation because they felt that members of these groups lacked the characteristics necessary for educational leadership. In a system that appears to depend on sponsorship for promotion, women and minorities seem less likely to receive the support of superiors than do white males. The existence of an old-boys network, whether real or imagined, has unfortunately caused many highly capable women and minorities to avoid administration or to simply leave education entirely because they perceive that their path to advancement will be determined more by local sponsorship than personal merit. As Richards (1988) argues: "Nowhere is the disparity between ideal and practice more damaging to the meritocratic charter of educational institutions than in the underrepresentation of women and minorities in administrative positions" (p. 160).

Organizational Socialization

Another consequence of the underrepresentation of women and minorities in educational administration is the impact that it has on behaviors and attitudes in the school workplace. For example, some have argued that because so few women and minorities have been promoted in the past, women and minority teachers are socialized to see little chance for advancement into administration (Ortiz & Marshall, 1988). Instead, members of these groups focus primarily on their work as teachers and on their interactions with colleagues. "Being well liked becomes another meaning of success to people in dead-end work" (Kanter, 1977, p. 59). Ortiz and Marshall (1988) report that whereas men are more likely to develop relationships with superiors, perhaps to obtain their sponsorship, women are socialized to look instead to their colleagues. Indeed, Ortiz (1982) reports that women who aspire to administration are cautious about revealing their ambitions and usually do so only after they are tenured.

Those women and minority members who actually enter administration face organizational problems that are often the result of their limited numbers rather than their gender or ethnicity. For example, due to their limited numbers, minority administrators are commonly assigned to minority schools where they often become professionally isolated and their opportunities for further sponsorship are drastically diminished (Valverde & Brown, 1988). Underrepresentation causes women administrators similar problems, as Shakeshaft (1986) writes: "Women principals and superintendents, because they are tokens and because they are not included or do not choose to be included in all-male activities, often report less colleagueship with male administrators and a deep awareness of 'loneliness at the top' " (p. 172).

Perhaps it is the loneliness experienced by women administrators that helps to explain the existence of a female-defined school culture that differs from traditional male organizational cultures in the areas of work environment, leadership, communication, decisionmaking, and conflict resolution. In other words, separation from the male-defined norms of their colleagues may enable women administrators to redefine the organizational culture within their own schools. Specifically, Shakeshaft's (1988) review of the literature indicates that female-defined schools tend to be more child-centered and less hierarchical and to allow more opportunities for shared decisionmaking than male-defined schools. Women administrators "take a more active stance towards instructional leadership" (Wheatley, 1981, p. 269) and are more likely to classify governance activities as maintenance rather than leadership (Clark, 1983).

Pitner's (1981) study of superintendents, for example, revealed that women superintendents tended to tour their buildings more often than males, and when they did, "females used their time to visit classrooms and teachers, keeping abreast of the instructional program, while males used the time to walk the halls with principals and the head custodians" (p. 288). Pitner found that female administrators tend to be more casual in dress, more flexible in their meeting agendas, and more informal with subordinates than their male counterparts, commonly allowing subordinates to maintain a first-name relationship. In addition, Pitner found that women superintendents spend more time with nonparent community members and professional colleagues than males, although this time is spent almost exclusively with other females.

Shakeshaft (1986) contends that the recent literature on female-defined schools clearly reaffirms the conclusion reached by Hemphill, Griffiths, & Fredericksen (1962) over a quarter of a century ago, which was that women should be favored over men for positions of administration "if the job of the principal is conceived in a way that values working with teachers and outsiders; being concerned with objectives of teaching, pupil participation, and the evaluation of learning; having knowledge of teaching methods and techniques; and gaining positive reactions from teachers and superiors" (p. 334).

In contrast to the prevailing perception of administration, as described by Ortiz and Marshall (1988), the concept of administration offered by Hemphill et al. (1962) emphasizes collaboration over competition, instruction over control. If conceived in these terms, school administration would probably become far more attractive to pupil- and subject-oriented teachers (while at the same time probably having little effect on the behavior of benefits-oriented teachers since it's unlikely that teaching's unique vacation schedule will ever be extended to school administrators). In other words, by redefining the role and responsibilities of the educational administrator, it might be possible to begin attracting more school leaders from the ranks of those dedicated professionals whose primary interest in instruction traditionally has caused them to avoid administrative positions. An increased interest in administrator preparation by this previously untapped pool of teachers is particularly important if we begin preparing "fewer—better" because it would enable preparation programs to be more selective in their admissions and thereby address a second concern of the *Leaders for America's Schools* report—the lack of quality candidates for preparation programs.

EDUCATIONAL REFORM AND FUTURE SCHOOL LEADERS

What then does the reform movement have to say about redefining present concepts of educational leadership? Although the first two waves of reform were relatively silent about the role of the school administrator, the recommendations of first-wave reports such as *A Nation at Risk* (NCEE, 1983) simply reinforced existing notions that school improvement was dependent on technical efficiency and hierarchical control. In contrast, reformers of the second wave began to question implicitly both educational administration's present orientation and its traditional career path. Recommendations from *Teachers for the 21st Century* (Carnegie Forum, 1986) and *Tomorrow's Teachers* (Holmes Group, 1986) reveal a deeper concern for the fundamental curriculum and instructional issues that confront our schools, and both reports offer a restructured profession in response. For example, the Carnegie Forum suggests, "giving teachers a greater voice in the decisions that affect the school" (p. 24), and the Holmes Group recommends "a staged career that would make and reward formal distinctions about responsibilities and degrees of autonomy" (p. 36).

At the pinnacle of the Carnegie Task Force's proposed teacher hierarchy would be a building-level committee of "Lead" teachers whose administrative responsibilities would include setting schoolwide performance criteria, the development of curriculum, instructional supervision, course scheduling and assignment, and even the hiring and dismissal of personnel. In other words, this cadre of Lead teachers would be responsible for making decisions, particularly in the area of instruction, that in the past have been reserved almost exclusively for administrators. Under this system, traditional administrative positions would remain primarily managerial in nature. Educational leadership would no longer reside solely with a single individual whose role responsibilities were almost entirely divorced from the classroom. Instead, participation in educational leadership would be broader based, with key administrative functions shared by a group of individuals, some of whom would remain intimately involved with classroom instruction. In essence, school administration becomes a bicameral form of leadership, with one group of teacher-administrators responsible for the technical core of instruction, while another group of administrator-managers is responsible for maintenance and control. This broadened concept of educational leadership would not only make the field of administration more attractive to instruction-oriented teachers but could allow alternative career paths to be developed for qualified nonteachers as well.

Alternative Paths to Administration

Using this broadened concept educational leadership as a basis for discussion, let us examine two proposed alternative administrator career paths for qualified nonteachers. The first is a proposal by the New York State Association of School Business Officials (NYSASBO, 1988) to create a separate certification for school business officials; the second is a proposed revision of requirements for the preparation and certification of school principals in New Jersey.

Jordan and Webb (1986) write, "The primary purpose of school business administration is to provide a service and support function. This administrative function is effective to the degree that adequate and appropriate goods and services are made available to students" (p. 171).

The responsibilities of the school business official usually include, but are not limited to fiscal planning and budgeting, accounting, data processing, facility maintenance and operation, risk management, purchase and supply, food services, and pupil transportation. Clearly, these responsibilities are primarily managerial in nature, providing service and support for the technical core of instruction. Nevertheless, existing certification in New York requires three years of teaching experience for a candidate to obtain a School District Administrator certificate. As the NYSASBO Certification Committee points out, under existing conditions:

> It is possible, and likely, that a candidate can get a School District Administrator certificate and function as a chief business official of a district without ever having completed one course in business or finance. It is also possible that a person could have two years of teaching experience, hold an MBA degree, have served successfully for three years as a civil service business manager, hold a doctorate in Educational Administration and still not meet current certification criteria. (p. 4)

These hypothetical examples are representative of the two basic licensing flaws described by Cooperman and Klagholz (1987), that is, the inclusion of individuals lacking basic skills and the exclusion of those whose basic competence is probable. The NYSASBO's proposal to create a separate School Business Administrator certificate seeks to address errors of the first type by requiring that school business officials be trained in both educational *and* business administration, and it addresses errors of the second type by allowing "candidates with proven business competencies and expertise greater access to the field of public school administration" (p. 5). Included within this pool of competent nonteacher candidates would be successful business managers from the private sector, as well as many of the Civil Service employees currently working in school districts around New York State. An existing shortage of qualified school business officials both in New York and nationally (NYSASBO, 1988) will only be magnified if the movement toward site-based management intensifies. Providing competent individuals with limited or no teaching experience to have greater access to the school business office seems a reasonable approach for dealing with potential shortages in this noninstructional component of administration. More challenging and potentially problematic is allowing individuals with limited or no teaching experience to have greater access to the principalship.

As early as the turn of the century, the primary responsibility of the building principal had begun to change from "principal" teacher to administrative manager (Jacobson, Reavis, & Logsdon, 1954). Issues of instruction increasingly gave way to concerns far more clerical in nature (e.g. record-keeping and maintenance of schedules), as principals were called on to manage the daily affairs of increasingly larger and more complex organizations. Nevertheless, the effective schools literature has been interpreted to suggest that the "effective" principal is one who is both an efficient administrative manager *and* an instructional leader. As a result, today's principal feels pressured to assume both roles yet experiences frustration over the ambiguity and conflict that this dual function creates.

In its call for changes in the preparation and certification of school principals, the New Jersey State Department of Education (NJSDE, 1986) begins by arguing that there is a need for a clearer concept of the work principals *ought* to perform. After an examination of the relevant literature the NJSDE concludes:

> The time has long passed when principals can realistically be expected to function as the "head teachers" or "teaching experts" of their schools. Indeed, instructional leadership must cease to be thought of as meaning personal teaching expertise. . . . The time has also come to recognize that it is teachers themselves who are and must be the teaching experts of their schools. (pp. 56, 57)

Clearly, the position expressed by the NJSDE is supportive of the reconceptualization of educational administration described earlier. The NJSDE recommends that principals receive "highly focused training and practice, not in how to teach, but in how to observe and evaluate teaching" (p. 67). The assessment of principal performance would depend on "generic management and leadership competencies implied by a conception of the principal as an organizational executive, rather than a teaching expert or a specialist in public school administration" (p. 68). Therefore, in addition to programs in educational administration, individuals could prepare academically for the principalship through training in business administration, public administration, management science, or organizational leadership. After obtaining the appropriate degree (MBA, MPA, etc.), aspiring principals would then have to, "acquire a practical familiarity with schools as organizations and with the work of teachers from the perspective of an executive" (NJSDE, 1986, p. 78). This "practical familiarity" would take the form of a carefully supervised administrative internship (see Milstein, Chapter 8, for a detailed discussion of an appropriate clinical sequence) and require the aspiring administrator to "know the business" (Peters & Waterman, 1982). This approach to preparation and licensure still values the importance of exposure to the classroom and classroom instruction by the aspiring administrator. What distinguishes New Jersey's proposed path to the principalship from traditional career routes is that it opens the door to a wider pool of nonteacher candidates, including: "Men and women of great leadership potential and solid track records, individuals who have already run substantial units and systems within the private sector, the military, perhaps higher education itself" (Peterson & Finn, 1988, p. 106).

Peterson and Finn (1988) address head-on what is perhaps the thorniest question in terms of providing alternative routes to administration: "Would the teachers in a school allow themselves to be led by one who had not come up through the ranks?" (p. 106). These authors conclude that teachers would accept the leadership of nonteachers if two conditions are met: (1) that teachers are themselves provided a career ladder that would allow them greater access to instructional decisionmaking, and (2) that nonteacher administrators become familiar with pedagogic issues so that they can provide knowledgeable support and assistance when needed. Once again, the conceptual underpinning of an alternative career proposal such as New Jersey's is dependent on a new vision of educational leadership that attempts to define more clearly the articulation of administrative and instructional responsibilities by broadening the existing level of participation. Obviously, the impact of this new vision of educational leadership (and the alternative career routes it creates) on the supply of and demand for high-quality school administrators cannot be determined *a priori*. Nevertheless, changes such as those taking place in New Jersey should be viewed as meaningful experiments that need to be encouraged and monitored carefully.

CONCLUSIONS

Let us review briefly what has been covered in this chapter. Data on administrator supply and demand nationwide suggest that currently there are far more certified individuals than available positions. Indeed, there are far more certified individuals than existing administrative positions, whether available or not. One response to this surplus is to simply prepare fewer aspiring administrators. Yet, even during this period of administrator glut, there are a considerable number of school districts that cannot attract or retain high-quality educational leaders. Among the factors identified as contributing to this problem are deficiencies in administrator preparation, responsibility overload due to underadministration, dissatisfaction with compensation, professional isolation, traditional career paths that exclude nonteachers, "old-boy" sponsorship networks and organizational socialization that have restricted the participation of women and minorities, monetary disincentives, and perhaps most important, the prevailing perception that the responsibilities of the school administrator are unrelated to the primary interests of teachers dedicated to instruction.

There is a growing body of literature to suggest that educational leadership is a critical determinant of educational quality. Yet, just as we are beginning to consider the UCEA's recommendation to prepare fewer, there are structural and technological changes occurring in the field to indicate that in the near future we will be needing more rather than fewer high-caliber educational leaders. Educational leadership has obviously reached an important juncture. Although I support preparing "fewer—better," this recommendation will be successful only if we first reconceptualize what educational leadership entails and who should be involved. For even if we prepare them better, if we simply prepare fewer of the same types of administrator candidates—candidates with the same preferences and orientations as in the past—we are not likely to address successfully the educational challenges of the next millenium. If the field is to become more attractive and accessible to a broader range of potentially high-quality candidates, then educational leadership must come to be viewed as being as concerned about fundamental pedagogic and instructional issues as it has been traditionally about issues of efficiency and control. Furthermore, educational leadership and the expertise required for obtaining it must come to be viewed as residing both in and out of the classroom. These changes would signal a redefinition of educational leadership that for women and minorities, pupil- and subject-oriented teachers, and nonteachers (regardless of gender or ethnicity) might make administration more attractive than it has been in the past.

Proposed revisions in administrator certification in at least two states indicate that a movement toward a new concept of educational leadership has already begun. Further evidence of change is offered by Ortiz and Marshall (1988), who report a dramatic increase in the number of women serving on local school boards. These authors believe that an increased participation of women in local school governance will presage a shift in traditional school board concerns from issues primarily managerial in nature toward a more instructional orientation. Assuming these changes make administration more attractive to a wider range of candidates, preparation programs that chose to prepare "fewer—better" could then be far more selective than in the past. But with increased selectivity should come a greater responsibility on the part of institutions of higher education to help their graduates locate field placements, particularly aspiring minority and female administrators. As preparation programs become more sensitive to market realities, they should take an advocacy role in administrator sponsorship. Marshall (1979) notes that because traditional field-related sponsorship is often more problematic for women than men, women tend to depend on their graduate preparation in administration as an alternative source of sponsorship. Unfortunately, sponsorship in many preparation programs often means little more than posting job openings on a bulletin board or helping students develop their résumés. Administrator preparation programs could play a significant role in redressing the marked underrepresentation of women and minorities in the field through the aggressive placement of their graduates. Although there are data to suggest improvements in the proportion of minority and women educational administrators over the past decade (see Jacobson, Chapter 3), these changes have come primarily in large urban districts. Through aggressive entry-level sponsorship, administrator preparation programs could help make important inroads in other geo/demographic areas as well—inroads that would offer minority and women candidates greater visibility and thus greater access to subsequent field-related sponsorship.

REFERENCES

Achilles, C. (1984). Forecast: stormy weather ahead in educational administration. *Issues in Education, 2,* 127-135.

Bliss, J. (1988). Public school administrators in the United States: An analysis of supply and demand. In D. Griffiths, R. Stout, & P. Forsyth, (Eds.), *Leaders for America's schools: Final report and papers of the National Commission on Excellence in Educational Administration* (pp. 193-199). Berkeley, CA: McCutchan.

Carnegie Forum on Education and the Economy. (1986). *Teachers for the 21st century.* New York: Author.

Clark, P. (1983). A leadership study of local education association presidents in Maryland. Unpublished Master's Thesis, University of Maryland, Baltimore.

Cooper, B., & Boyd, W. (1988). The evolution of training for school administrators. In D. Griffiths, R. Stout, & P. Forsyth (Eds.), *Leaders for America's schools: Final report and papers of the National Commission on Excellence in Educational Administration* (pp. 284-304). Berkley, CA: McCutchan.

Cooperman, S., & Klagholz, L. (1987). *Teaching experience and the certification of principals.* Trenton: New Jersey State Department of Education.

Cuban, L. (1988). *The managerial imperative and the practice of leadership in schools.* Albany: State University of New York Press.

Gilbertson, M. (1981). The influence of gender on the verbal interactions among principals and staff members: An exploratory study. In P. Schmuck, W. Charters, & R. Carlson, (Eds.), *Educational policy and management: Sex differentials* (pp. 297-306). New York: Academic Press.

Griffiths, D., Goldman, S., & McFarland, W. (1965). Teacher mobility in New York City. *Educational Administration Quarterly, 1*(1), 15-31.

Griffiths, D., Stout, R., & Forsyth, P. (1988). The preparation of educational administrators. In D. Griffiths, R. Stout, & P. Forsyth (Eds.), *Leaders for America's schools: Final report and papers of the National Commission on Excellence in Educational Administration* (pp. 284-304). Berkeley, CA: McCutchan.

Heller, R., Conway, J., & Jacobson, S. (1988, September). Executive Educator Survey. *The Executive Educator,* pp. 18-22.

Hemphill, J., Griffiths, D., & Federicksen, N. (1962). *Administrative performance and personality.* New York: Teachers College Press.

Holmes Group. (1986). *Tomorrow's teachers: A report of the Holmes Group.* East Lansing, MI.: Author.

Jacobson, P., Reavis, W., & Logsdon, J. (1954). *The effective school principal.* Englewood Cliffs, NJ: Prentice-Hall.

Jacobson, S. (1988). Effective superintendents of small, rural districts. *Journal of Rural and Small Schools, 2* (2), 17-21.

Jordan, K., & Webb, L. (1986). School business administration. *Educational Administration Quarterly, 22* (3), 171-199.

Kanter, R. (1977). *Men and women of the corporation.* New York: Basic Books.

Marshall, C. (1979). Career socialization of women in school administration. Unpublished Doctoral Dissertation, University of California, Santa Barbara.

Miklos, E. (1988). Administrator selection, career patterns, succession, and socialization. In N. Boyan (Ed.), *Handbook of research on educational administration* (pp. 53-76). White Plains, NY: Longman.

National Commission on Excellence in Education. (1983). *A nation at risk: The imperative for educational reform.* Washington, DC: U.S. Government Printing Office.

New Jersey State Department of Education. (1986). The preparation and certification of school principals in New Jersey. Trenton, NJ: Author.

New York State Association of School Business Officials. (1988). Licensing and certification of school district business administrators. Albany, NY: Author.

New York Times. (December 14, 1988). Chicago Gets Law Overhauling the City's Public Schools: B17.

Ortiz, F. (1982). Career patterns in educational administration: Women, men and minorities in educational administration. New York: Praeger.

Ortiz, F., & Marshall, C. (1988). Women in educational administration. In N. Boyan, (Ed.), *Handbook of research on educational administration* (pp. 123-141). White Plains, NY: Longman.

Peters, T., & Waterman, R. (1982). *In search of excellence.* New York: Harper & Row.

Peterson, K., & Finn, C. (1988). Principals, superintendents, and the administrator's art. In D. Griffiths, R. Stout, & P. Forsyth, (Eds.), *Leaders for America's schools: Final report and papers of the National Commission on Excellence in Educational Administration* (pp. 89-107). Berkeley, CA: McCutchan.

Pitner, N. (1981). Hormones and harems: Are the activities of superintending different for a woman? In P. Schmuck, W. Charters, & R. Carlson, (Eds.), *Educational policy and management: Sex differentials* (pp. 273-295). New York: Academic Press.

Richards, C. (1988). The search for equity in educational administration: A commentary. In N. Boyan, (Ed.), *Handbook of research on educational administration* (pp. 159-168). White Plains, NY: Longman.

Shakeshaft, C. (1986). *Women in educational administration.* Beverly Hills, CA: Sage.

Shakeshaft, C. (1988). Women in educational administration: Implications for training. In D. Griffiths, R. Stout, & P. Forsyth (Eds.), *Leaders for America's schools: Final report and papers of the National Commission on Excellence in Educational Administration* (pp. 403-416). Berkeley, CA: McCutchan.

State Education Department. (1982). *Public school professional personnel report: New York State 1981-82.* Albany, NY: Author.

State Education Department. (1987). *Public school professional personnel report: New York State 1986–87.* Albany, NY: Author.

University Council for Educational Administration. (1987). *Leaders for America's schools: The report of the National Commission on Excellence in Educational Administration.* Tempe, AZ: Author.

Tyack, D., & Hansot, E. (1982). *Managers of virtue.* New York: Basic Books.

Valverde, L., (1974). *Succession socialization: Its influence on school administrative candidates and its implications on the exclusion of minorities from administration.* Washington, D.C.: National Institute of Education, Project 3-0813. ERIC ED 098 052.

Valverde, L., & Brown, F. (1988). Influences on leadership development among racial and ethnic minorities. In N. Boyan, (Ed.), *Handbook of research on educational administration* (pp. 143–157). White Plains, NY: Longman.

Wheatley, M. (1981). The impact of organizational structures on issues of sex equity. In P. Schmuck, W. Charters, & R. Carlson (Eds.), *Educational policy and management: Sex differentials* (pp. 255–271). New York: Academic Press.

CHAPTER 12

An Epilogue: Where Is Educational Leadership Going?

James A. Conway and Stephen L. Jacobson
State University of New York at Buffalo

The purpose of this book has been to examine what we have called the third wave of the current educational reform movement—the reform of administrator preparation. It was our intention to present a variety of voices with each author offering a slightly different perspective on this most recent wave of reform. In this final chapter, we will bring these voices into harmony, summarizing the perspectives and underscoring the issues or challenges posed.

Our organizing framework for the book has moved from general descriptions of the *contexts of reform* to more particularized *undercurrents or issues* that have an impact on the reform movement, followed by even more specific *implications for leadership and preparation*, that is, for doing something about something. That very nebulous description at the end underscores one of the difficulties of creating a sense of harmony around this educational movement, for in many ways the complexity of the reform movement reflects the definitional complexity of *reform*. What does reform mean? Included among the meanings to be found in any standard college dictionary are the following:

1. To form again; to bring back or restore to an original state.
2. To change for the better; to free from previous faults.
3. To put an end to; to take away or remove entirely.

Clearly, reform implies change. It can be a re-forming of what is into something that more closely resembles what once was. It can be a re-forming of what is into something better, that is yet to be. Or it can simply be the end of what is. Although the point of transition may not be clear, reform implies both an ending (of what is) and a beginning (of what will be, even if what will be is the end of what is). This transition could be revolutionary (i.e., a drastic change in the existing condition) or, what is more likely in the context of education, evolutionary (i.e., a process of unfolding, growing, or developing).

Leaders in education must cope with the uncertainties of reform in order to determine who should be doing what, if anything, and for what ends. If there is disagreement as to whether *something is wrong*, there will probably be disagreement over the need to re-form. If there is disagreement over *what it is that is wrong*, there will probably be disagreement over what it is that needs to be re-formed.

The convoluted nature of leadership in an era of reform is captured well in Janusz Korczak's classic fable *King Matt the First* (1923). Matt, as a child king, tries to learn what a king is supposed to do. Matt wants to be known as the "Reformer King" so he visits with a neighboring regent to inquire about this. The regent tells Matt that a king does more than just wear a crown; he must also bring happiness to the people. Matt asks how one does that, and the regent says by making various reforms—but adds a caution—that it's a very hard thing to do. Matt leaves with a puzzled expression and thinks, "I am the Reformer King and I don't know what reforms are. But he says they are very hard" (p. 120). For many principals and superintendents, that captures the essence of their feelings—we are expected to implement reforms that we don't really understand, but that we know are very hard to do.

PART I: THE CONTEXT OF EDUCATIONAL REFORM

Reflecting on the first wave of the current reform movement, Farrar observed that its impact was far greater than earlier reform efforts due in large measure to a consensus among business, political, and educational leaders (as well as the public at large) that *something was wrong* with our educational system and that change was necessary. During the Sputnik era, we saw ourselves in a competitive struggle for space, and the nation responded to the challenge of conquering this new frontier. Now the perceived danger was economic survival. There was a new sense of urgency as first-wave reformers linked declining student performance to markets lost to competitors in the Far East and ultimately to an overall sense of national economic malaise. The stakes were perceived by most to be too critical to neglect. It was suggested that we were rapidly becoming a second-class nation—and nothing is more damaging to the American ego than to think that others will no longer listen when we speak. This psychologically felt crisis, fired by political and social forces, resulted in knee-jerk reactions such as recommendations for longer school days and more of them, with more homework to be completed between them. Old work ethic solutions were resurrected: "when things get tough" "pull yourself up by your own bootstraps,"—hard work—greater efficiency—more pay—carrots and sticks. But as Farrar points out, old solutions could not meet current challenges. She indicates that educational excellence was not amenable to either fiats from above or monetary incentives. So, instead, we moved to a second level of concern and looked at the problem as centered in and among the teaching force.

Reflecting on the second wave, Petrie observes that although there was agreement that something was wrong, there was considerable disagreement over *what it was*, and therefore, considerable disagreement over what needed to be re-formed. The first wave of reform could be characterized by what Tocqueville identified as a tendency peculiarly American, self-criticism. But what the blue-ribbon national committees apparently forgot was the word *self*. Teachers were not a significant part of this first movement. Rather, they were the focus of bashing because their "mediocrity" was considered a root cause of our purportedly poor educational system.

Petrie notes that second-wave reformers moved the context of reform to a different level of understanding by first questioning and then redefining basic assumptions of earlier critics about teachers and teaching, the processes of learning and teaching, and, most important, the context of those processes we know as "schools." First, if teachers are to be treated as *professionals*, rather than as *technicians*, then a new set of roles should be identified that differ from past traditions. Specifically, teachers would now be more concerned with the goals of education and with balancing means and ends, rather than simply trying to implement what others have defined. Second, if traditional assumptions about the teaching-learning process are transformed from the factory and/or therapist metaphors to an emerging view of joint meaning-making, then a different set of teaching practices must occur, with consequent expectations for reforming teacher preparation. Third, it would seem that schools and schooling have not heeded significant changes in the social and cultural contexts within which they exist, and as a result, they have been inattentive to their real or potential impact on teachers, children, and subject matter. Emerging from these challenged assumptions come a set of new expectations for educational leaders that highlight a need to cope with collegiality and accountability, autonomy and national assessments, new technologies and a renaissance of liberal education. These expectations give rise to the third wave of reform wherein consideration must be given to the dynamics of preparing these "new" educational leaders.

Jacobson places the National Commission on Excellence in Educational Administration in the historical context of administrator preparation in America. Perhaps because the composition of the commission was broad-based, it did not conclude with a unified voice. In fact, the potential ramifications of the commission's final recommendations were perceived as threatening by a considerable number of programs, professors, and many others in the field. For example, many preparation programs saw the outcomes as serving primarily the interests of the major research universities because one recommendation was to close small programs. On the other hand, large and small programs alike were challenged by the commission to consider what to teach and how. Professors trained in the 1950s are still entrenched in educational administration programs teaching the theory of the field. Jacobson raises the spectre that perhaps the teaching of theory has become a ritualized myth in current preparation programs. Perhaps educational administration is at a point at which it is facing what other social sciences encountered. For example, Campbell (1972) argues that psychology (as a related field of social science) has undergone considerable change during the past half-century or so, and much that was myth in psychology has since been refuted by science. But has that meant that the challenged beliefs fundamental to psychology have been transformed? "Not so!" argues Campbell. He points, for argument sake, to Frazer in *The Golden Bough* who,

> *assumed* that when a custom or belief was shown to be unreasonable, it would presently disappear. And how wrong he was can be shown simply by pointing to any professor of philosophy at play in a bowling alley: watch him twist and turn after the ball has left his hand, to bring it over to the standing pins. (p. 11)

Have professors become so enamored with theory that they have ritualized it as theory for theory's sake? In Griffiths's (1988) analysis, the theory movement was viewed as a positive force that helped to catapult educational administration from a practical art to a status approaching that of an academic discipline. On the other side, however, Greenfield (1984) saw this same movement as contributing to fragmented outcomes, often irrelevant if not disconnected from the world of practice.

Professors in all programs are often viewed as enmeshed in a theory-practice-research struggle, and in some cases the reactions have indicated an open hostility between theory and practice (Thomson, 1989):

> We have created two cultures in educational administration, with incompatible perspectives, divergent reward systems, and little agreement about the root causes of current deficiencies in the preparation and development of elementary and secondary school leaders. (p. 373)

In a similar sense, the practitioners have found themselves labeled as poorly prepared, managerial rather than leader-oriented, resistant to change, and confrontational as to teaching and teachers. It is not surprising, therefore, that the audiences of the commission have not heard the same message, or if they have, they have resisted it. Once again, reform is faced with a lack of agreement over what is wrong and what needs fixing (although there is no argument that *something* needs to be done).

In the second section of the book, the voices of four authors were heard as they examined some critical issues that cut across the contextual currents of reform.

PART II: THE UNDERCURRENTS OF REFORM

As we reflect on the Farrar, Petrie, and Jacobson pieces, we see a set of tensions identified that are affecting administrator preparation programs, the educational leaders they propose to produce, and even the school systems in which they will practice. All systems exist within a set of major but competing forces. If a system is able to control the pull of these competing forces, it will experience a dynamic balance. In the present state of affairs, these three writers have identified a number of political, social, demographic, economic, and philosophical tensions that have set our educational system to spinning, which in turn has increased the two major sets of forces acting on the system. In one direction, the system experiences a force to centralize, and as it spins, it pulls *inward* to provide a gravity for its members (centripetal forces). In the other direction, the spin creates movement *away* from the center as elements seek to escape and break free (centrifugal forces). If either force becomes dominant, the system may become a black hole as it swallows itself, sucking in all energy, or it may become totally random as elements break free in a wild spin through its universe. The delicate balance that holds the system in a dynamic growth state is critical.

Some of the tensions increasing the centripetal (centralizing) forces include top-down mandates for greater accountability and efficiency; demands for expenditure reductions; legislative bodies encouraging (even mandating) common sets of school outcomes; demographic changes such as declining school enrollments and an aging teaching workforce; a movement toward packaged staff development where all in the system are subjected to a common training regimen; a belief (as Jacobson points out) that there exists "One Best Model" for running schools effectively. Opposing these pressures to centralize are centrifugal (decentralizing) forces such as teacher expectations for increased autonomy and empowerment, as well as expectations that both teachers and administrators act as reflective practitioners who exercise professional judgments about educational means and ends. In addition, there are significant social and cultural forces acting on the system such as an at-risk population that is increasing in both size and complexity and a population that seems to respond negatively to the traditional "suburban" model of schooling.

These tensions or forces were further elaborated and clarified in this second part of the book. For example, Nyberg's analysis of power, empowerment, and authority suggests that emergent roles in education can act on the system in *either* a divergent (centrifugal) *or* convergent (centripetal) fashion, depending on underlying assumptions as to the nature of power. He gives credence to the notion that power is a variable-sum rather than a zero-sum game that is based on mutually enhancing social, psychological, and instrumental relationships. Although Nyberg suggests that power can take many forms, it is power as trust and mutual commitment that will enable education's principal actors to learn to work with one another in a school community by building a psychological commitment to cooperative, collegial relationships. When all is said and done, Nyberg implies that empowering teachers, students, and the community means sharing authority and enabling these significant others to act and act critically.

Nyberg's chapter relates well to the traditional knowledge content of educational administration and management. For example, his analysis of trust as a form of power is quite consistent with research on participative decisionmaking (Conway, 1984) and with Chester Barnard's (1938) concept of a "zone of indifference." It is less consistent with the meanings and limits of trust that Barber (1983) discusses. Barber develops an understanding of the meaning of trust as operating at three levels:

> The most general is expectation of the persistence and fulfillment of the natural and the moral social orders. Second is expectation of *technically competent role performance from those involved with us in social relationships and systems.* And third is expectation that partners in interaction will carry out their fiduciary obligations and responsibilities, that is, their duties in certain situations to place others' interests before their own. (p. 9) (Emphasis added.)

Once again the diametric tensions emerge. For Nyberg "trust and mutual commitment" are an empowering force and thus centrifugal. For Barber, however, trust is related to mutual confidence in positional competence that is potentially "standardizing" and thus a centripetal force. This tension suggests that a crucial aspect of professionalism is that all individuals permitted to practice be adequately prepared (Darling-Hammond, 1988). Although that expectation has been applied to teacher education programs by reformers of the second wave, it is equally appropriate to administration and is at the heart of this third wave (Darling-Hammond, 1988):

> So long as anyone who is not fully prepared is admitted to an occupation where autonomous practice can jeopardize the safety of clients, the public's

trust is violated. So long as no floor is enforced on the level of knowledge needed to teach [or administer], a professional culture in schools cannot long be maintained, for some practitioners will be granted control and autonomy who are not prepared to exercise it responsibly. (p. 38)

Nyberg and others may decry the apparent mindlessness of Hunter's Essential Elements of Instruction, but at least that synthesis of knowledge can be packaged and disseminated to remind teachers of the basic competencies of their professional practice. But what is the equivalent for administrators? *By what process are teachers assured that administrators will have positional competence necessary for trust and mutual commitment?* Is it to be by preparation programs with virtually no standards for admission? We recall that Jacobson cites evidence that the administrators of today consider their administrative preparation as inadequate. Then what is the professional (staff) development program equivalent to Hunter's Essential Elements of Instruction that will help them with the Essential Elements of Administrating?

Moving on to the restructuring of school governance, Lomotey and Swanson's analysis of rural and urban schools contrasts the cultures and structures of communities at the demographic extremes of American education. The authors raise important questions about the relative strengths and weaknesses of these disparate units of school governance: How big should a school or district be? How small? How comprehensive? How specialized? How standardized? How diversified? Given this diversity, what should graduate programs emphasize when preparing aspiring administrators who are moving to either end of this educational continuum? Should we continue to have programs that purport to prepare administrators who can operate at any level of the educational system and across such variant cultures? Or should we have more directed programs as in England and the Commonwealth countries? Have concerns for efficiency caused our programs to become too generic? Although these questions remain unanswered, Lomotey and Swanson point out that there are important commonalities between what "effective" building-level administrators in urban sites do and the work of "effective" rural superintendents (e.g., community relations and shared decisionmaking). In short, Lomotey and Swanson argue that administrators of school systems from opposite ends of the continuum have much to learn from studying one another.

Brown extends this debate by examining the significant but often ignored political dimension of educational leadership. He explicates the complexities of policymaking and political leadership in education by exploring the plight of the urban poor and disadvantaged. Although his discussion is restricted to urban America, the educational plight of minorities is equally appropriate to rural areas. Witness the emotional shame expressed by some for the passive indifference of white America to the racism and extremism of the Ku Klux Klan in the rural South as depicted in the 1989 movie *Mississippi Burning.*

Whether administering a rural, suburban, or urban district there is an essential need to understand the roots of discrimination and its social, psychological, and philosophical consequences. Furthermore, effective political leadership in education requires an experiential and cognitive background in what Burns (1978), Bass (1985), and Yukl (1989) describe as "transformational leadership."

It is interesting that some theorists view charisma as a necessary but not sufficient condition for performing as a transformational leader (Yukl, 1989):

> According to Bass (1985, p. 31), "Charisma is a necessary ingredient of transformational leadership, but by itself it is not sufficient to account for the transformational process." Transformational leaders influence followers by arousing strong emotions and identification with the leader, but they may also transform their followers by serving as a coach, teacher, and mentor. (p. 211)

The transformational leader is the "culture-changer" that Nyberg, Petrie, and Conway allude to in their chapters. The transformational process can be viewed as a unifying (centripetal) force that provides the organization a moral basis for action. Unfortunately, although some progress has been made during this past decade, we still have much to learn about the transformational process and transformational leadership (Yukl, 1989). In terms of administrator preparation, we need to know more about the process in order to identify individuals with the potential for transformational leadership, and then to enable these aspiring school leaders to realize their potential through instruction and practice.

The last undercurrent explored in this section was the impact of advanced information and communication technologies on schools. Swanson examined the political implications of transforming today's schools into tomorrow's learning centers. He sees technology as an integrating (centralizing) force that balances the decentralizing pressures created by demands for greater local autonomy. His strategy for change is predicated on an interorganizational collaboration that requires both leadership and understanding if empowerment and mutual benefit are to ensue. Notice that although Swanson's strategy reinforces Nyberg's concern for cooperation and mutual trust, its overarching objective is greater efficiency. Therefore, rather than "Tit for Tat," the strategy for change that Swanson endorses is short-range sacrifice for long-term gain. Yet this too is an underscoring of transformational leadership of the type studied by Roberts (1984) in a case analysis of a public school superintendent:

The superintendent in this study was deemed to be effective, because she was able to implement large, mandated budget cuts in a way that satisfied diverse stakeholders and still allowed progress in implementing desirable educational innovations. The teachers gave her a standing ovation for her efforts, even though the plan required program cuts and elimination of jobs. She was described as a "visionary" who had almost a "cult-like following" in the district. (Yukl, 1989; p. 225)

Yukl goes on to cite an incident that characterized both the transformational leadership of this particular superintendent as well as some of the essential elements of future educational leadership:

After a scheduled 40-minute presentation to district staff, teachers beseiged the stage to ask for more of her time to discuss the various initiatives the district was pursuing. Their requests turned into a four-hour dialogue with 800 people, in which the superintendent shared her hopes, her dreams, her past, her disappointments. Many people were moved to tears, including the superintendent. A critical point in the exchange came in answer to a question of how people could be certain that what she and the School Board promised would indeed occur. The superintendent's response was, *"Well, I guess you just have to trust us. I trust you."*

Dead silence followed as people drew in their breaths and held them for a moment or two. Upon being asked what this silence meant, people responded that the superintendent had proven her point. That was what the dialogue and the honesty were all about. She had trusted them with her thoughts, hopes, and feelings, and they in turn would trust her. *Mutual trust had created a bond between the superintendent and her audience.* (p. 226) (Emphasis added.)

PART III: ADMINISTRATOR PREPARATION AND EDUCATIONAL REFORM

In the third and final section of this book the chapters concentrate more specifically on administrator preparation and roles of leaders in this era of reform, change, and transformation. The nature of the chapters makes it prudent to treat them all together rather than serially, because all of them raise questions or offer suggestions about a common concern—the administrators of the future and their preparation.

Milstein devotes his attention to the theory-practice dichotomy and elaborates on a model for increasing the efficacy of clinical experience. His perspective, in contrast to Petrie's renaissance model, seems to make the assumption that the client has had a liberating education at the undergraduate level and is now entering into a theory-grounded, vocational education administrator program. He mentions four other approaches to a programmatic sequence: linear, dialectic, reflective practice, and developmental. There are, of course, other approaches as well as modifications of this basic list. Two alternatives that should also be considered could be labeled: apprenticeship (legal), and linear-iterative (medical). It may be of value to elaborate briefly on these two.

The Apprenticeship Approach

I recently learned that one of my tennis partners (whom, for our purposes, I will call Tom) entered the law profession through an apprenticeship process. As a young adult driver, Tom was stopped and cited for speeding. Protesting his innocence, he chose to take the case to court, and, moreover, he chose to defend himself. The arresting officer testified that the car Tom was driving was clocked at 65 mph in a 45 mph zone. Tom brought a witness who testified that Tom left the witness's home, which was a quarter of a mile from the point of infraction. Tom then asked the court to permit a demonstration. He asked a professional driver to accelerate Tom's vehicle for one-quarter of a mile and to indicate the speed reached. Without naming the vehicle, I can say that in five tries the professional driver was unable to get that old clunker to anything near the speed indicated by the arresting officer. Case dismissed! After that experience, Tom thought he would like to enter law. He found a firm that was willing to take him on as an apprentice, and he worked with that firm in increasingly more responsible roles. At the same time, he studied on his own and with the law partners (as coaches, teachers, and mentors) till he was ready to sit for the bar exam . . . which he passed.

That is not the typical route to the legal profession, yet it is an alternative. In many countries, the apprenticeship is still the primary route for entering educational administration. It is almost always the approach that private or independent schools use. A teacher might be assigned to a committee and find that he or she enjoys the activity, the responsibility, and the outcome. Gaining a sense of self-worth, the teacher soon becomes identified as one with administrator potential. In England that teacher might earn a post of responsibility, such as head of form, head of games, or perhaps department chair. Working with experienced administrators, the teacher begins to learn about the tasks, roles, skills, and craft of administering a school. With study (initially independent study), the teacher begins to learn about the "science" of administering a school. But perhaps most important, with practice the teacher begins to learn about himself or herself as an adult in a post of responsibility and whether or not that role is rewarding.

A few years ago that teacher would have moved through a series of posts including assistant head of a small school, then a larger one, to head of school and so on. That happens less today in foreign countries because courses of study for the various posts have been created and approved so that administration is now more taught than caught. This route to administration is almost always the case for our independent schools, however, where candidates are viewed in terms of their intellectual prowess and their demeanor for motivating teachers to perform consistent with the philosophy of the school. It may be that this alternative increases the likelihood of identifying those with transformational leadership qualities or with a different combination of intelligences (as Conway argues). Perhaps the apprenticeship approach should be resurrected and tested in our public schools, particularly as we consider the problem of administrator shortages anticipated by Jacobson in Chapter 11. Finn (1986) has argued that the ways principals are selected, trained, and certified are ill-suited to producing savvy, risk-taking, entrepreneurial educational leaders. On the other hand, unless the candidates come from the teaching ranks where they have proven themselves as first among equals, the apprentice approach might generate more managerial and manipulative administrators than educational or instructional leaders. In part, this is the argument against the New Jersey proposal for the development of an alternative career path to the principalship. Nevertheless, the apprenticeship approach to administration is something that warrants research and testing rather than emotional polemics.

The Linear-Iterative Approach

Petrie argues against the metaphor of the clinical-medical professions for the teacher-learning process, but there may still be utility to that metaphor for administrator preparation. In most medical colleges, students enter with an undergraduate liberal arts or science degree and then spend their first two years in concentrated study on the basic sciences needed for practice (e.g., biology, anatomy, physiology, chemistry). In their third and fourth years, medical students enter into clinical rotations where they learn through a systematic exposure to the major areas of practice (e.g., obstetrics, psychiatry, surgery, family medicine). Upon the successful completion of these clinical rotations, students are awarded a degree which asserts that they are a medical doctor. Now that they have had a taste of the possible areas of concentration, they choose one for focused clinical learning (internship or residency). This practical experience may last from 3 to 12 years. During that period, they practice as a medical doctor, gradually assuming greater responsibility as they pursue excellence in a particular field of practice, a specialization. What is most important in terms of possible applications to educational administration is that the education of the doctor-specialist does not cease at the end of the residency. Rather, the individual continues to study independently and participate in workshops to learn new procedures as they are developed. Indeed, individuals may even take time off from practice to teach and/or upgrade their skills. In other words, knowledge and skill acquisition in the linear-iterative approach is a continuous process of learning, testing, upgrading, discarding, reviewing, and evaluating. How might that play itself out for administrator preparation?

If we assume that leaders are widely diffused in schools and school districts (Barth, 1988) and that the various opportunities for leadership are understood by the educational actors, then we might consider the first end-point of preparation (the M.D. equivalent) as being an "educator" rather than a teacher certification. Specializations that an educator could then pursue might include pedagogy, curriculum development, evaluation, supervision, management, staff development, and so on. During the first two years of post-baccalaureate graduate work, the student would study educational sociology, philosophy, psychology, administration, and organizational sciences, followed by a year of clinical rotation in the specializations (i.e., teaching practice, administrator practice, curriculum practice, etc.). At this point, the aspiring educator would earn his or her "educator degree" (Ed.M. perhaps), after which the person would choose an area for concentrated study, interning in one or a combination of specializations. Perhaps most important to the educators' education would be a continuous commitment to the study of the field or fields of specialization through the review of research journals, participation in workshops teaching new techniques, advanced graduate study, and the like for the duration of their professional life.

This linear-iterative approach to educator preparation could help to bridge the schism that presently exists between teacher and administrator preparation. At our own institution, teacher and administrator preparation are quite disconnected. As in many other universities, these programs are offered by different departments, and there is little co-mingling among students from these programs. Occasionally a student in teacher education will find his or her way into an administration course, but rarely do administration students take courses in teacher education. Administrator certification in New York requires three years of teaching experience, so there is a tacit assumption that aspiring administrators need not spend time going back over what they should already know. Moreover, there is a pervasive attitude in administrator preparation that to become a successful administrator an individual must, "Stop thinking like a teacher!" Whatever thinking may have enabled the individual to be a successful teacher is now viewed as being potentially counterproductive in the world of administration. The implication is that teachers think too narrowly, perhaps focusing primarily on *their* pupils, or *their* subject matter, or *their* benefits (see Jacobson, Chapter 11, for a further discussion of teacher orientations). Administrators, on the other hand, must learn to think more broadly, concerning themselves with the success of the school at large. This attitude perpetuates the we-they adversarial relationship that characterizes much of the interactions between teachers and administrators in the field. In contrast to separate preparation programs for teachers and administrators, a linear-iterative approach to educator preparation would introduce teachers to administrative issues earlier in their training, while at the same time requiring administrators to keep abreast of pedagogic and curricular issues. This approach is much in line with the instructional managerial synthesis urged by Heller and Paulter in Chapter 9. Such a program would require either closer working relationships between existing departments or the creation of new institutional entities to breach the gap. The Buffalo Research Institute on Education and Teaching (BRIET) is one such cross-cutting attempt.

The goal of BRIET is to create a collegium of faculty whose mission will be to work toward the improvement of elementary and secondary school teaching and learning. What makes this effort unique is that it will draw faculty from across the three departments that comprise the University of Buffalo's Graduate School of Education as well as from the liberal arts and sciences and from the professional schools. In addition, a clinical faculty is being developed from among the most outstanding educational practitioners in western New York. This holistic approach to problemsolving educational preparation stands in sharp contrast to the more fragmented, isolationist traditions of both teacher and administrator preparation.

REFLECTION AND AN ENDING

So where does this put us? What is the ending, if any? We seem to be in agreement that something is presently wrong with administrator preparation; therefore we can agree that there exists the need to re-form. Unfortunately, we are uncertain as to what it is that is wrong. There are multiple issues, therefore there is disagreement over what it is that needs to be re-formed . . . yet reform is imminent, if not already past. Centrifugal (decentralizing) pressures of reform, such as experiments with site-based management and increased empowerment of teachers (parents, students, and administrators as well) may be more sham than reality if they continue to operate within centralized systems using traditional forms of accountability. Centripetal (centralizing) forces, such as the movement to replace administration's long-standing cult of efficiency with what Hills (1983) calls the "cult of effectiveness," may already be passé if they are unable to cope with the increasing problems posed by at-risk populations. It appears that America's educational system is at a juncture where creative design may have more meaning than reasoned replications. The need for change is an obvious thread throughout this book, but change to what and from what?

It is well recognized that schooling in this country has changed little in form and structure in its 200-plus year history. It may well be that we no longer need leaders who simply do more efficiently what has already been done but that we need to develop leaders who can think thoughts that have not been and then find ways to bring them to be. We need to discover what "good" educational leadership means, in "good" schools. We need to find ways to attract leaders, to help them enter our school systems and to help them succeed. We need theory to be presented so that it generates creative thought rather than stifles it—theory that is integrated into systematic study that works from practice, through practice, to practice. Practice must be the beginning *and* the end, perhaps at last appropriately found.

Although public school systems need to enter into collaborative commitments to cope with the complex contexts and changing conditions, it is equally appropriate that academicians and administrator preparation programs abandon their isolationist tradition and work in a similar fashion. We shall see reforms succeed more through mutual commitments, encouragement, and cooperation than through partisan criticisms and traditional Tit-for-Tat "professional" bashings. The process task is clear for programs and students alike: to discover and implement new forms of collaboration, to create new designs for organizing schools (and programs), and to make new meanings as the goals are mutually set and evaluated. A challenge indeed!

REFERENCES

Barber, B. (1983). *The logic and limits of trust.* New Brunswick, NJ: Rutgers University Press.

Barnard, C. (1938). *The functions of the executive.* Cambridge, MA: Harvard University Press.

Barth, R. (1988). On sheep and goats and school reform. In D. Griffiths, R. Stout, & P. Forsyth (Eds.), *Leaders for America's schools: Final report and papers of the National Commission on Excellence in Educational Administration* (pp. 185–192). Berkeley, CA: McCutchan.

Bass, B. (1985). *Leadership and performance beyond expectations.* New York: Free Press.

Burns, J. (1978). *Leadership.* New York: Harper & Row.

Campbell, J. (1972). *Myths to Live By.* Toronto: Bantam Books.

Conway, J. (1984). The myth, mystery and mastery of participative decision making in education. *Educational Administration Quarterly, 20*(3), 11–40.

Darling-Hammond, L. (1988). Accountability and teacher professionalism. *American Educator, 12*(4), 8–13, 38–43.

Finn, C. (1986, February 18). Better principals, Not just teachers. *The Wall Street Journal.*

Frazer, J. (1950). The golden bough: A study in magic and religion. New York: Macmillan.

Greenfield, T. (1984). Theories of educational organization: A critical perspective. *International encyclopedia of education: Research and studies.* Oxford, England: Pergamon.

Griffiths, D. (1988). Administrative theory. In N. Boyan (Ed.), *Handbook of research on educational administration* (pp. 27–51). White Plains, NY: Longman.

Hills, J. (1983). The preparation of educational leaders: What's needed and what's next? UCEA Occasional Paper #8303. Columbus, OH: University Council for Educational Administration.

Korczak, J. (1986). *King Matt the First.* (1st Pub. 1923) R. Lourie (trans). New York: Farrar, Straus & Giroux.

Roberts, N. (1984). Transforming leadership: Sources, processes, consequences. Paper presented at the Academy of Management, Boston.

Thomson, S. (1989). Troubled kingdoms, restless natives. *Phi Delta Kappan, 70*(5), 371–375.

Yukl, G. (1989). *Leadership in organizations* (2nd Ed.). Englewood Cliffs, NJ: Prentice-Hall.

Index